Winning Companies; Winning People

Making it easy for average performers to adopt winning behaviours

Winning Companies; Winning People

Making it easy for average performers to adopt winning behaviours

Colin Coulson-Thomas

Published by Policy Publications in association with Adaptation Ltd

Coulson-Thomas, Colin

Winning Companies; Winning People: Making it easy for average performers to adopt winning behaviours

ISBN 978-1-872980-72-0

First published in 2007 by Policy Publications Ltd in association with Adaptation Ltd

Every effort has been made to ensure that the information contained in this book was accurate at the time of writing. The publishers and the author cannot accept responsibility for any errors or omissions, however caused. No responsibility for loss or damage occasioned to any person acting, or refraining from action, as a result of the material in this publication can be accepted by the publisher or the author. Neither the publisher nor the author can accept liability for loss or expense as a result of relying on particular statements in the book. The book is sold on the clear understanding that the publisher is not involved in providing a professional service. If in doubt about any particular circumstances, or when considering the applicability of general guidance in a particular situation, readers are advised to seek reliable professional advice before taking any action based upon information provided in this book.

Policy Publications Ltd
Mill Reach
Mill Lane
Water Newton
Nr Peterborough
Cambridgeshire PE8 6LY
United Kingdom

www.policypublications.com

British Library Cataloguing in Publication Data
A CIP record for this book is available from the British Library
ISBN 978-1-872980-72-0

All rights reserved. No part of this book may be reprinted or reproduced or utilised in any form or by any electronic, mechanical, or other means, now known or later invented, including photocopying and recording, or in any information storage or retrieval system, except under the terms of the Copyright, Designs and Patents Act 1988 or in the case of reprographic reproduction in accordance with the terms of a licence issued by The Copyright Licensing Agency Ltd (www.cla.co.uk), without the prior permission in writing from the publishers.

© Colin Coulson-Thomas, 2007

Copyright notice

The right of Colin Coulson-Thomas to be identified as the author of this work has been asserted by him in accordance with the Copyright, Designs and Patents Act 1988.

Laid out, printed and bound in Great Britain by Printondemand-Worldwide Ltd

To Yvette, Vivien and Trystan Coulson-Thomas

Contents

About the author
Acknowledgements
Other books by Professor Colin Coulson-Thomas
Introduction

Chapter 1   *Setting the Scene*
Chapter 2   *Understanding the Business and Market Environment*
Chapter 3   *Visioning*
Chapter 4   *Creating a Winning Board*
Chapter 5   *Providing Strategic Leadership*
Chapter 6   *Corporate Governance*
Chapter 7   *Differentiation*
Chapter 8   *Winning Competitive Bids*
Chapter 9   *Pricing for Profit*
Chapter 10   *Developing Strategic Customers and Key Accounts*
Chapter 11   *Negotiating Partnering Relationships*
Chapter 12   *Managing Supply Chain Relationships*
Chapter 13   *Leading and Managing Change*
Chapter 14   *Corporate Transformation*
Chapter 15   *Corporate Communications*
Chapter 16   *Going Global*
Chapter 17   *New Ways of Working*
Chapter 18   *Managing Virtual Organisations*
Chapter 19   *Creating an Entrepreneurial Culture*
Chapter 20   *Entrepreneurial Purchasing*
Chapter 21   *The Knowledge Entrepreneur*
Chapter 22   *Exploiting Corporate Know-how*
Chapter 23   *Developing a Corporate Learning Strategy*
Chapter 24   *Integrating Learning and Working*

Chapter 25 *Maximising Benefits from IT and E-business*

Chapter 26 *Boosting Workgroup Performance and Salesforce Productivity*

Chapter 27 *Launching New Products*

Chapter 28 *Working with Consultants*

Chapter 29 *Using Management Methodologies, Tools and Techniques*

Chapter 30 *Creating a Competitive Company*

Chapter 31 *Achieving Commercial Success and Personal Fulfilment*

Appendix A: *Winning Companies; Winning People Research Programme*

Appendix B: *Winning Business Research and Best Practice Programme*

Appendix C: *Courses, Workshops and Masterclasses*

Index

Also available from Policy Publications

About the Author

Prof Colin J Coulson-Thomas is an authority on business, director and board development and transforming key process and corporate performance. He counsels individual directors and senior managers and has advised over 100 boards on improving board and/or corporate performance. He also leads the Winning Companies; Winning People and winning business research and best practice programmes and has reviewed the processes and practices for winning business of over 100 companies. Colin helps boards and entrepreneurial teams to create and exploit knowledge, differentiate their offerings and develop their businesses. A regular speaker at major corporate events and international conferences, he has given around 300 presentations in some 35 countries.

An experienced chairman of award winning companies, Colin has also been Professor of Direction and Leadership at the University of Lincoln since 2005. He draws upon his experience as the Process Vision Holder of major market transformation projects at home and abroad when advising boards on corporate direction, transformation, learning and knowledge entrepreneurship. Colin currently serves on the Professional Accreditation Committee and Board of Examiners of the UK Institute of Directors and the Corporate Governance and Risk Management Committee of the Association of Chartered Certified Accountants.

Formerly chairman of ASK Europe plc for eight years, Colin served for ten years on the Board of Moorfields Eye Hospital, and for six years as Deputy Chairman of the London Electricity Consultative Council. He served two terms on the Council for Professions Supplementary to Medicine as representative of HM Privy Council, nine years on the National Biological Standards Board, five years on the Council of the Foundation for Science and Technology and four years as Corporate Affairs Adviser to the British Institute of Management. He is a past Chairman of the Crossbencher parliamentary liaison programme, a past Chairman of the Bow Group and a past Chairman and past President of the Focus Group.

Colin has served on various other corporate boards and the governing bodies of representative, professional, learned, and voluntary institutes, societies and associations, including as chairman and president. He led the European Commission's COBRA initiative which examined business restructuring across Europe, was the principal author and co-presenter of the 'employment and training' module of the 'CBI Initiative 1992', and is the principal author of the 'Induction Package for New TEC Directors'. As well as chairing the Judges for the e-Business Innovations awards, he has also been a National Business Award and Sword of Excellence Award judge and a member of the European Commission's Team Europe.

From 1994-97 Colin was the Willmott Dixon Professor of Corporate Transformation, Dean of the Faculty of Management and Head of the Putteridge Bury campus at the University of Luton, and a Senior Associate at the Judge Institute of Cambridge University. He was Hooker Distinguished Visiting Professor, McMaster University, Canada in 1995; and Visiting Professor, East China University of Science & Technology, Shanghai in 1996. Between 1997 and 2000 he was a Visiting Professor at the Management Development Institute, Delhi. His academic experience also includes some five years as Head of the Centre for Competitiveness and a Professor of Competitiveness at the University of Luton. He is currently a Visiting Professor at the University of Bedfordshire.

Colin has led various change management, re-engineering and transformation projects and surveys of entrepreneurial/boardroom issues, attitudes and practice for the Institute of Directors, Institute of Management, Institute of Personnel Management, Government Departments and the NHS. Practical lessons derived from these surveys and his work with entrepreneurs and boards are summarised in: *Creating Excellence in the Boardroom* (McGraw-Hill, 1993), *Individuals and Enterprise* (Blackhall Publishing, 1999), *Shaping Things to Come* (Blackhall Publishing, 2001), *Winning Companies; Winning People, the differing approaches of winners and losers* (Kingsham Press, 2007), and *Developing Directors, a handbook for building an effective boardroom team* (Policy Publications, 2007).

Colin's other publications include *Creating the Global Company: Successful Internationalisation* (McGraw-Hill, 1992), *Transforming the Company* (Kogan Page, 1992, revised edition 2002 & 2004), *The Future of the Organisation: Achieving Excellence through Business Transformation* (Kogan Page, 1997 and 1998), *Developing a Corporate Learning Strategy* (Policy Publications, 1999), *The Information Entrepreneur* (3Com, 2000), *Pricing for Profit* (Policy Publications, 2002) and *The Knowledge Entrepreneur* (Kogan Page, 2003). He is the editor of *Business Process Re-engineering: Myth & Reality* (Kogan Page, 1994), and executive editor (all Policy Publications) of: *The Responsive Organisation: Re-engineering new patterns of work* (1995), *The*

Competitive Network (1996), *Winning Major Bids* (1997), *Developing Strategic Customers & Key Accounts* (1998), and the 'Winning new Business in ...' series of reports (1999-) and co-author of *Winning New Business* (Policy Publications, 2003).

Colin was educated at the London School of Economics (Trevennon Exhibitioner), London Business School, EAESP - Fundacao Getulio Vargas (Brasilian Government Scholar), and the Universities of Aston, Chicago (Deans List) and Southern California (Graduate School Distinction). He obtained first place prizes in the final examinations of three professions. Colin can be contacted by telephone: +44 (0) 1733 361149; fax: +44 (0) 1733 361459; email: colinct@tiscali.co.uk; or via http://www.coulson-thomas.com or http://www.adaptation.ltd.uk

Acknowledgements

I would like to thank my colleagues at Lincoln Business School, Adaptation Ltd, Cotoco Ltd, Policy Publications Ltd and The Networking Firm.

I am particularly grateful for the support of both Cotoco Ltd and its managing director Don Fuller.

Over a period of years I have served upon several boards in the private, public and voluntary sectors. At most of the board meetings I have attended I have learned something from my fellow directors.

I also owe a special debt of gratitude to Yvette, Vivien and Trystan Coulson-Thomas to whom this book is dedicated for their understanding while I write and consult.

Colin Coulson-Thomas
Mill Reach
Mill Lane
Water Newton
Peterborough
Cambridgeshire
PE8 6LY
United Kingdom

July 2007

Other recent books by Professor Colin Coulson-Thomas

(1992) *Creating the Global Company, successful internationalization*, McGraw-Hill, London

(1992) *Transforming the Company, bridging the gap between management myth and corporate reality*, Kogan Page, London

(1993) *Creating Excellence in the Boardroom, A guide to shaping directorial competence and board effectiveness*, McGraw-Hill, London

(1993) *Developing Directors, building an effective boardroom team* (First edition), McGraw-Hill, London

(1994 & 1996) *Business Process Re-engineering, Myth & Reality*, Kogan Page, London

(1995) [Principal Author] *The Responsive Organisation, re-engineering new patterns of work*, Policy Publications, Bedford

(1997 & 1998) *The Future of the Organization, achieving excellence through business transformation*, Kogan Page, London

(1999) Developing a Corporate Learning Strategy, the key knowledge management challenge for the HR function, Policy Publications, Bedford

(1999) *Individuals and Enterprise, creating entrepreneurs for the new millennium through personal transformation*, Blackhall Publishing, Dublin

(2000) *The Information Entrepreneur, changing requirements for corporate and individual success*, 3Com Active Business Unit, Winnersh

(2001) *Shaping Things to Come, strategies for creating alternative enterprises*, Blackhall Publishing, Dublin

(2002) *Pricing for Profit, the critical success factors*, Policy Publications, Bedford

(2002 & 2004) *Transforming the Company, manage change, compete and win*, Kogan Page, London

(2003) *The Knowledge Entrepreneur*, Kogan Page, London

(2003) [Joint] *Winning New Business, the critical success factors*, Policy Publications, Bedford

(2006) [Co-authored with Peter Bartram] *How to Make Your Case in the Media*, New Venture Publishing, Brighton

(2007) *Winning Companies, Winning People, The differing approaches of winners and losers*, Kingsham Press, East Hampnett

(2007) *Developing Directors, A handbook for building an effective boardroom team*, Policy Publications, Peterborough

All recent books and reports by Colin Coulson-Thomas can be ordered from the bookshop of The Networking Firm: http://www.ntwkfirm.com/bookshop/

Details of related Policy Publications titles can be obtained from http://www.ntwkfirm.com/policy-publications/

Information on the critical success factors identified by Prof. Coulson-Thomas' research can be obtained from http://www.winningnewbusiness.biz/

Further information on related bespoke benchmarking services can be obtained from http://www.ntwkfirm.com/policy-publications/benchmarking.htm

Information on support tools that can incorporate identified critical success factors and winning ways can be obtained from http://www.cotoco.com

Introduction

Average performers at a range of important tasks can be helped to adopt the winning ways of high performing superstars. The productivity of key workgroups and corporate performance can be transformed to deliver commercial success for organisations and personal satisfaction for individuals.

It sounds too good to be true, but this book shows how it can be done. The book draws upon: (i) an extensive research programme that has identified critical success factors and winning behaviours for important activities; and (ii) practical experience of helping innovative companies to incorporate them into work processes and job support tools that enable users to emulate the approaches of high achievers.

Have you ever wondered why some people are so much more effective than others who undertake similar tasks in equivalent circumstances? What do the high performers do differently? The Winning Companies; Winning People research programme examines how people operate in important areas such as building relationships, bidding, pricing, purchasing and exploiting know-how.

Over 4,000 organisations from smaller firms to major corporations have already participated in the continuing research programme led by the author. Some 2,000 of these have contributed to studies to identify critical success factors and winning behaviours for key business development activities. The differing behaviours of winners and losers are summarised in this book and the critical success factors that have been identified are set out in over twenty research reports that are also published by Policy Publications (see www.policypublications.com).

The findings are remarkably consistent across sectors, professions, corporate nationalities and different sizes of organisation. Areas examined range from communicating to visioning. Because most success factors are attitudinal and behavioural, investigating teams can distinguish the approaches of high performers or winners from the practices of low achieving losers.

The investigation and this book represent good news for people and organisations who would like to raise their game. For those with ambitions to build successful businesses and achieve their full potential it provides a compendium of the differing approaches of winners and losers and examples of what can be done to help under-achieving people adopt the approaches of their more successful peers. Individuals, entrepreneurs, managers, coaches and consultants can also use this book as a tool to identify losing behaviours that need to be addressed.

In many sectors leading competitors have similar offerings, adopt prevailing technologies and systems, recruit from the major business schools, fall for current management fads and employ the same or similar professional firms. Yet examine a particular area of operation and huge variations of performance are evident. Why is this?

Individual studies within the Winning Companies; Winning People research programme rank participant's attainments in relation to outcomes achieved from the most to the least successful. The approaches of high and low achievers – for example, those in the top and bottom quartiles of accomplishment – are then compared to isolate critical success factors that explain the differences of attainment.

Over 100 exercises have now been undertaken by the author to build critical success factors into processes and practices for winning business. Identified winning ways can be quickly adopted. Every participant in the research programme could boost performance by embracing additional critical success factors and adopting more winning approaches.

People don't jump out of bed in the morning eager to rush into the office to struggle and fail. They want to do well. When critical success factors and winning ways are explained to small groups they understand and adopt them. The challenge for larger organisations has been to find a cost-effective way of getting significant numbers of people in scattered locations to quickly emulate winning ways.

This book will show that help is at hand. A new generation of practical job support tools promises to transform workgroup productivity and corporate performance (see www.cotoco.com). Because they make it very easy for people to do difficult jobs in a winning way they can be rapidly deployed without the problems normally associated with 'the management of change'. They represent a cost-effective and superior alternative to a range of activities from traditional training to consulting interventions.

Winners don't work harder or cheat. They approach challenges and opportunities differently. In summary, pioneers are building critical success factors into the processes for key activities and adopting cost effective ways of helping people to emulate the winning ways of high performing superstars.

Overall, the research findings and winner-loser comparisons are intriguing. Companies that excel at certain activities usually perform badly at others. Were companies to adopt winning ways across the board overall productivity and personal satisfaction would increase by an unprecedented amount.

There are important implications for directors and boards. The investigating teams have found massive expenditure on activities that do not relate to critical success factors and winning behaviours. Almost every company visited during the research programme was found to be devoting considerable resources to similar initiatives that would make little if any difference to outcomes achieved in areas covered by the investigation.

The directors of many companies do not appear aware of critical success factors and successful approaches to key activities. Most companies are also poor judges of their relative performance, and unaware of why they are not more successful. Some also struggle to identify their superstars and winning behaviours that others should adopt.

There is a huge opportunity to improve individual and corporate performance. Even high performers could do so much better. For example, in relation to competitive bidding the superstars in the top quartile of achievement are only very effective at less than half of the identified critical success factors.

The core research data bases have been constructed so that in addition to the guidance available in this book and individual critical success factor reports bespoke benchmarking reports can be generated that offer comparison with average and high performers and highlight areas to concentrate upon to match the achievements of superstars (see www.policypublications.com). In future, for those adopting the approaches set out in this book winning or losing can become a matter of choice.

Chapter 1
Setting the Scene

Have you ever wondered why some individuals and groups out perform others who are undertaking equivalent activities in other companies in a similar situation? Why do some businesses expand, while others that appear to be in the same boat plateau and contract? Are there certain business and management practices that lead on the one hand to growth and development and on the other hand to stagnation and decline? Do the most successful operators know things that others are not aware of? Do they adopt different approaches?

In many sectors of the economy competing companies appear to be offering similar products and services, and using the same or equivalent technologies, processes and systems. They recruit similar people, often from the same universities and business schools, employ the services of the same or similar consultants, and they invariably fall for the same management fashions and fads. Yet over time some workgroups do better than others and some businesses prosper while others wither. Why is this? What do the leaders of successful workgroups and companies - or winners - do differently from losers who struggle and fail?

There are various rules of conduct aimed at equipping individuals to lead a moral life and achieve success. 'Self help' books feature prominently on airport bookstands. But what about achieving success for one's workgroup or even one's corporate organization? Are there equivalent rules or principles that, if adopted, might increase the chances of commercial success?

The author's continuing research programme has been considering the questions just posed for over 20 years (see appendix A). It examines areas that are critical to competing and winning such as improving performance, managing change, competitive bidding, building customer relationships and creating and exploiting know-how. The purpose of this research is to determine what boards and management teams need to do - and also what they should not do - to lead, innovate, pioneer, discover, compete and win.

This book and another by the author 'Winning Companies; Winning People, the differing approaches of winners and losers' (Kingsham Press, 2007) provide a brief overview of the major findings to date in areas critical to business success. The book also includes various checklists that can be used to help assess whether one's approaches and those of colleagues or clients falls into the 'winner' or 'loser category'.

The book is intentionally concentrated. The aim is to present a compendium of concise summaries of research findings into the differing approaches of successful and unsuccessful companies for students, directors, managers and entrepreneurs with ambitions to build successful businesses and realize their full potential.

The author's intention is to provide an authoritative, positive, realistic and inspiring 'go for it' book for ambitious directors, managers, business school students, entrepreneurs, and all those who want to achieve both commercial success and the personal fulfillment that comes from competing and winning.

There is a long established success literature for individuals. Titles on the bookstands mentioned above range from the thought provoking and profound to the simplistic and lightweight, but there are far fewer accessible, holistic and research based approaches based upon a comparison of what effective and ineffective corporate directors, managers and entrepreneurs actually do. Many of the books that consist largely of assertions, 'gut feel' and 'writing from the heart' fail to identify the activities that actually make the difference between winning and losing.

The present book is based upon differences between the approaches and conduct of winners and losers - or leaders and laggards - as revealed by the above mentioned research programme led by the author. It contrasts and compares how those who are successful (winners) and those who struggle and fail (losers) actually set about important activities such as winning business, buying, building customer relationships and creating and exploiting know-how.

The critical success factors that have been identified are set out in a series of research reports (see appendices A and B). The more recent reports specifically relating to winning business are set out in appendix B. The attitudes and approaches underlying or associated with these critical success factors are summarised in the following chapters of this book. For those interested in applying key lessons of the research programme within their own business appendix C gives details of various course, masterclass, seminar, presentation and workshop modules that are available and from which bespoke sessions can be created.

This book aims to be accessible but balanced. The intention is to present research findings in an easily digested form for busy readers.

Most of the chapters contain comparisons of the differing approaches of winners and losers. These are intended to show people what to do and what not to do to succeed in an area that is important for business success, for example building effective boards, winning new business, partnering or corporate learning.

The author has been leading the performance improvement, transformation and winning business research and best practice programmes since 1988 and there is a considerable body of work to draw upon. Details of various books, reports and articles which summarize the findings of individual studies are given in the author's book: 'Winning Companies; Winning People, the differing approaches of winners and losers' (Kingsham Press, 2007).

Appendix A provides an overview of the author's research programme. This book will synthesize the key lessons from this body of work into a comprehensive summary of winning and losing approaches to business development. The implications for director and board development are covered in a companion volume by the author: 'Developing Directors, a handbook for building an effective boardroom team' (Policy Publications, 2007). This includes certain winner-loser comparisons relevant to the work of directors and provides guidance on how to develop more competent directors and build more successful boards.

In total, over 4,000 companies and knowledge-based businesses (e.g. professional firms) have participated in research projects led by the author. In the last decade, each of the research projects has ranked the outcomes achieved by participants and compared the approaches of those who are in the top and bottom quartiles or above and below the average or mid-point in the range of achievement, depending upon the number of participants and statistical considerations for determining the reliability and validity of findings.

Figure 1 shows the main areas covered by the research programme, the items in italics being the names of some of the books and reports that summarise the findings in the fields concerned. Areas examined range from establishing the strategic direction of a company to managing performance. Outputs include methodologies for transforming performance, introducing new ways of working, re-engineering processes and re-engineering supply chain relationships using e-commerce technologies.

As mentioned above, the stream of research relating to winning business - shown at the top of Figure 1 - is described in appendix B. From time to time books and reports that have been published are updated as new findings are processed. At the time of writing a new

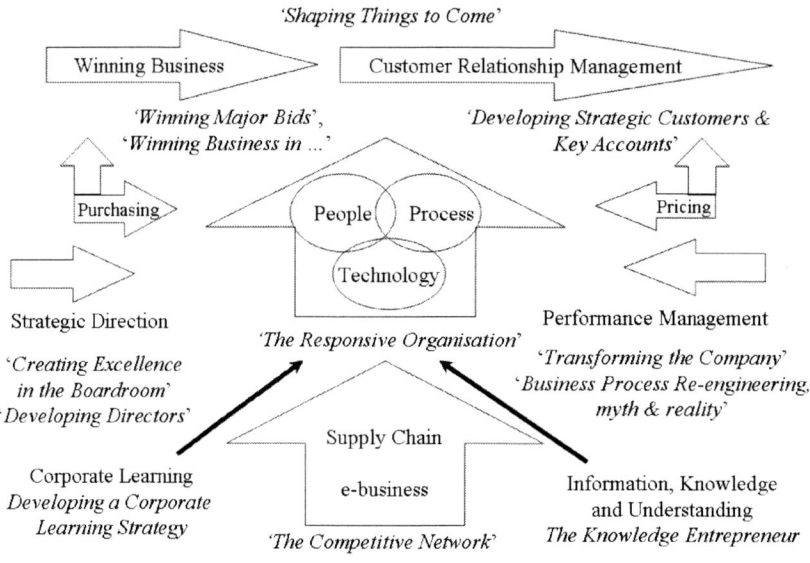

Figure 1: **Colin Coulson-Thomas Research Programme ('*Winning Companies; Winning People*')**

and updated summary of key findings relating to transforming corporate performance is being produced. Details of the latest research reports can be found on www.policypublications.com.

Significantly for the readership of this book, while there are sector specific issues to address in most business sectors, its core messages - and the main differences of attitude, approach and behaviour of winners and losers - have been found to apply independently of sector and company size. Encouragingly also are the findings that many of the critical success factors and winning approaches are independent of each other. Hence success – as one might expect from the research methodology – increases with the number of them that are put in place.

In the studies that have been undertaken typically only a quarter - or at most a third - of the businesses examined were either a 'winner' or a 'leader'. Most of the teams examined were losers or laggards. Many well known or 'blue chip' companies are firmly in the loser or laggard category for certain of the activities studied, despite much effort to improve their general performance. Generally consulting inputs, corporate initiatives and other activities to boost results have missed the critical success factors in the areas concerned. Many interventions the author has encountered have actually introduced losing ways.

In most of the companies visited during the research considerable resources were being devoted to areas that are not relevant to competing and winning. At the same time quick and easy ways of improving performance by simply putting the critical success factors in place and adopting winning approaches were ignored and overlooked. One can only speculate that losing behaviours and wasteful expenditures attract vested interests that benefit from their continuation.

Intriguingly, many well-known corporations that win in some areas are found to be losers in others. If this were not the case and certain businesses only displayed winning behaviours in all of the areas examined most of the world's output could be controlled by a handful of giant enterprises. However, many companies that appear well placed to prosper seem ignorant of the critical success factors identified in the research reports and remain unaware of whether or not they are adopting winning or losing approaches.

In some of the areas examined, even the most successful companies – those in the top quartile – are only very effective at less than a half of the critical success factors that have been identified and set out in a series of research reports (see the sources of further information at the end of each chapter and www.policypublications.com). Hence, the research findings are very encouraging. There is enormous scope for improvement in all the businesses examined so far.

To date opportunities have been identified to improve the performance of every survey participant by introducing a change of attitude, behaviour or approach independent of systems and/or process changes. The lead-time for benefiting from improvements can be as short as the time taken to approach and undertake a particular activity in a winning way. Many people start behaving as winners from the moment a more successful approach is explained to them and understood.

The research programmes continue (see www.coulson-thomas.com) and winning approaches have been adopted and tested in many operational environments. They have also been embedded in tools and techniques described in later chapters of this book and the author's book 'The Knowledge Entrepreneur' (Kogan Page, 2003). The author has recently completed a programme of Masterclasses for boards and management teams of ambitious companies, so hopefully the text will be practical and attuned to current issues and contemporary realities.

The readership for whom the book is intended embraces company directors, mangers in businesses of all sizes, consultants, professionals, business school students, entrepreneurs and business advisers who have had enough of retrenchment, downsizing, playing games, cosmetics, distractions, spin and management fads, and who want to get real and succeed through adopting positive, pro-active and evidence based approaches.

One of the core themes of the book is that personal fulfillment and business success increasingly need to go hand in hand. Businesses can no longer sustain success at the expense of their people. It is therefore hoped that the book will be bought both by individuals who wish to transform their prospects and quality of life, and become personally more successful, as well as those setting out to transform organizations and the fortunes of particular businesses.

The book is all about how to become a 'winner', someone who is both successful and fulfilled. It is intended to be honest rather than escapist. It endeavours to avoid peddling hyped concepts, panaceas or single solutions. Instead, it highlights the combination of elements and the attitudes, approaches and behaviours needed to succeed. At the heart of what needs to be done is putting additional critical success factors in place and adopting the winning ways of high performers.

Losers tend to avoid rolling up their sleeves and taking steps to adopt critical success factors and enable their people to emulate winning ways. Instead of sorting the fundamentals they seek single solutions to problems and become lost in a world of trendy management concepts, and fashionable fads and panaceas. They are lured by, and become preoccupied with, ideas that are interesting for their own sake.

Rather than think for themselves, losers are attracted by those who appear positive and claim to have answers to questions that concern them. Because of distractions and avoidance of getting too deeply involved they may need to be subjected to a degree of hype and a relatively high level of generalization before their attention is captured.

Even when losers recognize what they want and have a genuine desire to change, they are usually uncertain as to how to bring it about. They experience anguish and frustration when people and events do not turn out as they might have hoped.

Losers tend to be preoccupied with their own aspirations and requirements and largely oblivious to what is going on around them. As a result they may either miss or ignore the requirements for the successful management of new forms of organization, different ways of working and more collaborative relationships. Ultimately they fail to transform either themselves or their organizations.

Winners are different. They keep their feet on the ground and are more willing to address the critical realities of the situation they are in, such as whether critical success factors and winning ways are in place. They recognize that the solution of a problem may require a combination of elements.

Distractions are avoided. Winners would not cross the street for an interesting idea that was not relevant or capable of implementation. They are attracted by those who focus upon critical success factors and concentrate upon what is important. They become engaged when they perceive the relevance of what is being suggested and the specifics of what needs to be done are addressed.

Winners consciously set out to make their aspirations a reality. They are prepared to address the fundamentals and are not daunted by challenges or ambitious goals. They expect reverses and disappointments and are not distracted or inhibited by them.

Our winners track and understand what is happening in the business environment and think through the implications for themselves and their customers. They are aware of the attitudes, qualities and approaches required to successfully manage alternative forms of organization, ways of working and types of relationship. They accomplish sufficient personal and corporate transformation to remain relevant and vital.

The book will show how companies can compete and win and how businesses can work with individuals to enable them to achieve both commercial success and personal fulfillment. While aiming at the serious corporate governance, business development, personal success, management of change and entrepreneurship markets it also seeks to address contemporary work-life balance concerns. Life is simply too precious to squander time on losing activities.

Because it is research based the book will also hopefully ring true as an honest account of the differing attitudes and behaviours of winners and losers. Corporate leaders might wish to circulate the book to management colleagues or to management course participants as the basis for subsequent discussion.

We live in a world of opportunities and problems that could be addressed by imaginative solutions. There is enormous scope for economic and social entrepreneurship. Success and failure are increasingly a matter of choice. Go for it.

Checklist:

- At this stage do you view yourself and/or your colleagues as winners or losers?
- Do others view you and/or your colleagues as winners or losers?

- Does the company have a compelling reason for existing? What would the world lose if it ceased to exist tomorrow?
- Does the company have clear and agreed vision, goals and values?
- Who within the company has thought through what the vision and these goals and values mean for its relationships with people, whether as customers, suppliers or business partners?
- Is there an overview of what the company is trying to achieve in terms of its various objectives?
- Are all the objectives expressed in terms of measurable outputs?
- Have the key processes that are necessary to achieve desired outcomes been identified and have critical success factors for these activities been identified and put in place?
- Have relevant roles and responsibilities been allocated, and the required resources been lined up?
- Have high performers and what they do differently been identified? How do they compare with high performers in other organisations?
- Are average performers helped to adopt the approaches of their more successful colleagues and external peers who are more succeseful at the activities they undertake?
- To what extent are you and management colleagues frustrated with what has been achieved in the area of improving key workgroup and corporate performance? What are the symptoms of non-achievement?
- Is there a process in place within your company to root out the underlying causes of gaps between aspiration and achievement?
- Is the nature, and full extent, of the performance improvement and/or corporate transformation challenge fully appreciated?
- Has thought been given to whether particular critical success factors, winning ways or other change elements are missing from the transformation jigsaw puzzle?
- How genuine is the desire to change in each functional component and business element of your organization?
- Is there an agreed vision of a more flexible and responsive 'end point' organization in which people are helped to understand complex issues and do difficult jobs?
- To what extent have the changes which have been introduced into your company to date influenced attitudes, values and behaviour? Which if any changes are getting in the way of what needs to be done?

- Crucially, are people equipped, empowered and motivated to do what is expected of them?

Chapter 2
Understanding the Business and Market Environment

Some companies appear ambushed or taken by surprise by external events. They find themselves ill prepared to react to both challenges and opportunities. Other businesses are much more alert to what is happening in the business and market environment in which they operate. They track issues, anticipate events and monitor competitive activities.

So what do the winners do differently in relation to understanding the business and market environment? To answer these questions research teams led by the author have examined the corporate experience of over 2,000 companies (see appendix A). The results are summarized in the author's forthcoming book on transforming corporate performance and in 'Transforming the Company, Manage Change, Compete and Win', while the steps that boards can take to question and challenge prevailing assumptions are set out in 'Shaping Things to Come' a handbook for creating a better future*. In this chapter we look specifically at findings relating to understanding the business and market environment.

Let's start with unsuccessful boards or 'losers'. They are often unaware of impending challenges and pressing requirements to change. They simply do not see them. They tend to be largely oblivious to developments in the market places in which they operate. They also do not anticipate or look ahead, and they are not alert to threats and opportunities. Hence, when they do wake up to what is at stake they may have little time in which to adapt even if they had the will and means of doing so.

Losers just hunker down. They make cosmetic references to environmental and social concerns in annual reports and accounts. They stick to what they know and feel comfortable with and plough ahead regardless, hoping any problems they encounter will blow over. If they do stop and take stock of where they are it is generally infrequently. Whatever changes are made tend to quickly become permanent features.

Opportunities can also be resisted if responding to them would require changed practices and behaviours. New requirements may be perceived as distractions until such times as they become so pressing and potentially lucrative that they can no longer be ignored or avoided. Some only act when legislators or competitive activity requires them to do so.

In contrast, the boards of successful companies or 'winners' have more acute and sensitive antennae. They look out for the weeds that can foul propellers. They are aware of what is happening around them and in the business and market environment. They are also entrepreneurial. They view problems as arenas of potential opportunity and take the initiative in shaping the future, challenging assumptions to create new options and choices.

Winners identify and monitor economic, political and technological trends, and assess their likely impacts upon both themselves and their customers. They then consider what if anything they should do in response. Such exercises are undertaken on a regular basis, and at least once a year. Resulting actions are subsequently reviewed and if need be challenged and amended as events unfold.

Because they read the road ahead, winners generally give themselves sufficient time to register, react and adapt. Changes are made quickly as and when they are needed. They are often implemented before they are imposed or otherwise formally required.

People in winning companies address problems rather than conceal, ignore or avoid them. Hence, they do not build up to a point at which they are either insurmountable or appear to be. Steps are taken one at a time. A series of adjustments over time – some small others more fundamental - may allow winners to cope with radically altered circumstances.

Smart companies have an issue monitoring process (IMP) and undertake formal issue monitoring and management. If not undertaken more frequently this could be an annual exercise to which all board members, key personnel and even customers, suppliers and business partners might be asked to contribute. It should also precede any annual budgeting or planning.

IMP participants are asked to identify major issues, trends and developments in the external business environment, and consider: (i) how will they impact upon firstly the company and secondly its customers and suppliers; (ii) what the company needs to do in response at local, operating unit and group levels; and (iii) how it might be able to help customers and suppliers to respond (i.e. possible business opportunities).

Support tools such as those we will examine in later chapters can be used to share the results of issue monitoring and management and competitor analysis with key workgroups such as bid teams and key account managers. Winners take practical steps to make it very easy for people who can benefit from IMP findings to access and use them as and when they are required.

Experienced users of IMP find that it is difficult to track more than ten issues at any one time, and better to concentrate effort on a smaller number of the more significant issues. To aid comprehension the summary of each issue, its impacts and what needs to be done in response should, ideally, be no more than a page. Those reporting issues should be asked to think through their implications and make practical recommendations for action to confront challenges and seize opportunities.

Significant positive developments and negative issues need to be continuously managed. If left unchecked even minority interests can grow like waterway weeds and block navigation. Proactive approaches can generate considerable goodwill. For example, BP-Amoco acknowledged the risks of global warming ahead of other oil companies and announced its intention of securing specific reductions in carbon dioxide emissions over a defined period.

★ *Further Information*

Information on the forthcoming companion volume on transforming corporate performance will be available on www.policypublications.com

'Transforming the Company, Manage Change, Compete and Win' by Colin Coulson-Thomas and published by Kogan Page can be ordered by Tel. 01903 828800; Fax. 020 7837 6348; E-mail: orders@lbsltd.co.uk or on-line at www.ntwkfirm.com/bookshop

'Shaping Things to Come, strategies for creating alternative enterprises' by Colin Coulson-Thomas can be ordered from Blackhall Publishing (Tel: 00 353 1 2785090; Fax: 00 353 1 2784446; email: blackhall@eircom.net) or from the online bookshop www.ntwkfirm.com/bookshop

Checklist:

- Are you and/or your colleagues winners or losers at understanding the business and market environment?

- Do others regard you and /or your colleagues as winners or losers?
- Does the company monitor business, technological, political, environmental, social and other issues, trends and developments in the business and market environment continuously?
- Does the company's vision, and related goals and values reflect the issues, trends and developments that are being tracked? Has the vision been communicated and shared?
- Is the company aware of the views of customers, employees, suppliers, business partners and other 'stakeholders' on issues, trends and developments that are being tracked?
- Has the company carried out any form of SWOT analysis to examine strengths, weaknesses, opportunities and threats?
- Has it determined how these and issues, trends and developments in the business and market environment will impact upon its operations and activities and those of its customers?
- What does the company plan to do in response?
- Have clear and measurable objectives been derived from the vision, goals and values relating to key issues, and is there an agreed strategy for their implementation?
- Are there clear roles and responsibilities for adressing key issues and responding?
- Have 'vital few' priorities been established, and have likely barriers and obstacles been identified?
- Are people motivated to respond and deliver, and have they been equipped and empowered to take the necessary actions?
- Have the cross-functional processes and the inter-departmental linkages necessary to deliver appropriate corporate responses been identified and appropriate critical success factors, winning ways and support tools put in place?

Appendix to Chapter 2 : Issue monitoring and management

Smart people are awake and aware. They keep an eye on factors affecting their current activities and future prospects. Organizations need alert and intelligent systems and procedures for: (i) understanding what is happening within the context or environment in which they operate; (ii) assessing what the impacts of the most significant trends and developments are likely to be; and (iii) determining what could or should be done in response. The following questions should be posed:

- Are you and your colleagues fully aware of what is happening around you? What steps do you take to identify and track potential threats and significant opportunities?
- Does your organization systematically monitor the impact of external changes upon itself and its customers, suppliers, business partners and own people?
- Does your company understand the major issues, trends and developments affecting each of the markets in which it operates? Is it aware of the likely calendar of any events of particular relevance to its operations, activities and prospects?
- Have you identified the boundaries of current knowledge? Where is the greatest progress being made, or does it need to occur, in terms of the development of new knowledge and improved understanding?
- In which of these areas is your organization active? Where could it make the greatest contribution to the creation and exploitation of new know-how?
- What is happening in the economic, social, political and technological environment that could have a significant impact upon your organization and its key stakeholders?
- In particular, how is the emergence of the 'information age' and 'knowledge society', and the globalisation of markets for information, knowledge and understanding, likely to affect it?
- Does your organization have access to the information, knowledge, and relationships required to effectively identify, monitor and assess relevant trends and developments?
- What are the possible impacts and future implications for your organization of any identified trends and developments likely to be?
- Have you and/or your colleagues assessed the potential consequences for its operations and people? Have the results of this analysis been shared with those who are most directly concerned?
- How will customers, prospects, suppliers and business partners be affected? What are the implications for their relationships with your organization?
- In relation to customers and prospects, what new needs or additional requirements might be generated? Which of these represent business opportunities?
- What obstacles and barriers are being removed, and what new ones are being created? What are the implications for future threats and opportunities?

- What does the organization need to do in response at local, unit, national and international levels? Who will monitor and coordinate the various reactions?
- What other people and/or organizations are likely to be similarly affected? Do they have compatible interests, shared concerns and complementary capabilities? What scope is there for collective action?
- Are effective processes in place for involving all relevant parties in the determination and implementation of what needs to be done in response to identified threats and opportunities?
- Does your organization participate in collaborative arrangements for making effective and collective representations at local, regional, national, European and international levels?
- Do outputs from your organization's issue monitoring and management processes feed into its planning and direction setting processes?

Inputs into an issue monitoring and management process should be practical, succinct and honest. Obstacles, barriers and risks should be reported rather than concealed. Issues should neither be played down nor exaggerated. Everyone involved should be encouraged to 'tell it as it is'.

Chapter 3
Creating a Compelling Vision

Are your people, and those with whom you deal, clear about what your organisation is endeavouring to achieve? In this chapter we will examine what leaders of the most successful companies do differently when setting about the strategically important task of visioning.

A stretching, distinctive and compelling vision that paints a picture of a future, desired and attainable state of affairs can engage and motivate. A clear vision is of value internally and externally. Internally it motivates people to achieve and focus their efforts, while externally the vision should differentiate a company from its competitors.

The board is primarily responsible for formulating and agreeing a company's strategic vision and ensuring its implementation. In some companies particular individuals have been given the specific task of ensuring that a corporate vision remains current and vital. These keepers of the vision attract various job titles. At USA.net someone known as the Chief Visionary was appointed to undertake the role.

A vision should capture the essence of what a company is all about. At the start of the new millennium Steve Ballmer became CEO of Microsoft. His predecessor Bill Gates a co-founder of the company assumed the title of chairman and chief software architect. The latter role allowed Gates to return to his roots and the activities he most enjoyed. It also reflected the importance of a strategic vision in the development of new technologies.

Some visions motivate more than others. Staff at the BBC became much more engaged when the public broadcaster's vision was changed from 'to be the best managed organisation in the public sector' and became 'to be the world's most creative organisation'. A vision and a mission statement should balance the needs of both individuals and the organisation along the lines of Amazon's 'Work Hard, Have Fun, Make History'.

Internally and externally, the common and shared element of a vision should be a unifying factor. It should hold a diverse, complex and network form of organisation together and provide its people with a sense of common purpose. Yet while a vision can inspire, it can also result in disillusionment and distrust if it is incomplete or incapable of achievement, and there is a gap between aspiration and attainment.

So what do the winners do differently in relation to visioning? To answer this question the research programme led by the author (see appendix A) has examined the corporate experience of over 2,000 companies. The results are summarized in the author's forthcoming book on transforming corporate performance and in 'Transforming the Company, Manage Change, Compete and Win', while exercises that boards can undertake to develop new offerings and distinct strategies are set out in 'Shaping Things to Come'*. Winners and losers are distinguished by their visions.

The corporate visions of losers are often little more than words on paper. Most are instantly forgettable. A bland statement produced during an off-site 'planning day' is printed on a card and distributed to staff. Although it may make occasional appearances in corporate brochures it is rarely referred to. Whatever 'visioning exercise' was undertaken is viewed as a one-off event. The outputs may linger on in unchanged form long after they have ceased to reflect what is possible, current or desirable.

Loser companies often lack a distinctive or compelling reason for existing. They are one of a kind or breed. They are not noticeably special or unique. People find it difficult to justify why they should join a 'loser' company, work with it, use its services or invest in it. Perhaps the initial underlying business concept lacked originality. Maybe it simply mirrored what competitors were already doing.

The wider world tends not to care when losers falter. External parties may have little interest in keeping such an enterprise alive. The corporate herd continues as individual stragglers fall by the wayside. Even failure may go largely unnoticed. While employees lose their jobs customers may be able to obtain very similar products and services from other suppliers.

Many of the key players within loser companies are uncertain and insecure. They lack self-confidence and have little self-esteem. Other people have little interest or faith in them. They themselves are not really sure what they are about. In difficult circumstances they may not have sufficient inner conviction or do enough to keep the enterprise alive. They throw in the towel and are relieved when shot of onerous responsibilities.

Losers can appear dull, resigned and subdued. They drift. They seem to lack drive, personality, heart and soul. Senior managers in corporate losers become preoccupied with 'fitting in', 'hanging onto customers', 'papering over cracks' and surviving. After a time they lose sight of corporate objectives and lose touch with past dreams and their inner selves.

In contrast, winners are confident, vibrant and driven. They fizz and are clear about what they are seeking to achieve. They are much more likely to have articulated a unique rationale. They endeavour to root their visions in real customer requirements. When it is described, people react. They usually understand it and they appreciate what is special about it.

Managers in winning companies feel important and wanted. They ensure that employees and business partners know what they have to do to bring a vision about. The vision lives and motivates because while it may be challenging it is also regarded as relevant and exciting. People are proud to be associated with it.

Winners stand out. They strive to be different. From the moment she first arrived in New York Madonna endeavoured to meet the people who mattered. She registered and was remembered. Her single-minded determination to build her personal brand has made her a global icon. Richard Branson's ballooning exploits have helped to keep his name in front of the public and entrench his reputation as a business leader who is different from the traditional 'suit'.

Winning businesses connect. They also contribute. Their people try to make them special and unique. Customers may find it difficult to obtain similar goods and services elsewhere. They would certainly notice and be inconvenienced if the enterprise failed. Like investors they want it to do well.

When a winner stumbles other people catch their breath. They are concerned. Because it's role and contribution is important to them a variety of 'interested parties' including customers, suppliers and business partners might be willing to provide temporary support during difficult times. Because business fundamentals and the critical success factors for competitiveness are in place investors may be willing to provide additional funding to allow a winning company to ride out an occasional storm.

Winners never rest on their laurels or become complacent. Their people are restless. They search, test, learn and apply. Directors of winning companies are much more likely to regularly review their vision, purpose, key corporate goals and strategies during board meetings to ensure they are still current and relevant. If they are found wanting people throughout the organisation make whatever changes are necessary to reflect altered conditions and evolving requirements.

They are also much more confident, and less likely to 'cut and run' in crisis situations. Obstacles, difficulties and the unknown invariably confront those who venture ahead of the pack. People in winning companies derive self-worth and inner strength from the knowledge that their organisation is valued and needed. Senior managers do not need to play games or pretend the know things. They trust their instincts and are not afraid to be themselves.

Eternal parties who deal with winners know where they stand with them. While they may be flexible and prepared to bend so far in the search for accommodation they are unwilling to compromise cherished principles and core values. They also avoid promising more than they can deliver.

Winners are determined. Like a predator they play to their strengths and can also be patient when waiting for the right moment to go after an opportunity. They acknowledge and confront challenges. In difficult times they are open and honest with those whose support they seek. They tell it as it is and share rather than conceal reality as they understand it. As a consequence, they are more likely to receive help when they ask for it.

★*Further Information*

Information on the forthcoming companion volume on transforming corporate performance will be available on www.policypublications.com

'Transforming the Company, Manage Change, Compete and Win' by Colin Coulson-Thomas and published by Kogan Page can be ordered by Tel. 01903 828800; Fax. 020 7837 6348; E-mail: orders@lbsltd.co.uk or on-line at www.ntwkfirm.com/bookshop

'Shaping Things to Come, strategies for creating alternative enterprises' by Colin Coulson-Thomas can be ordered from Blackhall Publishing (Tel: 00 353 1 2785090; Fax: 00 353 1 2784446; email: blackhall@eircom.net) or from the online bookshop www.ntwkfirm.com/bookshop

Checklist:

- When it comes to creating a compelling vision are you and/or your colleagues winners or losers?
- Do others regard you and /or your colleagues as winners or losers?
- Does the company have a distinctive vision that is rooted in the reality of customer requirements?
- Does it involve the development of new and distinctive marketplace offerings?
- Will customers be offered alternatives and genuine choices?

- Has the vision been agreed by the board, and communicated and shared with the people of the company, and with its customers, suppliers and business partners?
- Do people remember the vision? What does it mean to them?
- What would you do differently if you had not heard of the vision?
- Is there a clear, comprehensive and realistic strategy for implementing the vision?
- Is the strategy a document in a filing cabinet or a working process?
- Is it to be implemented through quantifiable objectives that are consistent with the goals and values of the company?
- Do all those with the responsibility for delivering each objective know what is expected of them?
- Have they the motivation, skills and necessary discretion to 'make it happen'?
- Have the resources and other implications of implementation been thought through?
- Have the implementation 'helps and hinders' been identified?
- In particular, have all the necessary management and business processes been established and relevant critical success factors, winning ways and support tools put in place?
- What is being done to identify all those activities within the organization that are either not compatible with, or not contributing to, the objectives of the organization?

Chapter 4
Creating a Winning Board

The boards of many companies axe jobs, cripple prospects and destroy shareholder wealth. Enron was advised by leading professionals, used fashionable approaches and invested in the latest technologies. Yet it all went wrong. What did the corporation's directors overlook? What do boards of successful companies do differently?

The leading performance improvement and transformation research programme led by the author (see appendix A) has examined why some companies grow while others stagnate. The experience of over 2,000 enterprises reveals that the prime responsibility for wide gaps between potential and achievement, and between intentions and outcomes, lies in the boardroom. In this chapter we consider the attitudes and approaches that distinguish between successful boards (winners) and unsuccessful boards (losers).

The essence of the difference in approach and behaviour between effective and ineffective boards, and the critical success factors for competing and winning that have been identified suggest that: (i) the corporate governance debate has done little to improve the contribution of many boards; and (ii) a different balance may need to be struck in many boardrooms*.

Corporate performance depends primarily upon what boards actually do and how their members behave. Winning boards are distinguished by the attitudes and conduct of their members. Corporate governance arrangements are often a symptom rather than a cause of board effectiveness.

The board should be the heart and soul of a company, the source of its ambition and drive. Whether or not a company competes and wins, sustains success and remains relevant usually depends upon its board. Without a sense of purpose, a sound strategy and the will to achieve, well endowed corporations wither and die.

Winning boards display the will to win and are driven to succeed. Their actions demonstrate they care. They understand what is happening in the business environment and marketplace. They anticipate events. They confront realities, take a longer-term view and provide strategic leadership.

Directors of winning boards assume personal and collective accountability for their actions. They understand the distinction between direction and management, and their directorial duties and responsibilities.

Winning boards concentrate upon the external, strategic and business development aspects of corporate governance. They strive to benefit shareholders by delivering additional value to customers. They provide and communicate clear direction, a distinctive vision, a compelling purpose, achievable goals and clear objectives.

Winners focus upon the critical success factors for competing and winning. They develop additional income streams, new capabilities and fresh intellectual capital. They invest in director development and the professional selection, appointment and induction of new directors. Their chairmen consciously build effective boards of competent directors.

In comparison, 'loser' boards lack will, drive and heart. Their members mouth generalizations and are easily distracted by pleasantries and trivia. They avoid responsibility and blame others for disappointing results. Their perspective is essentially defensive and short-term.

The directors of losing companies are preoccupied with their own status and remuneration. They confuse the roles of director, manager and shareholder. They concentrate upon internal, policing and stewardship aspects of corporate governance, and engage in spin and damage limitation exercises to protect their reputations.

'Loser' directors confuse operational and strategic issues, and muddy personal and corporate interests. Many charming individuals who effortlessly assemble portfolios of independent directorships instinctively know when to look the other way and can be relied upon not to rock the boat. Insecure chief executives seek out their services.

Board members of loser companies fail to engage, excite or motivate people. They respond to developments rather than influence events. They focus almost exclusively upon financial measures of performance and the control of costs. They make little effort to review and improve their own effectiveness.

The boards of both winner and loser companies attract articulate and highly paid people. However, they distinguish themselves particularly in their respective approaches to managing change, leading transformation and creating future opportunities.

Winning boards inspire, energise and motivate. They avoid rhetoric, blather and hype and address specific issues. They are determined, pragmatic and positive. They strive for success rather than survival. Instead of rationalizing disappointment they learn from it.

Winners are also proactive. They approach those they would like to do business with. They set out to become business partners rather than commodity suppliers. They are also selective. They focus upon areas that make a difference. They understand that change can disrupt valued relationships, and only change what needs to be changed.

Winners support and enable the achievements of others. They trust reliable people and take calculated risks. They delegate and encourage entrepreneurship. They ensure their people are equipped with the tools to do what is expected of them. In comparison, losers are self-interested and fear the unknown. They play it safe and avoid commitments.

'Losers' mouth platitudes, spread themselves thinly, and bark up the wrong trees. They also react, imitate and copy. They jump on band-waggons and adopt me-too approaches. They duck issues, fall for fads, embrace panaceas and search for single solutions.

Winners think for themselves and reflect before they act. They read the road ahead and assemble what they need to succeed. They adopt simple solutions and differentiate their companies' approaches, products and services. They shape the future by creating bespoke offerings, additional choices and new markets.

Finally, winning boards are self-aware. They monitor their own performance. They are open, welcome questions and invite feedback. They critique themselves and encourage challenge. They choose pragmatic colleagues and competent advisers.

Further Information

★'Developing Directors, A handbook for building an effective boardroom team' is published by Policy Publications in association with Adaptation and can be ordered from 00 44 (0)1733 361 149 and http://www.policypublications.com/developingdirectors.htm

'Developing Directors' identifies the knowledge, skills and personal qualities required by directors and defines the competent director and the effective board. It looks at the route to the boardroom and how to become a director, and how directors are and should be prepared. Developing the boardroom team, evaluating board performance and practical next steps are also considered.

The handbook is packed with exercises and checklists which have been specifically designed for boardroom participation. For those concerned with understanding and addressing the fundamentals the book also examines the development challenge, the roles of directors and boards, the distinction between direction and management and factors affecting team work in the boardroom.

'Developing Directors' is designed for chairmen and directors, consultants and trainers charged with the task of developing dynamic boardroom teams to lead the organizations of today. It draws upon the author's extensive experience of working with directors and boards, and provides practical advice on identifying and developing the qualities, competencies, and approaches needed for greater directorial contribution, board effectiveness and corporate success.

'Shaping Things to Come, strategies for creating alternative enterprises' by Colin Coulson-Thomas can be ordered from Blackhall Publishing (Tel: 00 353 1 2785090; Fax: 00 353 1 2784446; email: blackhall@eircom.net) or from the online bookshop www.ntwkfirm.com/bookshop

Checklist:

- Are the organisation's directors winners or losers?
- Do others regard the members of the board as winners or losers?
- In relation to its collective approach, decsions, activities and impact would you describe the board as a 'winner' or a 'loser'?
- Who is responsible for ensuring that the board is effective and composed of directors that individually and collectively are competent?
- Does the board evaluate its own effectiveness at least once a year?
- What does the board do to benchmark itself against other boards?
- Is the nature of the board and how it conducts its operations appropriate to the situation and circumstances of the company?
- Is the board aware of its accountabilities to various stakeholders?
- Does the board fully understand the requirements of the various stakeholders in the company?
- Have the cross-functional and inter-organizational processes that deliver these requirements been identified and relevant critical success factors, winning ways and support tools put in place?
- Are the individual members of the board aware of their legal duties and responsibilities as directors?
- Has the board identified a distinctive purpose for the company, and agreed and shared a compelling vision?
- Has the board agreed and shared clear goals and values, established measurable objectives and put a performance management framework in place?

- Have the 'vital few' actions that must be done been identified, and roles and responsibilities relating to their achievement been allocated?
- Does the board pay sufficient attention to the implementation of objectives and policies?
- Are the enablers, critical success factors and resource requirements for implementation in place?
- Are the people of the organization motivated, empowered and equipped with the necessary skills and support tools to make it happen?

Chapter 5
Providing Strategic Leadership

The critical importance of the board was established in the last chapter. Director and board development represents a huge arena of opportunity. Direction is a separate but complementary activity to management and establishes the framework of aspirations, goals, values and policies within which the people of an organisation operate. Yet while large investments are made in management training director and board development is largely overlooked in many companies and public bodies.

A companion volume I have written, 'Developing Directors; a handbook for building an effective boardroom team'* which is also published by Policy Publications provides guidance, exercises and checklists for creating an effective board of competent directors. In this chapter we will look at what directors and boards that provide strategic leadership do differently from those that do not.

Whether or not a particular board is perceived as an overhead cost or a source of focus and inspiration, and regarded as an obstacle or an enabler, will reflect its own view of its role. Too many boards concentrate upon 'staying alive', and responding to good or bad news, rather than proactively guiding their organizations towards the achievement of corporate goals.

The reality of the boardroom is often very different from the requirements for successful corporate governance. The very people who should be the fount of corporate drive and purpose are frequently plagued by insecurity and doubt.

The actual operation of boards is clouded by myth, uncertainty and misunderstanding. Here are some examples:

- Many directors are uncertain as to their directorial duties and responsibilities. Others experience a conflict between the different roles which they may have. An executive director could be a director, a manager and an owner, and in each role might be expected to have a distinct perspective on certain issues.
- In many companies, the allocation of responsibilities between the board and management is unclear. This can lead to confusion, both in the boardroom and throughout the senior management team.

- New members of a board are typically selected on account of being thought to possess directorial qualities. Once appointed, however, if executive directors are assessed at all, they are likely to be evaluated in terms of their managerial performance in running a department or activity rather than their directorial contributions to the business of the board.
- In few companies is there a clear path to the boardroom. The qualities sought in new directors are rarely made explicit. Hence, many managers with directorial ambitions find it very difficult to prepare for membership of the board.

Boards must focus on opportunities to make the greatest contribution to the achievement of strategic corporate goals. Too often there is an almost exclusive preoccupation with matters that could be described as 'nice to have'. While desirable in themselves they will not make the difference between winning and losing.

The board itself, in terms of its own role-model behaviour, may be partly to blame for the disillusionment that is found in many companies as a result of the growing gap between initial expectations of corporate change programmes and what is actually being achieved. The failure of 'actions to match words' is the source of much misunderstanding and distrust, as follows:

- Under pressure to perform and survive, the focus of many (particularly UK and US) boards has been visibly internal and short term, while the messages that have been communicated to managers have encouraged them to develop longer-term relationships with external customers.

- While directors advocate the transition to a team-based form of organization, the effectiveness of many boards has been limited by poor teamwork. Improved communication, open discussion, regular meetings and a shared or common purpose can help ensure that a board works effectively as a team.
- Many boards that call for a 'focus upon the customer' have not initiated activities to identify the key business processes that deliver customer satisfaction or provided customer facing staff with support tools that would enable them to undertake bespoke responses to the requirements of individual customers. Boards are defining goals without ensuring that the mechanisms are in place to achieve them.
- While the rhetoric of many boards stresses the need to put the customer first, their ordering of business objectives and the

reward systems of their companies result in managers concentrating upon other priorities.
- Boards talk about 'continuous improvement' and the need to develop people, while failing to identify and address their own deficiencies. Many boards do not even recognize the need for improvement. Dissatisfaction is accepted simply because of an inability to determine how it might be addressed.
- Among those who advocate 'benchmarking' and the merits of the 'learning organization', there is little evidence of experimentation with new ways of organizing boards. Peer reviews by other boards, or the benchmarking of other boards, is rarely undertaken.

Directors of loser companies often fail to distinguish between operational and strategic matters. They get lost in the detail and are reluctant to delegate responsibilities to an effective management team. Such board meetings as are held tend to be rambling, unstructured and unfocused. Attendees may be largely unaware of their duties and responsibilities as directors and oblivious of significant developments and what is really important.

Winners establish an effective board. This gives them an edge in difficult circumstances. Competent directors are aware of their duties to the company itself and they endeavour to act in its best interests and the interests of stakeholders. Looking ahead enables them to identify obstacles and opportunities. For example, they may anticipate a drop in turnover and periods of peak borrowing requirements in time to take corrective action.

Regular meetings and accurate minutes enable specific responsibilities to be allocated and subsequent actions monitored. Losers avoid confrontations. Their meetings have a tendency to become polite rituals. Winners are much more willing to challenge, critique and probe. They question colleagues and hold people to account.

One means of introducing a form of peer review at a senior level is to appoint two or more independent directors to a properly constituted corporate board. Among smaller companies losers tend to avoid this step. Their reasons for caution are as varied as the extra costs involved and the risk of losing control. As a result, the principals of the business may confuse their respective roles as shareholder, manager and director.

People who are not subject to checks and balances sometimes 'go off the rails'. External parties may sense danger when they encounter a board consisting entirely of founder entrepreneurs who are still active in a business and who insist upon calling most of the shots. Those who initially established an enterprise may not be the best people to take it forward to the next stage of development.

Customers, employees, creditors, business partners and investors may all be reassured by the very existence of a balanced, confident, capable and committed board. The active involvement of effective directors may result in a premium being attached to share valuations, particularly when certain individuals have the skills and experience to encourage and support the further growth of a company.

Boards of losers undertake annual reviews of performance and competitiveness to identify problem areas. They concentrate upon the discussion of past performance and formulate general objectives that are imposed upon the people of the organization. When outcomes fail to match expectations results are fudged, concealed or rationalized, or spin is used to make them appear better than they really are.

In contrast, the directors of winners engage in regular reviews and continually monitor corporate performance. They focus upon resolving issues and taking steps to improve future competitiveness. They are also realists. They know that if there is a gap somewhere in the length of a hedge at least one sheep in the flock will find it. If there is a weak point, the cows will break through.

The direction and guidance that directors of winners give is simple, clear and specific, and they themselves act as role models. They operate as they expect others to behave. They assume accountability for their actions, conduct and decisions and they encourage accurate reporting and honest feedback.

Losers tend to regard observing the principles of good corporate governance as an end in itself. They think in terms of current structures rather than future opportunities. So long as the right committees are in place and their members turn up for meetings directors are thought to earn their fees.

Winners are more concerned with what the board and its committees actually do, for example to release talent and build and mobilize the capability to deliver greater value to more customers and hence achieve corporate objectives. They provide strategic leadership and support internal entrepreneurs. They ensure their companies remain vital and competitive.

Losers tend to follow others and be reactive. They also look over their shoulders, benchmark and copy. As a consequence they lose control of their destinies. They are insensitive, unaware and fail to anticipate events. Crises catch them unawares and they struggle to respond. Their lack of foresight puts them under time pressure and their inflexibility limits their options.

People in losing companies simply process items that fall into their in-trays. Business development teams respond to incoming invitations to tender. They wait for others to approach them. They reply to those who suggest deals, arrangements and joint venture or take-over proposals without first considering and clarifying their own objectives. Board meetings consider draft replies to the initiatives of others.

Losers can be a salesperson's dream. They agree to meet people who approach them with services to sell even though they may not have identified a requirement for what they are offered. They fall for sales patter and divert resources to distracting activities.

Smooth talkers can lead losers by the nose. Flattery can be used to persuade them to seek a listing.

Yielding to pressure or going with the flow is felt by losers to be easier than weighing up the options. Better alternatives are not considered. Steps taken may not be in the best long-term interests of the people involved. Observers may wonder whether the board or external advisers are calling the shots.

As we will see in other chapters, winners are more pro-active. They set out to systematically identify the organizations they would most like to have as customers, suppliers or business partners. They analyse the aspirations, strategies, requirements and capabilities of their targets and make a direct or indirect approach to them. They initiate contacts, suggest discussion topics, craft tailored offerings and submit proposals with advantages for all the parties involved.

There are other differences to look out for. Losers are tempted and distracted by personalities and surface appearance. They make the pursuit of the visible and the formulation of acceptable rhetoric a key element of policy, exaggerate achievements and talk up future prospects.

Losers conceal any divergence between aspiration and achievement, and often avoid grasping nettles and confronting harsh realities. They also close gaps between aspiration and achievement primarily by lowering expectations; and rationalize their failure to deliver, for example by stressing how difficult it is to achieve a successful corporate transformation. Losers are driven by insecurity to want and demand fast results; and remain frustrated and vulnerable to probing questions by auditors, shareholders and investors.

As we will see in the next chapter winners are more willing to probe, ask questions and challenge fundamental assumptions. They seek to penetrate surface appearance in order to understand the reality beneath. They avoid rhetoric and focus policy upon the reality of actual achievement. They give a balanced account of what has been accomplished and endeavour to make accurate and responsible forecasts.

In addition, winners acknowledge and make explicit gaps between aspiration and achievement and assess, address, manage and endeavour to close them by taking steps to raise achevements rather than reduce aspirations. In so doing they are not afraid to tackle difficult issues, take tough decisions and address realities.

Winners survive and learn from setbacks and persist in striving to achieve what they have set out to accomplish. While recognizing that some customers and investors may be impatient they are prepared to devote the time it may take to achieve a desired outcome. As a consequence of these and other behaviours examined in this book winners obtain the satisfaction and fulfilment of accomplishing much of what they set out to achieve.

Further information

*A companion volume 'Developing Directors; a handbook for building an effective boardroom team' explains how the reservoirs of latent potential that exist in many organisations can be tapped by director and board development. It addresses a desire for better board and corporate performance as well as contemporary concerns over corporate governance standards.

'Developing Directors' is published by Policy Publications in association with Adaptation and can be ordered from 00 44 (0)1733 361 149 and www.policypublications.com/developingdirectors.htm

'Shaping Things to Come, strategies for creating alternative enterprises' by Colin Coulson-Thomas can be ordered from Blackhall Publishing (Tel: 00 353 1 2785090; Fax: 00 353 1 2784446; email: blackhall@eircom.net) or from the online bookshop www.ntwkfirm.com/bookshop

Checklist:

- In relation to providing strategic leadership is the board a 'winner' or a 'loser'?
- Do others regard the members of the board as winners or losers?
- Does the board provide strategic leadership?
- Does it provide people with a distinctive and compelling vision?
- Are they enabled to live the vision?

- Have the aspirations of the company's business development prpogramme and corporate change and other programmes been clearly articulated?
- Have they been considered and agreed by the board? Is the board an instigator and driver or a rubber stamp?
- Does the board and its members display the characteristics of 'winners' or 'losers'?
- Does it inspire trust and encourage innovation?
- Does it back initiative and responsible risk taking?
- Have the boards aspirations, and resulting goals and objectives, been expressed in operational and measurable terms?
- Who within the company shares these aspirations? Are people equipped with the understanding and tools to turn aspirations into achievements?
- How aware is the top management of the company of gaps between aspiration and achievement?
- How willing are the directors and senior managers to confront reality?
- Is there agreement on the nature and extent of the gaps that have been identified?
- To what extent have any gaps between aspiration and achievement been publicly acknowledged and shared with the people of the company and other 'stakeholders'?
- Does the culture and reward system of the company encourage openness and trust, or avoidance and concealment?
- Are there areas in which the company has a conscious, if unstated, policy of rhetoric or concealment?
- Have the dangers and possible implications of such policies been thought through?
- Are the general and specific reasons for the existence of a gap between aspiration and achievement understood?
- How tolerant is the organization of mistakes?
- Has a 'helps and hinders' analysis been undertaken to identify specific barriers and obstacles to progress, and what needs to be done about them?
- Has the company's board and management team thought through how it should divide its effort between managing expectations and managing achievement?
- Who balances the make-up of the various elements in the company's business development and corporate renewal or transformation programme?
- Does the company fall prey to the lure of the fast result?

- Is the company considering a fundamental reassessment of some aspect of its corporate development and corporate transformation programme?
- Is this being undertaken for appropriate and valid reasons?

Chapter 6
Corporate Governance: Challenging conventional wisdom and shaping things to come

Too many boardrooms are like chapels of rest, the only signs of life being the ticking of corporate governance checklists. A handbook for ambitious directors* written by the author argues that if boards are to add more value and create a better tomorrow they must challenge conventional thinking and current practices. This chapter examines some further differences between successful and successful boards.

Many boards are failing to deliver. They are rubber stamping rather than shaping things to come, picking over the past rather than creating the future. Debates focus upon details and trappings within the rules of an existing game. Assumptions are not challenged. Efforts are not made to create a new game that might deliver more value to customers and shareholders and greater satisfaction to employees.

In a world of benchmarking and preoccupation with prevailing fashions and fads certain behaviours, approaches and practices are assumed. People with similar backgrounds to their peers go with the flow. They look over their shoulders at others and imitate and copy them. They use the same or similar tools, techniques, systems and processes. Not surprisingly they come to similar conclusions as their competitors.

Different suppliers produce very similar offerings aimed at the same and largest customer segment their analyses identify, even though the many smaller segments of the market ignored might collectively constitute an overwhelming majority of people whose requirements could have been better addressed by alternatives. Cosy consensus, inertia and intellectual laziness prevent many companies from providing new and better options. Fundamental questions need to be asked in boardrooms.

A systematic investigation of the differing approaches of successful companies (winners) and their unsuccessful competitors (losers) has assembled sets of questions that directors can use to challenge prevailing assumptions and create new offerings that provide greater choice for consumers and communities. 'Shaping Things to Come' is a handbook for bringing more creative thinking into the boardroom★.

The essence of good corporate governance is to achieve an appropriate balance between a number of critical factors, for example performance today and the capability to compete and win in the future. The investigation of how directors actually behave reveals that the practices and unchallenged assumptions of many boards are likely to condemn them to presiding over a losing company.

Striking a different balance, for example between activity and reflection or between action and reaction is often the key to greater boardroom effectiveness and marketplace success. Thus, whereas many losers appear to value activity for its own sake, reflection was much more evident among the members of successful boards. Often losers are so busy that they simply do not have time to think.

The concern of losers to be seen to be active and to be 'doing things' is evident in their approach to change. They exhibit an unquestioning and naïve faith in the benefits of change. Very often changes appear to be made for changes sake, for fear that a lack of restructuring or re-organisation might be taken as an indication that they are 'asleep on the job'.

Winners strive to achieve a balance between change and continuity. They recognize that while some change may be desirable, indeed inevitable, it can also be stressful and disruptive of valued relationships. Continuity is important in areas such as purpose and service. Customers who are unsure of what to expect may become unsettled, and they might take their custom elsewhere.

Looking at the balance different groups strike, for example between change and continuity or complexity and simplicity is also the key to creating new offerings. Thus many consumers - from members of re-enactment groups to purchasers of classic brands and houses with Georgian features in conservation villages - may favour continuity and might prefer aspects of the past. Others might desire products with fewer features that are easier to understand and use.

Losers are also more pre-occupied with reacting to the competitive moves of others, following fashions and jumping upon bandwagons. In comparison, winners are more likely to be proactive, for example when seeking ways of helping their customers and delivering more value to them. They take the initiative and approach prospects they would like to do business with, and work with them and business partners to explore new possibilities. They are not afraid to venture out in front, explore and discover.

Whereas losers are also pre-occupied with their own agendas and the achievement of corporate objectives, winners are more concerned with achieving a balance between individual and corporate interests. If changes have to be introduced they will strive to ensure they benefit the people concerned as well as help achieve corporate goals. They recognize that relationships which are mutually beneficial to all parties involved are more likely to last.

Directors, particularly independent directors, should question, probe and challenge. Is the right balance being struck in the above and other areas examined? Is there too much focus upon fads while insufficient attention is paid to the fundamentals - the core building blocks of corporate success, the critical success factors for competing and winning? Is the board addressing surface symptoms or the underlying substance?

Losing boards of struggling companies engage in spin to explain and rationalize events where winners would identify and address root causes. A balance has also to be achieved between packaging and assembling the elements that make up the package. Within the mix that makes some directors competent and certain boards effective the willingness to pose critical questions that others overlook or are reluctant to ask can be a crucial ingredient.

To increase the likelihood of becoming a winning company, consciously build an effective board of competent and questioning directors. Avoid the distractions of trappings. Invest in director and board development. Be professional when selecting, appointing and inducting new directors. Go for those likely to shake the cage.

Some individuals add value, others are parasitic or distractions. Aspiring winners should avoid the bloodsucker brigade and devious courtiers. Don't let your board become a form of outdoor relief for the semi-retired. Select practical and competent contributors. Find candidates who are quiet thinkers and will do what is right.

Further Information

★'Shaping Things to Come, strategies for creating alternative enterprises' (ISBN: 1 901657 87 6, £27.50) by Colin Coulson-Thomas can be ordered from Blackhall Publishing (Tel: 00 353 1 2785090; Fax: 00 353 1 2784446; email: blackhall@eircom.net) or from www.ntwkfirm.com/bookshop

Guidance on director and board development is given in 'Developing Directors, A handbook for building an effective boardroom team' which is published by Policy Publications in association with Adaptation and can be ordered from 00 44 (0)1733 361 149 and www.policypublications.com/developingdirectors.htm

Checklist:

- In relation to providing good governance is the board a 'winner' or a 'loser'?
- Do others regard the members of the board as winners or losers?
- Is the board achieving an appropriate balance between activity and reflection; between 'internal' and 'external' issues; between 'today' and 'tomorrow'; and between the interests of different groups of stakeholders?
- Do the policies and activities of the board benefit both the organisation and its people?
- Are the right questions being asked in the boardroom? In particular, is the board focused upon critical success factors for competing and winning?
- Is the board committed to ensuring that critical success factors and the winning ways of high performers are built into key processes?
- Are directors focused upon realities, fundamentals and root causes, or are they distracted by spin, fads and surface appearance?
- Are they prepared to challenge fundamental assumptions?
- Do the directors get lost in excessive complexity or do they aim for simplicity and transparency?
- Where issues and developments are intinsically complex do the directors take practical steps to help people to understand complex matters and undertake difficult tasks?
- Are members of the board proactive or do they largely react to events?
- Are high performers inside and outside of the organisation identified, and are efforts made to identify what they do differently?
- Does the board take steps to enable key work groups within the organisation to emulate the approaches and winning ways of high achievers?
- Does the board introduce changes for change's sake or do the directors only change what needs to be changed while consiously preserving what is valuable?
- Do the directors operate behind prison bars that have been created in their own imaginations?

- Are they imitating and copying others, or are they creating new opportunities and choices?

Chapter 7
Differentiation: Strategies for creating alternative enterprises

From time to time most boards are impatient for more sales. Directors grumble about the lack of interest shown by targeted prospects in corporate offerings, poor media coverage or disappointing reactions to presentations. But why should anyone be interested in their company's activities? What is distinctive about what they provide or do?

Research into the differing approaches of successful and unsuccessful companies (see appendix A) has resulted in guidance* for challenging cherished assumptions and creating new offerings that provide customers with additional choices. In this chapter we learn that businesses must be distinctive and differentiate their offerings to survive.

Many advertisements, mail shots, brochures and press releases fail to capture the attentions of their recipients or excite their imaginations. We are interrupted by sales calls and inundated with junk mail. Proposals and prospectuses all seem the same. People sell to us rather than help us to buy by highlighting what is different about their offerings.

Consider your own company. Can you quickly communicate what it does? What is special or unique about its offerings? Do pitches for new business or requests for additional funding register and succeed? Do your colleagues' presentations bite? Does your corporate literature stand out? Is your presence noticed at exhibitions?

Does your company struggle to differentiate its offerings? If so, consider what the world would lose if it ceased to operate. What is different about its purpose, goals, values, brands, image and reputation? Does it offer new options and choices?

Above all, does your business supply its customers and offer its prospects goods and services that they cannot get elsewhere. If your company were to close down how much inconvenience would its customers really suffer? Could they obtain similar offerings from your competitors?

Many struggling enterprises or losers find it difficult to motivate their people, stand out and justify premium prices. They lack a compelling rationale and distinctive purpose. Their offerings and messages to the marketplace are largely indistinguishable from those of other suppliers. In short, many losers are bland, faceless or boring.

There is little excuse for this sorry state of affairs. There are countless possibilities for differentiation, and also endless opportunities for consumer, social and knowledge entrepreneurship. 'Me-too' approaches, copying and imitation lead to squeezed margins and consumer indifference. Increasingly, market leadership goes to those who create, pioneer and discover.

Although trading conditions may sometimes be tough and competitive pressures can be severe, smart companies or winners balance cost cutting with innovation. They break out of commodity product traps by differentiating their offerings. They deliver additional value to justify higher prices. They provide alternatives and address unmet needs.

Ambitious entrepreneurs do not wait for an economic upturn. Winners generate additional income streams by creating bespoke products for individual customers and establishing new markets. They bring their proposals and business plans alive with interesting angles, unusual approaches and novel offerings. They intrigue prospects, attract customers and secure venture capital or place new shares by being different.

Cautious suppliers play it safe. Losers tend to follow the herd. They seek refuge in large numbers and aim at the biggest market segments. They try not to make exceptions for particular customers in order to avoid 'systems problems' or increased transaction costs.

More courageous suppliers find that technological advances are making it easier to address individual needs. Mass customization is possible in ever more sectors. The Internet offers a cost-effective way of reaching scattered members of minority interests, people with common passions, shared obsessions and complementary aspirations. There may be enough of them to justify the creation of new and distinct offerings.

Increasingly, customers also like to stand out. More of them are demanding goods and services that reflect their individuality and personal requirements. They may be prepared to pay a higher price for customization through particular modifications, the addition of requested features or a more distinctive design.

Questions should be asked to determine whether the board of your company is adopting the losing approach of encouraging conformity and uniformity or behaving like the more successful winners and stimulating challenge and diversity. For example:

- How much emphasis is placed upon conforming to a corporate culture, exhibiting role model behaviour, benchmarking, competitor analysis and sharing received wisdom?
- In comparison, how much importance is placed upon innovation, individual expression, diversity, differentiation, entrepreneurship and aspiring to be distinctive, memorable and relevant?
- Do people dare to question and dissent from prevailing opinions? Do formal reviews and development activities explicitly embrace the personal qualities and skills needed to be different, craft novel offerings, and create genuine choices?
- Are people equipped with the tools needed to challenge prevailing activities and assumptions?
- Are innovations, departures from the norm and breakthroughs that create distinctive value rewarded?
- Do incentives encourage people to become more effective at playing current games, or do they inspire them to create new and alternative games?
- Are new people explicitly recruited to 'enrich the gene pool' and increase diversity?
- To what extent are the company's people, processes, knowledge, working environments and supporting infrastructure conducive of reflection and learning, distinctive and a source of differentiation from competitors?

There are many ways of creating genuine alternatives. For example, we could strike a different balance between delivery time and distinctiveness. Many of us would not make the trade-offs that certain suppliers decide on our behalf. Enthusiasts for custom-built cars forgo fuel economy from lower wind resistance and opt for designs that turn heads. Some consumers might prefer a more accessible product that has fewer features but which is easier to use and understand. Could they be offered a utility version?

Corporate communications should highlight what is special about an enterprise and it's activities. Do your company's people have special competencies? Do they work and learn in novel ways? Does it have exclusive access to - or ownership of - particular know-how or unusual approaches? Do its products and services provide memorable features?

Winners take steps to help customer facing staff to differentiate their offerings from those of competitors and explain the benefits and advantages of their products and services. Job support tools can be used for these purposes, and in later chapters we will examine the experience of companies that have equipped their sales teams and customer relationship managers with tools that make it easy for differentiators to be both grasped and communicated.

Does your company help prospects to understand its unique capabilities and buy its offerings? Does it use accessible tools (see www.cotoco.com) to assess requirements, configure and price solutions, and generate proposals? Do its people design personalized products and services? Can customers create their own offerings and 'try them out' in virtual worlds.

Differentiation requires a willingness to explore and discover. Winners are much more likely to be pioneers who dare to question. They reject bland consensus, middle ways and lowest common denominators. They think outside of the box.

Further Information

*'Shaping Things to Come, strategies for creating alternative enterprises' (ISBN: 1 901657 87 6, £27.50) by Colin Coulson-Thomas can be ordered from Blackhall Publishing (Tel: 00 353 1 2785090; Fax: 00 353 1 2784446; email: blackhall@eircom.net) or from www.ntwkfirm.com/bookshop/

The importance of differentiation is apparent in critical success factors for winning business set out in the 'Winning New Business' resource pack, winning business reports covering individual sectors and seven professions and related and the bespoke winning business benchmarking reports which can be obtained from Policy Publications: Tel: +44 (0) 1733 361 149, Fax: +44 (0)1733 361459 or online from either www.policypublications.com or www.ntwkfirm.com/policy-publications/

Checklist:

- In relation to differentiation do you view yourself and/or your colleagues as winners or losers?
- Do others view you and/or your colleagues as winners or losers?
- Does the organisation have a compelling reason for existing?
- What is unique, special or distinctive about it?
- Why should anyone outside of the organisation be interested in it or what you and your colleagues do?

- What is unique, special or distinctive about what you and your colleagues do?
- Can the organisation charge a price premium for its offerings?
- If the organisation stumbled who would be concerned, and who might wish to help?
- What would the world lose if the organisation ceased to exist?
- Would any one outside of the organisation notice or care?
- Could customers obtain similar products and services from other suppliers?
- Has the company provided them with additional options and choices?
- If there are differentiators, do the people of the organisation understand them?
- Are the people of your organisation equipped to quickly communicate the essence of what it is about and what is unique, special or distictive about it
- Are they helped to be different and provided with support tools that enable them to respond in a bespoke way to individual customers?
- Do the tools help them to understand the advantages of the company's offerings in comparison with those of competitors?

Chapter 8
Winning Competitive Bids

Most businesses would like to secure a higher proportion of the contracts they bid for. Bidding is a tough game. Competitive markets and falling barriers to entry strengthen the negotiating position of buyers. As more contracts are put out to competitive tender and new entrants are invited to bid, the prospects of winning a particular opportunity can fall.

As expectations rise, invitations to tender are also becoming more demanding. Proposals get larger and more expensive to prepare. The cost of lost bids have to be recovered out of a squeezed margin on those won. Companies that win too few bids are driven out of business. Enterprises need to succeed in competitive bid situations.

Yet some companies - according to a flow of reports from the Winning Business Research and Benchmarking Programme (see appendix B) - are much more successful than others at winning business. Studies undertaken cover sectors such as construction, engineering, manufacturing, IT and telecoms, and seven professions ranging from lawyers and accountants to engineering and management consultants.

The findings - which we examine in this chapter - are consistent and compelling. The approaches of the 'superstars' or winners enable them to regularly outperform the 'also rans' or losers included in bid races to 'make up the numbers'. Understanding the critical success factors for winning competitive bids and how high performers operate, and building them into winning business processes and job support tools (see also chapters 26 and 27) greatly increases the prospect of increasing overall win rates.

A wide gulf exists between winners and losers. They appear distinct species with very different attitudes and approaches. 'Losers' are undisciplined, unimaginative and reactive. They pursue far too many opportunities, and focus primarily upon their employers' concerns and priorities.

Members of 'loser' bid teams respond mechanically to invitations to tender. They are pre-occupied with the practicalities of producing proposals, such as obtaining cost information and CVs. They find themselves under pressure to meet submission deadlines. Yet they ignore tools that could speed up their basic activities and free up thinking time.

'Losers' 'hold back' and only commit significant effort when a prospect is 'seriously interested'. They describe their jobs in terms of 'submitting bids'. As winning business professionals they actually spend their days losing potential business as most proposals sent in are rejected. In businesses with below average success rates bid team members are left to 'get on with it'. Senior managers are rarely involved in individual opportunities.

'Losers' measure success by the number of proposals submitted. They make little effort to learn from experience or best practice. Rejection letters enable them to 'close the file' and move onto the next proposal. Above all, they don't mind loosing. Failure is accepted as the norm, and rationalised with phrases such as 'you can't win them all'.

'Winners' are very different from losers. They are far more confident and proactive. They identify prospects with growth potential that would make good business partners. They take the initiative and approach those they would most like to do business with.

'Winners' ruthlessly prioritise available opportunities. Turning down some invitations to bid allows more effort to be devoted to those retained. Construction company Henry Boot suffered a fall in turnover as a result of being more selective, but profitability significantly improved.

'Winners' want their customers and prospects to do well. They become absorbed in their problems and opportunities and focus responses and structure proposals upon prospect needs, priorities and selection criteria.

When winners do respond it is with commitment and clear objectives. They think through the outcomes and relationship they would like to achieve. They hit the ground running, and allocate sufficient resources early on to build up an unassailable lead.

Senior managers in the more successful companies participate in pitches. The visible and active support of senior management can be decisive in close contests. Redwood Publishing wrote its Managing Director into a proposal submitted to BT and won the business.

'Winners' try to understand how buying decisions are made. They identify and address the selection criteria being used. They consider the personalities involved and remain sensitive to changing buyer concerns throughout the purchasing process. They work hard to establish empathy, build trust, and match, the culture of prospects.

Wang successfully demonstrated 'cultural fit' prior to becoming a supplier of support services to Dell.

Where possible, 'winners' automate the more mechanical aspects of proposal production. Eyretel commissioned a laptop-based tool (see www.Cotoco.com) to enable its sales reps to access presentational information, configure and price solutions, and generate proposals. Time freed up is used to tailor responses, differentiate offerings and build relationships.

At the end of the day, 'winners' want to win. They are gutted when they lose. Win or lose, they regularly review their processes and practices, and debriefs are held to learn from both successes and failures.

The results of the Winning Business Research and Benchmarking Programme suggest the winners could do even better. The 'super bidders' - the 4% who win more than three out of four of the competitive races they enter - are only very effective at less than half of the 18 critical success factors identified by the report 'Winning New Business, the critical success factors'*. Quite simply, there is enormous opportunity for most businesses to significantly improve their 'hit rate'.

The gap between 'winners' and 'losers' can be bridged. 'Win rates' are directly related to how many of the 18 key factors a company is good at.

So what should you do to increase your win rate? As a first step, get hold of the 'Winning New Business, the critical success factors' report and/or the 'winning business' report for your industry or profession*. These spell out the relevant critical success factors. The individual reports also contain best practice case studies and commentaries by industry experts.

A related bespoke benchmarking service is also available, which allows you to compare your company's performance with both average and high achievers. The bespoke report that is generated highlights where your business is most behind the most successful bidders.

Review the skills of members of your company's bid teams. Another report produced by the Winning Business Research and Benchmarking Programme, 'Bidding for Business, the skills agenda' has identified the top twenty skills required for successful bidding and how to acquire them*. Thirty bidding tools are also available in the form of 'The Contract Bid Manager's Toolkit'*.

Consider how sales support tools could help put your message across. The problem of recruiting and training sales staff in the rapidly changing telecommunications sector was constraining

Eyretel's growth. The sales support tool developed by Cotoco reduced the sales cycle by up to 50% and the original investment was returned within four months by just one order. This and other applications are examined in a 'Win More Business' CD-Rom that has been produced by the Winning Business Research and Benchmarking Programme team★.

Finally, regularly subject your processes and practices to an independent review. Even though there is enormous potential for improvement, many companies re-engineer almost every process except that for winning business. For example, another report 'Pricing for Profit'★ from the Winning Business Research and Benchmarking Programme team shows how some companies achieve higher prices than others for similar offerings (see the next chapter). You can avoid being a 'loser' by consciously setting out to become a 'winner'.

★Further information

Information on the Winning Business Research and Benchmarking Programme and details of 'Winning New Business, the critical success factors', 'Bidding for Business, the Skills Agenda', 'The Contract Bid Manager's Toolkit', 'Pricing for Profit', the 'Winning New Business' CD-ROM and the 'Winning Business' series of reports can be obtained from Policy Publications: Tel: + 44 (0) 1733 361149; Email: colinct@tiscali.co.uk or from www.ntwkfirm.com/bookshop/

Details of the 'Winning New Business' resource pack, winning business reports covering individual sectors and seven professions, and related workshops can also be obtained from the publisher www.policypublications.com. It can also be obtained from http://www.winningnewbusiness.biz/

Companies can also now assess their own approaches to bidding. The research team can generate bespoke benchmarking reports for companies that would like to compare their practices with their peers and high performing winners. Details of these and other services can be obtained from www.ntwkfirm.com/policy-publications/benchmarking.htm

Checklist:

- In relation to competitive bidding do you view yourself and/or your colleagues as winners or losers?
- Do others view you and/or your colleagues as winners or losers?

- What proportion of the organisation's turnover is obtained by a process of competitive bidding?
- Do you and/or your colleagues examine trends in bidding practice?
- Is more or less business being put out to competitive tender?
- Is the organisation becoming more or less dependent upon competitive bidding?
- Is the organisation's bid process documented and understood?
- When was it last reviewed to ensure that critical success factors for competitive bidding and the winning ways of bid superstars are in place?
- Is your organisation's approach to bidding active or reactive?
- Is sufficient effort put in early on?
- Do bid teams understand the business environment in which prospects operate?
- Do they understand the values and benefits which prospects expect to gain, the factors they consider when buying, and cost of ownership issues that are taken into account?
- Do they understand propect buying processes and the roles played by particular individuals in purchase decisions?
- Are they able to persuade potential customers to invite your organisation to bid?
- Are they able to establish the superiority of the organisation's offerings over those of its competitors?
- Do they establish person-to-person relationships with potential customers?
- Do they offer support or anciliary services?
- Are proposals structured around the selection criteria of prospects?
- Do bid teams learn from successes and failures?
- Is knowledge of what works captured and shared?
- Are sales and bid teams equipped with support tools that make it easy for them to help prospects understand and acquire what they need?
- Do such tools automate the more routine and repetitive aspects of bidding?

Chapter 9
Pricing for Profit

Why is it that some companies are able to charge more than their competitors for what at first sight might appear essentially the same or a very similar product? In this chapter we will examine how to command premium prices for your offerings.

Pricing decisions impact directly upon sales revenues and profitability. Charge too much and orders are lost, while charging too little erodes margins and may give the impression that offerings are of low quality.

Obtaining and sustaining higher prices ought to be a top priority of entrepreneurs. Yet often they agonize over perfecting what is sold and then take quick pricing decisions based largely on guesswork.

So how should businesses set prices? Hitherto pricing has been shrouded in mystery. Firms have either been reluctant to reveal their approaches or – particularly when less successful – they have been sensitive to the lack of rigour involved.

The author has persuaded 73 companies to reveal their pricing strategies, tactics and practices. The firms surveyed provided data on 127 factors that could affect pricing decisions. The findings set out in the report 'Pricing for Profit'* reveal that more effective pricing could boost the profitability of many companies.

Comparing the companies that are most successful at using pricing to achieve business objectives such as growing market share or improving profitability (the winners or leaders) with the least successful (the losers or laggards) reveals stark differences between the two groups. For example, leaders make more use of all nine tools and techniques examined. Over twice as many make "very extensive" use of competitor analysis. Leaders are ahead by two to one or more in their use of break-even analysis, economic value analysis and price sensitivity measurement.

The winners or leaders understand the strategic importance of pricing and are more attuned to factors such as perceived value that affect price sensitivity. Overall, sales management, marketing, sales force personnel and finance are the groups most involved in pricing. However, leaders involve a wider range of departments in pricing decisions and members of the sales team play a more significant role.

Marketing and sales should contribute to pricing as they ought to be close to customers. But left to themselves they may be tempted to 'buy' orders. Offering discounts may be regarded by losers as a softer option than differentiating, tailoring and delivering extra value to justify a higher price. However, excessive discounting can reduce profitability.

The most successful companies – our winners - rely upon evidence rather than hunch. Thus before pricing products as a line rather than individually they would calculate whether an increase in profit overall would exceed the costs of implementation and any reductions in profit on individual products that might occur.

Leaders attempt to sell on value as opposed to price. They are more likely to segment a market-place and take a long-term view, for example using 'penetration pricing' to enter a new market. When laggards look ahead it is often for defensive reasons, for example our losers may cut prices to hold onto market share.

The cost drivers of leaders and laggards are very different. Leaders are five times more likely to increase volume to achieve economies of scale. In contrast, laggards are more likely to reduce product costs to allow price cuts or special discounts. Leaders are more realistic when allocating costs and more likely to understand the direct and indirect costs attributable to a particular product or service.

Overall leaders adopt a very different approach to building their businesses. They focus on each market segment, differentiate their offerings, and look for ways of increasing quality and delivering improved customer service. Investing in these areas allows them to build sales volume, reduce unit costs and become more competitive.

Leaders keep their pricing structures simple and transparent. Increasing an offering's economic value and the extent to which it is unique or special enables them to price for value. Differentiated, tailored and exclusive offerings attract a premium.

Laggards put the most emphasis upon cost cutting, while leaders strive to add value to their core offering, develop a reputation for service and use pricing to build closer relationships with strategic customers and key accounts. They are more willing to enter into partnering arrangements.

Pricing tactics should support business development strategy. Thus prestige pricing can enhance perceived value.

Within an economic region such as the euro zone cross-border buying and Europe-wide purchasing are increasing the demand for pan-regional (e.g. European) prices. Companies can resist downward pressure by developing clear benefits in each market and segmenting customers into ring-fenced pan-regional groups.

Too often pricing is handled in an ad hoc and uncoordinated way. A balance may have to be struck between the centralized response demanded by major customers, and the decentralization needed to respond to local market conditions.

Automating the more routine aspects of pricing can reduce the risk of errors and free up time for creating bespoke responses. Companies such as Eyretel use a job support tool for this purpose (see www.cotoco.com). Smart firms also monitor trends and developments that may impact on prices. For example, they are alert to possible price hot spots that might trigger consumer militancy.

Overall, winners put greater effort into pricing. They use more techniques and a wider range of sources of price information. They keep their finger on the pulse of customer, user and industry opinion, and review their approaches, strategies and tactics as situations and circumstances change.

Further Information

*'Pricing for Profit... the Critical Success Factors' by Colin Coulson-Thomas is published by Policy Publications. To order: e-mail colinct@tiscali.co.uk or call +44 (0) 1733 361149. The report can also be ordered from www.policypublications.com and www.ntwkfirm.com/bookshop/

Checklist:

- In relation to pricing do you view yourself and/or your colleagues as winners or losers?
- Do others view you and/or your colleagues as winners or losers?
- Does the organisation reap the benefits of effective pricing?
- Are a wide range of viewpoints, and particularly those who are close to customers and prospects, taken into account when pricing decisions are taken?
- Is the perceived value of the organisation's offerings understood?
- Are the factors which have the greatest influence upon price sensititivity understood?
- Are colleagues selling on value as opposed to price, segmenting the marketplace, taking a longer-term view and keeping price structures simple?
- Are costs kept low to facilitate price flexibility?
- Do sales teams differentiate, bespoke responses and add more value to obtain a price premium?
- Is appropriate use made of pricing tactics such as differential, prestige, penetration and pre-emptive pricing?

- Are steps taken to protect market share and enhance perceived quality?
- Are achieved prices and key accounts protected?
- Is individual customer profitability increased by adding value to the organisation's core offer and providing special pricing for key accounts?
- Are pricing decisions informed by using appropriate sources of information, including customer feedback, customer focus groups and industry associations?
- Are appropriate analytical tools such as competitor analysis, face-to-face research and activity based costing used?
- Have customer facing staff been equipped with appropriate pricing support tools?
- Are pricing strategies, policies and tactics proactive and regularly reviewed?

Chapter 10
Developing Strategic Customers and Key Accounts

Having won a valuable new customer the next challenge - which we will examine in this chapter - is to build a relationship that will result in a flow of repeat orders and follow-on business. To do this requires effective customer and/or account management, and critical success factors for building strategic customer relationships should be built into the appropriate processes and support tools.

A research team led by the author has examined how companies develop strategic customers and key accounts. The resulting report* identifies a variety of critical success factors that distinguish 'winners', the companies in the top quarter of achievement that realise the benefits of strategic customer relationships, from the 'losers' in the bottom quarter that do not. It draws upon the experiences of 194 companies with a combined turnover of over £70 Billion.

The investigation by a research team led by the author reveals general dissatisfaction with performance. Less than one in six of the participants consider themselves 'very effective' at increasing profitability through strategic relationships and fewer than one in seven are happy with the way they develop them. Yet, a clear majority of the respondents believe the proportion of their sales due to key accounts will increase beyond the current level of over two thirds.

The survey also reveals a wide gulf between the attitudes, approaches and results of the 'winners' and 'losers'. For example, 'winners' consider three times as many of the key processes identified by the investigating team to be 'very important', and are five times as likely to be intending to make use of emerging technologies.

'Losers' tend to live for the moment and are driven by the prospect of immediate business. They apply the 'key account' label to their most important current customers, and when dealing with them focus upon their own requirements. They use their customers to achieve their own short-term targets. Within such companies key account relationships are left to sales and marketing staff who play 'me-too' and 'catch-up with competitors'.

The 'losers' mouth generalisations about the importance of building closer relationships with customers, but do little to make them happen. They avoid commitment and integration. Open book accounting and direct electronic links are 'no go' areas. They are also very reluctant to bend standard procedures. Little effort is made to categorise accounts or 'do things differently' to help particular customers.

'Losers' use a range of traditional sales and negotiation techniques that fail to recognise 'buyer power'. Terms of business are used as a selling tool. Not surprisingly, losers are taken to the cleaners by customers who - on learning that they have become a 'key account' - respond by demanding price reductions.

The contrast between 'winners' and 'losers' is particularly stark when it comes to locking out the competition (or locking customers in). The 'winners' rank 11 out of 17 'lock out' factors examined by the research team while the 'losers' do not rank any. Quite simply the bottom quarter of companies in the survey sample do not appear to be taking any steps to protect their key accounts. No wonder they fail to realise strategic relationship benefits.

In contrast, 'winners' look ahead and take a lifetime view of relationships. They consider future potential when categorising accounts. They value their customers and are prepared to put themselves out for them. They are open and build personal relationships. Their focus is upon customer requirements and buyer expectations. They understand their customers' businesses, industries and buying processes and look out for opportunities that might benefit them.

'Losers' are sometimes exposed when particular individuals change jobs. 'Winners' encourage a broader range of contacts at multiple levels between their own staff and those of key account customers. At the same time, senior management are involved in important negotiations. They are prepared to differentiate and depart from the norm in order to deliver greater value and benefit their customers' businesses. Traditional sales techniques are largely ignored, as 'winners' influence buying rather than overtly sell.

Rather than mouth generalisations, 'winners' concentrate upon specifics. They are prepared to commit, to extend partnership to the terms of business, and to integrate processes and systems. Not surprisingly they realise the many benefits of strategic customer relationships that elude the 'losers'.

Overall, the research findings reveal that while there is a wide spectrum of effectiveness there is also considerable potential for improvement. Even the winners could do much better.

So what needs to be done? In many companies account managers have prime responsibility for customer relationship management and business development through cross selling and winning new accounts within sectors for which they are responsible. Sales directors and members of the sales team should start by defining or reviewing the role of account and/or key account managers and agreeing their responsibilities in relation to those of colleagues in order to identify and address any gaps, overlaps and boundary issues.

A profile of the competencies and 'role model' behaviours required by an effective account manager should also be developed and agreed, and individuals assessed against the agreed profile to identify personal and team development needs. Important next steps are to:

- Define and agree a key account development plan format and process, a customer relationship management process, and a process for winning business in competitive situations.
- Develop or acquire the approaches, tools and techniques account managers will require to cross sell and win and retain accounts. These include the 30 tools in the 'The Contract Bid Managers Toolkit', the 20 skills in 'Bidding for Business, the Skills Agenda' and the systematic model approach to key account management set out in the report 'Developing Strategic Customers & Key Accounts'*.
- Provide whatever training is required by the account managers, individually or as a group. Collaborative arrangements can supplement skills, experience and reference sites in areas of relative deficiency.
- More importantly – and often a more cost effective option – equip key account teams and customer facing staff with support tools that make it very easy for them to engage with customers, assess their requirements, differentiate offerings from those of competitors, develop and price solutions, prepare proposals and cost justifications, and generally help them to understand and buy.
- Allocate existing customers and eligible prospects to individual account managers. The allocation should reflect the sectors in which the individuals and the company and its partners have particular expertise and distinctive strengths. Rules, arrangements and terms covering the availability of, access to,

and use of partner know-how and staff by account managers for business development, customer support and service delivery purposes may need to be negotiated.
- Set and agree revenue and profitability targets for each sector/account manager, and develop sector specific business development and marketing plans, account development plans for all existing key accounts, and account capture plans for all eligible target accounts.

The Winning Business Research Programme led by the author (see appendix B) has produced reports on the critical success factors for winning business in particular business sectors and various professions, and account managers can use these to identify 'best practice' approaches. Specific sector and cross sector applications, offerings, events and marketing materials may also need to be developed.

Sales and business development teams should establish mechanisms for capturing, sharing and learning from positive and negative experiences. Joining a network such as the Business Development Forum may allow account managers to learn from the experiences of their peers. Deficiencies should be addressed. Thus arrangements could be negotiated with non-national partners to support the winning of international accounts.

Each account manager should be responsible for prioritising new business opportunities and prospects, allocating and managing available business development resources, and achieving account and sector business development and profitability targets. The assignment of customers to account managers will ensure a single point of contact, and help to create a holistic insight into the totality of customers' business needs.

Finally, sales directors must ensure that an appropriate performance management framework is in place. In addition to regular measures of customer satisfaction, retention and loyalty, performance indicators should address certain lessons of the research investigation★. For example:

- How much time do account managers spend in the office as opposed to with customers and prospects?
- Do senior staff and colleagues in other areas actively support relationship building with key accounts?
- What forms of interdependence with customers and integration of systems and processes have been achieved?

- Are account managers and other staff learning from and with strategic customers?
- Are risks and opportunities being shared?
- Are partnering relationships being built and open book accounting practiced?

The latter questions are important. The growth of partnering, spread of e-commerce, and desire for strategic alliances were identified by respondents to the 'Developing Strategic Customers & Key Accounts' survey as the three most important issues they face. Cautious companies that avoid risks by staying with what they know and adopt legalistic and protective approaches are likely to end up as low margin commodity suppliers. Playing 'win-lose' games ensures they lose.

Those who are flexible, innovative, willing to accept challenges, and ready to adopt new ways of working and learning earn higher returns. 'Winners' are willing to adopt a partnership approach. They share visions and risks. They strive for 'win-win' outcomes by agreeing mutually beneficial objectives. They remain relevant and add value.

'Winners' are prepared to commit to continued and measured improvements in whatever they supply or provide. Savings achieved are shared between the parties concerned. If required, they practice 'open book' accounting. They also recognise that differences can and do arise. However, within the partnering relationships they foster there are simple and quick processes for handling disputes at the lowest possible levels. Their earn respect and engender loyalty. Their relationships last and prosper.

Further Information

★'Developing Strategic Customers & Key Accounts', 'The Contract Bid Managers Toolkit', 'Bidding for Business, the Skills Agenda', the 'Close to the Customer' series of briefings, related reports in the 'Winning Business' series and bespoke key account benchmarking reports can be obtained from Policy Publications: Tel: +44 (0) 1733 361149; Email: colinct@tiscali.co.uk or from www.policypublications.com and www.ntwkfirm.com/bookshop/

Companies can also now assess their own approaches to building customer relationships. Using the developing strategic customers and key accounts database the research team can generate bespoke benchmarking reports for companies that would like to compare their practices with their peers and high performing winners. Details of these and other services can be obtained from www.policypublications.com and from www.ntwkfirm.com/policy-publications/benchmarking.htm

Information on the use of support tools for building relationships with customers can be obtained from 00 44 0870 748 1400 or www.cotoco.com

Checklist:

- In relation to developing strategic customers and key accounts do you view yourself and/or your colleagues as winners or losers?
- Do others view you and/or your colleagues as winners or losers?
- Is the vision of the company, and are its goals and values, rooted in the customer?
- How differentiated is the company from its competitors in the marketplace?
- How bothered or inconvenienced would the company's customers be if the company ceased to exist?
- How customer-focused is the board? Where do the customers rank in relation to other stakeholders?
- What steps does the company take to identify customer requirements and measure customer satisfaction?
- How much of the value sought by the ultimate customer is delivered by the company, and how much is delivered by other members of the supply chain?
- What do the customers of the company really think about it?
- Is customer value at the top of the list of key management priorities?
- Is reward linked to the delivery of value and satisfaction to customers?
- Has the company identified those key management and business processes that deliver the value sought by customers?
- Are the critical success factors for building strategic and key account relationships understood?
- Is future potential taken into account when decisions of whether or not to treat a customer as a key account are taken?
- How effective is the company at harnessing and applying its resources to meet the needs of the individual customer?
- Who is, and who is not, adding value for customers?
- Are customers regarded as 'outsiders', or as colleagues and business partners?
- Is the company prepared to practice open book accounting and enter into partnering relationships?

- What processes and practices are in place to learn from customers?
- How much effort is put into building close working relationships with customers, and other members of the supply chain?
- Are steps taken to lock customers in and keep competitors out of key accounts?
- Are multiple points of contact, on-line links and joint activities encouraged?
- How easy is it for customers and prospects to assess their requirements, understand what they need and buy?
- Are customer facing staff equipped with easy to use support tools for building relationships with individual customers?
- Are they enabled to differentiate the company and its offerings

Chapter 11
Negotiating Partnering Relationships

Some companies focus so much upon competing that they overlook the importance of collaboration. In the last chapter we considered how to build closer relationships with important customers. In this chapter we will also examine the importance of working with other organizations. For example, business, channel and supply chain partners could collaborate in the production of sales support tools.

Shared costs and increases in productivity and performance across a wider range of joint activity can significantly enhance financial returns. The chances of cooperation may be boosted by conscious effort to create a partnering relationship, in which mutually beneficial outcomes are negotiated and benefits are shared.

Winning business teams setting out to build relationships with customers and potential business partners sometimes assume a degree of harmony between organizations that may not exist. The various parties to new business and partnering negotiations may not be of one mind. The negotiation challenge may be to move from confrontation to collaboration by helping those involved to articulate their interests, understand contrary positions and conclude mutually acceptable accommodation.

Detailed and final negotiations can open up a Pandora's Box of arguments and lead to disagreements, disputes and confrontation between contending viewpoints. Latent conflicts may be brought to the surface. Supply chain partners may display protective behaviour. Different interests may seek to use meetings for their own ends. New ways may need to be found to handle disagreements and reconcile differing requirements.

Sensitive negotiators recognize that people may have different perceptions of the desirability, direction and consequences of certain outcomes. Some may feel strongly about certain issues. Old debates, clashes of personality, divisions within the boardroom or tensions between sales channel partners may be brought to the surface.

Within many markets there is a legacy of distrust and much scope for misunderstanding between negotiating parties and head offices and operating units. Some may harbour suspicions that particular groups are seeking to benefit from changes at the expense of others.

Certain partners may feel they are being asked to absorb an unfair proportion of budget cuts or make a disproportionate contribution.

Winning business and partnering negotiators should endeavour to identify differing expectations and perspectives and anticipate potential flash points. There might be varying degrees of misunderstanding between national cultures and distinct minorities within an international organization or marketplace. The greater the diversity between the different parties to a negotiation the more likely it is that outcomes may need to reflect local situations.

Possible arenas of confrontation need to be recognized and likely conflicts addressed. New business and corporate communications can themselves become a source of distrust and tension, especially when words are not consistent with deeds. People may perceive a gap between rhetoric and reality. For example, corporate messages might stress the need to adopt a longer-term approach to the building of partnering relationships with customers while directors take short-term actions to cut costs.

The author's research programme (see appendices A and B) has examined the approaches of a wide range of organizations in many sectors and identified critical success factors for managing change, competing and winning*. The findings reveal that successful companies or 'winners' display attitudes and behaviours for building relationships and partnerships that differ from those of 'losers' or businesses that struggle.

Successful and unsuccessful companies pursue very different approaches to avoiding disputes, handling confrontation and encouraging collaboration. People associated with 'loser' companies are cautious collaborators. They stress the time, effort and expense required to establish and build relationships, and they often conclude that the likely results do not justify the investment required.

In making such choices losers act as though working with others is an option rather than a necessity. At heart they are reluctant to share and would prefer to operate alone. They keep to themselves in an attempt to avoid becoming entangled in rivalries and drawn into disputes.

When negotiating losers pursue divisive strategies and seek to benefit at the expense of other parties. They sometimes foment conflicts in order to achieve sectional interests.

Some losers prize their independence so much they pass up opportunities to grow that would require them to work with colleagues and business partners. Collaboration is seen as a constraint upon their freedom of action.

Losers settle into familiar ways of operating. If existing arrangements and practices appear to work reasonably well they are reluctant to consider alternatives that might offer additional benefits.

Winners are more willing to work with colleagues and are more likely to be prepared to co-operate with other complementary suppliers. They see and seek the advantages of collaboration. It might enable them to learn and develop. It may allow them to offer a wider range of services to their customers and pursue a broader range of opportunities.

Winners are usually receptive to approaches from others. They are open to new ideas. They welcome suggestions for improvements and innovation. They actively search for potential business partners and explore possibilities for joint initiatives or collective action.

Once contact is established winners do not mind the confrontation and argument that may need to create mutual respect and a meeting of minds. They endeavour to find common ground, resolve conflicts and promote shared interests and goals.

Collaboration extends to 'external' parties. As companies outsource and focus upon core competencies they may hive off or transfer various activities to specialist suppliers. As a consequence combinations of complementary organisations work together in supply chains rather than operate alone as single entities to deliver value to customers. Each concentrates upon what it does best. A company that endeavours to do everything itself may become a 'jack of all trades and master of none'.

Consortium responses to invitations to tender for complex and large-scale projects are also increasingly common in certain sectors. Only by working together may the respondents be able to assemble the capabilities required. Companies that collaborate with business partners may significantly improve their prospects of winning a major contract.

It helps if aspiring collaborators have compatible interests and complementary capabilities. When they need to work with others losers tend to seek out potential collaborators with similar characteristics to themselves. As a consequence, they sometimes find in crisis situations that the whole is not necessarily greater than the sum of the parts. Like drunks endeavouring to prop each other up they compound each other's weaknesses.

If the parties endeavouring to co-operate are very different they may not have enough in common to cement a relationship. On the other hand, if they are so alike as to add little to each other's capabilities collaboration may not be justified. Winners are more likely to understand that lasting relationships often involve dissimilar but complementary partners that allocate roles and responsibilities according to comparative advantage.

Losers tend to be essentially selfish where relationships are concerned. They seek to co-operate on their terms, and they often put the bare minimum of effort into maintaining them.

Within relationships losers hold back emotionally and intellectually and endeavour not to become too deeply involved. They are wary and may even undertake cost-benefit assessments. When negotiating they endeavour to 'score points' and adopt win-lose approaches.

Collaborative 'partnerships' can take various forms. Whether an informal arrangements or a formal joint venture, such relationships can be of great importance. Opportunities can be addressed and significant amounts of new business won as a result of co-operative action. The consortium bid for a major contract, with each member focusing upon an area of core expertise is increasingly acceptable and may be encouraged.

Winners work hard at reaping the benefits of co-operation. They commit the effort required to establish and regularly review collaborative processes and practices. For example, they may put practical arrangements in place to clarify the ownership of customers, prevent poaching and protect intellectual property.

Winners also recognise that if internal and external relationships are to grow and deepen they should be acceptable and mutually beneficial to all the parties involved. Instinctively, when negotiating they look for win-win outcomes.

Winners also avoid rushing. Some parties will take longer to adjust and integrate than others. Winners also understand the dynamic nature of associations and arrangements. Time, effort and care may need to be devoted to them if they are to become more intimate.

Winners willingly commit. They become involved. They are flexible and understanding, and prepared to do things differently to accommodate particular and legitimate interests. They are also not 'fair weather friends'. They can be relied upon in crisis situations.

Collaboration should not be pursued at any cost or become a distraction. Some losers devote great effort to achieving 'teamwork' that may conceal or sideline differences and gloss over concerns in order to achieve a bland consensus.

Winners adopt a more entrepreneurial approach. They encourage open and frank discussion. They become demanding collaborators and partners. On occasion they may create waves in order to make faster progress.

Overall winners recognise that a lack of tension may mean the absence of ambition. The quiet organization may be asleep. Their drive and desire to innovate and push back the boundaries of what is possible may provoke confrontation between those favouring the status quo and those who desire to move on. The need for activities and processes for building mutual understanding, reconciling differences and building collaborative relationships is understood and addressed.

Discussion, informed debate, a willingness to challenge and a degree of confrontation is sometimes desirable. It can prevent complacency, spur innovation and lead to higher performance. Disputes are usually better in the open - where efforts can be made to resolve them - than hidden when they can fester.

It may be possible to avoid some conflicts by ring fencing certain activities or giving one or more of the protagonists greater autonomy. Involving different parties in discussions at proposal or concept stage may give them an opportunity to flag up areas of possible difficulty. Although their participation might delay a decision, implementation may be speeded up due to the greater perceived legitimacy of the process and likely outcomes made more acceptable.

Possible mechanisms can range from an ad hoc discussion forum or inter-unit team to a partnering agreement or issue monitoring and management. A process may also be required for handling dysfunctional conflicts. This could provide a framework for identifying common ground, isolating points of difference, and assessing and addressing the root causes of disputes. Organizational boundaries may need to be redrawn, roles and responsibilities reallocated, processes re-engineered and strategies reviewed.

Winning new business and customer relations teams can play a key role in moving from a climate of confrontation to a culture of collaboration. They can identify supporters and opponents of change and endeavour to ensure each understands the others viewpoints and legitimate concerns. They can put feedback loops in place and encourage senior managers to listen. They can assess tolerance for diversity and whether sufficient discussion and debate is occurring.

Business development teams and key account managers should work to achieve mutual respect and the credibility of two-way communications. Colleagues should be encouraged to match words with deeds. They need to distinguish between disruptive opposition and constructive questioning and encourage the latter.

Finally, customers and business partners should also be encouraged and helped to raise concerns, express viewpoints, explore issues, reconcile opinions, foster collaboration and share learning. Open relationships based upon trust and mutual respect are conducive of mutually beneficial co-operation.

★Further Information

Information about the forthcoming companion volume on transforming corporate performance will be available from www.policypublications.com

'Transforming the Company, Manage Change, Compete and Win' by Colin Coulson-Thomas is available from Kogan Page: Tel. 01903 828800; Fax. 020 7837 6348; E-mail: orders@lbsltd.co.uk or on-line at www.kogan-page.co.uk

'Developing Strategic Customers & Key Accounts', 'The Contract Bid Managers Toolkit', 'Bidding for Business, the Skills Agenda', the 'Close to the Customer' series of briefings, related reports in the 'Winning Business' series and bespoke key account benchmarking reports can be obtained from the publisher, Policy Publications: Tel: +44 (0) 1733 361149; Email: colinct@tiscali.co.uk or from www.ntwkfirm.com/bookshop/

Companies can also now assess their own approaches to building relationships. Using the developing strategic customers and key accounts database the research team can generate bespoke benchmarking reports for companies that would like to compare their practices with their peers and high performing winners. Details of these and other services can be obtained from www.policypublications.com and from www.ntwkfirm.com/policy-publications/benchmarking.htm

Information on the use of support tools for building relationships with channel and other partners can be obtained from 00 44 0870 748 1400 or www.cotoco.com

Checklist:

- In relation to partnering and collaboration do you view yourself and/or your colleagues as winners or losers?
- Do others view you and/or your colleagues as winners or losers?
- Is the organisation willing to enter into partnering and collaborative arrangements?
- Does the board and senior management team encourage openness and healthy debate with partner organisations?
- Does this extend to open book accounting?
- Are mutually beneficial outcomes sought during the course of negotiations?

- Are the aspirations of the various parties shared and compatible?
- Are all parties encouraged to be open about what they are seeking to achieve?
- Do they share agreed mutual objectives?
- Are they willing to share risks and returns?
- Are they committed to continued and measured improvements?
- Are benefits or savings shared between the parties?
- Are there direct links between the parties and are they collaborating in joint developments?
- Has a simple, quick and low level dispute resolution procedure been put in place?
- Are the people of the organisation trained, equipped and enabled to build collaborative relationships?
- Have they been equipped with easy to use tools for building relationships with channel and other partners?
- What steps are taken to protect intellectual capital when working with staff of partner organisations?
- How appropriate is the negotiating and approval process for concluding new collaborative relationships?

Chapter 12
Managing Supply Chain Relationships

How effective are you at working with other businesses? Following on from research findings we considered in the last chapter, should you be learning to collaborate as well as compete? Early industrial tycoons used to grow their firms by 'integrating along the supply chain' or grabbing more of what other companies did. Some verged on megalomania and aspired to take over just about anything that moved.

Today's commercial world is very different. Customers and investors look for 'focus'. They expect businesses to concentrate upon what they do best. Non-core activities are outsourced. Firms that spread themselves too thinly risk becoming 'Jack of all trades and master of none'.

Customers are also more demanding. They want the best. The emphasis has switched to differentiation and specialisation, doing a smaller number of things supremely well and developing a reputation for excellence in a particular field.

In business, sport and the arts an ever-higher share of the available rewards accrue to those who are outstanding. Average performers are marginalized while the super-stars clean up. As markets become more complex and competitive there are just not enough hours in the day to keep up with everything.

Inevitably these developments mean we have to change how we operate. We can no longer afford to keep to ourselves or go it alone. A greater proportion of the value consumed by end customers is now delivered by collective endeavours.

Co-operation with other firms enables businesses to broaden offerings with complementary products, add services to justify premium prices or reach new customers. Like it or not, companies have to work ever more closely with business partners. In many markets good supply chain relationships - the subject of this chapter - are a critical success factor.

The reputations of brands reflect customers' total experience. A failing at one point can undermine excellence elsewhere. Hence, the importance of working together to ensure consistency of service and create a positive spiral of mutual re-enforcement.

Managing supply chain relationships should be high on the entrepreneur's agenda. An investigation led by the author* reveals that visionaries use them to create new business opportunities while competitors wedded to existing practices go under. Successful companies (winners) reshape their organisations, introduce new channels and establish new markets through more intimate relationships with customers, suppliers and business partners.

Despite the opportunities many businesses lack ambition. They tinker with existing processes and adopt me-too practices rather than innovate. The creativity displayed when crafting new offerings is not matched by similar imagination when they consider how to get these into the hands of customers.

Of course change for its own sake should be avoided. As we will see in the next chapter it can be disruptive of existing relationships while new ones take time and effort to establish. Significant change should be for a strategic purpose, and one that can be shared by supply chain partners. The focus should be upon the customer, for example offering them additional choice or more tailored products and services.

Providing alternatives to existing provision can help to differentiate a business from its competitors. If more customers demand distinct or bespoke offerings supply chain partners must deliver greater variety at lower costs and more quickly. Ways of reducing waiting time might range from joint R&D and taskforces to seamless processes and direct electronic links.

On-line ordering, just-in-time responses, the ability to track orders and 'help-desk' support can all help to lock customers in. Maybe invoices and reports could be delivered electronically in formats to suit individual customers. Contracted in experts might be able to provide additional specialist services.

Collaboration can speed up international expansion. For example, it is difficult to become a global software player without a strong market position in North America. A local presence may be required. This might involve giving further percentages to yet more partners, but the smaller proportion retained may be of much larger income streams.

Micro-businesses - even individual craft workers in the jungle – can reach a global clientele via the Internet. Working with website management, transaction processing, fulfilment and debt collection partners frees them from the distractions of hiring people, finding premises and putting support processes in place. Instead, they concentrate upon their individual passions and play to their particular strengths.

Winners innovate. They create new ways of doing businesses and additional routes to potential customers. Maybe airline passengers and travellers on intercity train could order goods from an electronic catalogue and pick them up on arrival at their destinations. People could collect items selected on an office PC from reception when they leave to go home.

A particular role within a supply chain may both create a new source of competitive advantage and represent a wider business opportunity. For example, a service such as handling warranty repairs could be opened up to suppliers of non-competing products. A further partner could be brought in to run an interest group or offer end customers discounts on related items.

So long as rewards exceed costs and image and reputation are enhanced rather than compromised additional service providers can improve the competitive positioning of a supply chain. Yet few such groupings manage their affairs as a whole and actively seek new members, even though competition is increasingly between networks of collaborating partners rather than individual companies.

Some companies develop multiple supply chains as they further segment their customers and diversify their channels to market. Each additional relationship can complicate the task of securing agreement. Supply chains can fragment as well as coalesce. Participants need to be alert to potential fissures and forces for fragmentation.

Particular partners may seek to cut out intermediaries and secure a more direct route to an end-customer, perhaps via e-business over the Internet. Others may review their core competencies and consolidate their relationships. A whole network might be made redundant by the replacement of a physical market place by an electronic market space.

Supply chains do not obviate the search for advantage and profit. Today's collaborator may become tomorrow's competitor. Relationships should be regularly reviewed. Are they meeting end customer needs? Do they enable participants to specialise and build up their core skills?

Inevitably differences will arise. The trick is not to avoid or ignore them. Frustration, misunderstanding and resentment may build to a level that alienates one or more business partners. The whole chain is only as effective as it weakest link. A low-level dispute resolution process should be put in place to tackle issues before they escalate and entrenched positions are taken.

Losers sometimes naively exaggerate their own worth to others. Companies should be realistic about the value of their own contribution within a supply chain. Is it visible to end customers? How might their changing requirements, emerging trends and new technologies affect it? New attitudes, skills and capabilities may be required to deal with future challenges.

Particular attention should be paid to the likely impact of economic cycles and technological developments with the potential to change the shape of markets and create new ones. Businesses need to think about the implications for their relationships with supply chain partners and any new ground rules that are likely to apply.

Smart entrepreneurs build partnering relationships with both customers and suppliers. Winners start with requirements, what end-customers would really like. They identify gaps in their own capabilities and their partners' collective capacity to deliver. While acknowledging their deficiencies they do not loose sleep over them. Instead they cooperate with complementary providers of whatever they lack.

Cooperation with others may involve letting go of certain activities and possibilities. This can be difficult for entrepreneurs who feel they are losing part of 'their' opportunity. Many losers instinctively dislike sharing.

In reality, many business founders soon face pressure from investors to be 'true to themselves'. They are asked to focus upon their unique qualities and personal strengths and bring in people with complementary skills, or even hand over the reigns to professional managers. In essence, putting new supply chain relationships in place is specialisation at the enterprise level.

When they negotiate effective collaborators flush out the key business objectives of the various parties involved and agree 'win-win' outcomes that are mutually beneficial to all concerned. Winners recognise that relationships which are too one-sided do not stand the test of time.

If cost savings and productivity gains are shared business partners have more of an incentive to work together. It is usually to everyone's advantage to act in the best interests of a supply chain as a whole. It may be helpful for the parties to formally contract to achieve certain targeted improvements over time.

Increasingly, winners are likely to use support tools to help supply chain partners to collaborate. B&Q uses a support tool to make it very easy for current and prospective suppliers to understand and satisfy its quality requirements. Cisco Systems uses a range of tools to support its channel partners.

Resilient relationships are based upon openness and trust. This may extend to open book accounting to dispel suspicions of 'excess profits'. Everybody usually benefits if all business partners do well. The attention of parties that secure inadequate returns may wander. Collective success can generate the funds to invest in technology upgrades and other means of securing continuing competitive advantage.

Further Information

★'The Competitive Network' report and methodology shows how to combine e-business with re-engineering to build value creating supply chains and win new markets. Details and information on the related 'The Responsive Organisation' re-engineering methodology 'for introducing new ways of working can be obtained from Policy Publications: Tel: + 44 (0) 1733 361149; Email: colinct@tiscali.co.uk or from www.policypublications.com or www.ntwkfirm.com/bookshop/

Information on the use of support tools for building relationships with channel and supply chain partners can be obtained from 00 44 0870 748 1400 or www.cotoco.com

Checklist:

- In relation to managing supply chain relationships do you view yourself and/or your colleagues as winners or losers?
- Do others view you and/or your colleagues as winners or losers?
- Do the perspectives of colleague embrace business and supply chain partners?
- Are business partners considered as insiders or outsiders?
- Are colleagues secretive or open with partner organisations?
- Have partner objectives been made explicit and addresses?
- Does the company seek mutually beneficial relationships that deliver 'win-win' outcomes?
- Are all partners clear anout the value sought by end customers and what they can do to deliver this value?
- Have critical success factors and winning ways been built into supply chain processes?
- Is information about what high performers do differently shared across partner organisations?
- Are the winning ways of high achievers captured and shared?
- Have people in partner organisations been supplied with appropriate support tools to collaborate and also engage with end customers, explain offerings to them and help them to buy?

- Are these kept up to date?
- Can partners customise them and incorporate information about their own and related offerings?
- Do supply chain partners participate in the development of new products and services?
- Are supply chain partners learning together and from each other?
- Have steps been taken to lock in key supply chain partners?
- Are risks and returns shared?

Chapter 13
Leading and Managing Change

When considering performance improvement, business development, re-engineering and transformation options, boards need to achieve a balance between change and continuity, and focus upon areas of greatest opportunity. As situations alter and circumstances change, capabilities, processes and working practices need to be reviewed. For many, change is an inevitable consequence of their roles and responsibilities. It may be both necessary and desirable, and the management of it is now a lucrative area for consultants.

However certain changes are more welcome than others, and some people are much better at managing them than their peers. In some companies managers may be assessed and rewarded according to the amount of change they bring about. However, directors, boards and senior managers should tread warily as change can be disruptive and costly. It can distract people who should be focused upon other priorities.

When mismanaged change can be stressful and destructive. Few changes affect everyone in the same way, and the impacts of certain changes may not be immediately apparent. There might be hidden and longer term consequences. Board members may be divided between those who are for or against particular changes. People who are indifferent or ambivalent may simply 'go with the flow'.

Despite much rhetoric about 'change management' and nimble, responsive and flexible organizations, many business leaders periodically downsize, regularly restructure and inexorably destroy shareholder wealth. The research programme led by the author (see appendix A) has sought to find out why there is such a wide gulf between intentions and outcomes. The findings set out in the author's forthcoming companion book on transforming corporate performance★ and in 'Transforming the Company' identify what needs to be done.

Frustration is the inevitable consequence of how many people set about managing change. Many unsuccessful companies or losers introduce far too many changes. People are unsettled and important relationships are disrupted. Problems are allowed to fester until a point at which dramatic restructurings may be forced by the pressure of events.

Smart boards make adaptation and change a way of life. Winners read the road ahead and try to anticipate changes that may be required. They identify and approach those whose help they might need. They are proactive rather than reactive, and retain control. They introduce required changes when there is the greatest chance of success.

Much will depend upon the purposes of change and the capacity of the people involved to adapt. Directors should question the rationale for proposed changes, and ask whether an impact analysis has been undertaken of their likely implications. Are the potential consequences for employees, customers, suppliers, business partners and investors adequately assessed?

When deciding what to change, don't confuse operational and strategic issues, or your personal interests with those of the organisation. Build an effective board of competent directors who understand the distinction between direction and management. Surround yourself with open-minded, pragmatic and competent contributors who will consider proposals for change dispassionately and objectively.

Particular attention should be paid to the interests of customers. When new models are introduced will the spare parts needed for earlier products still be available? Introducing changes without considering their costs or consequences can do great harm to reputations and relationships. Customers sometimes have more regard for a company's offerings than its managers.

An 'end-to-end' perspective is required. People need to think through the likely consequences of changes for colleagues and business partners. Altering a task at one point in a process, or introducing a new activity, may cause problems for those operating elsewhere, either within the same process or in a related or dependent one.

Allies and opponents need to be identified. Some champion change. Others undermine it. Change can disorientate and disrupt, even when it is beneficial. People may also only be able to take so much of it. Organisational leaders need to think carefully about how much change they can handle before negative consequences wipe out desired gains.

Change for change's sake should be avoided. A degree of continuity may be required. People in smart organisations led by winners build upon an existing reputation and safeguard core values. Steps may need to be taken to protect what is important and prevent the compromise of cherished beliefs. What are the anchor points of the business? What is the cement that holds its people together?

There are other questions to consider. Might changes result in the loss of strategically important knowledge and understanding? Is sufficient effort devoted to building longer-term relationships with customers, suppliers, investors and business partners? How easy is it for people to speak up against change?

Directors should distinguish between goals, values, objectives, policies and activities that need to be changed and those that should be continued. Too many people passively 'follow the herd'. Once a clear majority appears to favour a particular course of action they climb aboard the prevailing bandwagon.

Think also about longer term and strategic impacts. Imitating and copying others can be dangerous. People can sometimes be naïve or mistaken regarding their best long-term interests. Preferences and priorities can change. Nothing is more frustrating than finding certain options have been lost because a decision cannot be reversed.

Boards sometimes attempt to change too much. Is there sufficient continuity for people to have a sense of identity, belonging, direction and purpose? Are conscious efforts made to provide enough continuity for people not to feel threatened and insecure?

Certain rules of thumb emerge from the 'Transforming the Company' study. Present a compelling case for change. People should only be expected to make demanding changes for good reason. The visions and rationales offered by many boards are excessively general. Inspire and motivate with a distinctive vision, compelling purpose and clear objectives. Accentuate the positive. Sell the benefits, but avoid blather and hype.

Think through 'what's in it' for those involved. People should be encouraged and enabled to work and learn in whatever ways best enable them to harness their full potential and give of their best. Individuals differ in how they react to certain situations and opportunities. Thus working from home may not be suitable for those who are not inwardly directed or self-motivated.

Effort should be concentrated where it is most likely to make a difference. Justifiable changes are more likely to be those that focus upon the critical success factors for achieving key corporate objectives and delivering greater customer and shareholder value. Winning business is particularly important for ambitious companies.

People need to be motivated, prepared, and equipped to achieve the changes they are expected to bring about. However, while general 'change' programmes are becoming more common bespoke initiatives and specific tools to help individuals bring about particular changes are few and far between. More effort needs to be devoted to them.

While small groups often quickly adapt, getting larger numbers of people across many locations to alter their behaviours has traditionally been more of a challenge. This need no longer be the case. The job support tools considered in chapters 26 and 27 were introduced without 'management of change' initiatives. People quickly grasped that the tools would make it easier for them to do difficult jobs and they were rapidly adopted.

However, not all interventions are as benign and helpful as support tools. Think carefully too about how much change your team can handle. Change can disorientate even when it is beneficial. After a point negative consequences may wipe out desired gains. At the same time, don't underestimate the potential of your colleagues. Be prepared to trust them and, when it is reasonable to do so, take calculated risks.

Changes occurring all around us represent challenges and opportunities. Boards should consider who are likely to be 'gainers' and 'losers' from significant trends and developments and assess whether new or alternative offerings would mitigate undesirable impacts or enable people to take fuller advantage of emerging possibilities. Those affected might represent a lucrative potential market for products and services tailored to their particular interests.

As a business grows its directors may be unable to become directly involved in the many and varied activities that more bespoke and imaginative responses to a greater variety of requirements demand. Organisations need to transform themselves into incubators of creative solutions and communities of entrepreneurs. Teams should be enabled to bring about whatever changes are required to enable them to achieve their objectives and deliver value to *their* customers.

Those who endeavour to bring about ambitious and fundamental changes should expect to encounter setbacks. Persist. Be confident, determined, pragmatic and positive. Value constructive criticism and invite feedback. Don't rationalize disappointment. Learn from it. Achieving transformational change is often easier and usually more satisfying than rationalizing, managing and suffering the consequences of failure.

Further Information

* Information about the forthcoming companion volume on transforming corporate performance will be available from www.policypublications.com

'Transforming the Company, Manage Change, Compete and Win' by Colin Coulson-Thomas is available from Kogan Page: Tel. 01903 828800; Fax. 020 7837 6348; E-mail: orders@lbsltd.co.uk or on-line from www.ntwkfirm.com

The skills needed by directors for leading and managing change are examined in 'Developing Directors, A handbook for building an effective boardroom team' which is published by the publisher, Policy Publications in association with Adaptation and can be ordered from 00 44 (0)1733 361 149 and also online from www.policypublications.com/developingdirectors.htm

Checklist:

- In relation to leading and managing change do you view yourself and/or your colleagues as winners or losers?
- Do others view you and/or your colleagues as winners or losers?
- Have the supporters and opponents of change been identified?
- What is being done to understand the viewpoints of those who appear to be opposed to change?
- Do members of the board and senior management team have the capacity to listen?
- How tolerant are they of diversity?
- Is open and vigorous debate encouraged?
- Do the company's key players have the respect of people throughout the organization?
- Do they themselves always behave as role models?
- Why should anyone believe the company's messages?
- Who cares if they are believed?
- What will be lost if they are not believed?
- Is the business and change strategy of the company credible?
- What evidence is there of senior management commitment to it?
- Where does it rank in the list of their priorities?
- Is day-to-day action consistent with the 'words'?
- What can be learnt from those who appear to lack commitment?
- Are managers able to distinguish between a healthy level of questioning and disruptive opposition?
- Do they encourage collaborative activity and shared learning?

- Do people understand why change is needed and what they can do to help bring it about?
- Are they equipped and enabled with appropriate support tools to do what is required?
- Do they feel they are enabled to make a difference?
- Do they have opportunities for personal growth?
- Are their unique contributions recognised?
- If achieved, will the changes that are sought deliver both commercial success and personal fulfilment?

Chapter 14
Corporate Transformation

Some companies succeed. They adapt to changing circumstances, and they remain relevant and vital. Their people manage change, compete and win.

Other companies struggle and stagnate. They adopt fashionable approaches. They buy the latest technologies. They introduce generic or re-engineered processes, and they are advised by leading professional firms. Yet they still fail.

In the last chapter we looked at the leadership of change. In this chapter we consider how to handle situations in which more radical action is needed, i.e. more than evolutionary adjustment or continuous improvement is required

Have you ever wondered why some companies are less successful than others in similar circumstances at introducing transformational change? What are these people overlooking or doing wrong? What do the winners do differently? To answer these questions the research programme led by the author (see appendix A) has been examining the corporate transformation experience of companies for more than a decade.

As mentioned in chapter 1, research teams have examined key processes such as those for winning business, building relationships and creating and exploiting knowledge. The outcomes achieved by survey participants are ranked from the most to the least successful, and the approaches of the 'winners' or most successful are compared with the 'losers' or least successful to isolate the factors that make a difference. The results summarized in the author's forthcoming book on transforming corporate performance* and in 'Transforming the Company, Manage Change, Compete and Win' suggest most of the critical success factors are attitudinal and behavioural.

Encouragingly, there is enormous scope for improvement. Typically, even the most successful companies are only very effective at less than a half of the critical success factors examined. This suggests there is enormous scope for improving the performance of key processes. By adopting winning behaviours many companies could achieve step change increases in performance in important areas of corporate operation.

Let's look at some overall differences between the behaviours of those in key positions who fail and succeed respectively at bringing about a fundamental transformation of their organizations.

First, we will examine the losers. They are indecisive and oblivious to the needs of others. They are cautious, wary of commitments and fail to inspire and motivate. They are also reactive. They respond to events and often fail to anticipate the need to change.

Losers as we saw in chapter 5 are indifferently led. Boards confuse operational and strategic issues. They offer bland rhetoric and spin rather than a compelling vision and clear direction. When they do act it is often in peripheral areas. They overlook what is important and the biggest opportunities for performance improvement.

Some companies put enormous effort into attempting to change people's fundamental attitudes, values and beliefs. The overwhelming majority of such initiatives fail. Yet, independently of values and beliefs, putting critical success factors in place and adopting winning ways can greatly increase the prospects of success.

Winners face realities. Those who have successfully used job support tools to transform the performance of particular workgroups tend to take their people as they are and simply make it easy for them to do difficult jobs. People are helped to emulate the approaches of high performers, and what works quickly gets adopted.

However, despite the impressive achievements of early adopters, losers are generally wary of new possibilities such as those offered by a new generation of support tools. Those who could most benefit from them ignore them

Losers hoard information. They are reluctant to delegate and trust. Although driven by their own agendas they often end up playing other people's games. They adopt standard approaches and are rigid and inflexible. They imitate and copy others rather than think for themselves.

Losers are great talkers. They mouth generalizations and confuse activity with progress. They are complacent, secretive and defensive. They try to do everything themselves and they resist new and external ideas.

Losers train by sheep dipping. Individual needs are not addressed. Immediate priorities take precedence over longer-term aims. A combination of attitudes, approaches and priorities locks change losers into a negative spiral of decline towards commodity product supplier status.

Winners in the challenge to change, transform and re-invent are very different from losers. They recognize that certain changes can be stressful and can disrupt valued relationships. They only alter what they need to change. Those affected are told why change is necessary.

Winners have a longer-term perspective. They become trusted business partners by enhancing their capabilities, deepening relationships, developing additional options and remaining relevant.

Winners are confident, positive and pro-active. They articulate compelling and distinctive visions. They build and release talent. They equip their people to make whatever changes need to be brought about.

Winners explore, pioneer and discover. They encourage enterprise and innovation. They trust other people, and share information and opportunities with them where this is likely to prove mutually beneficial.

Winners address the specific realities and practicalities of what they need to do to manage change. They inspire and motivate. They avoid wasted effort and concentrate upon the areas of greatest opportunity. They understand their customers and put themselves out to develop tailored responses to their requirements and bespoke offerings.

While open to ideas, winners select people, business partners and opportunities with care. They are persistent but pragmatic, and determined but adaptable in pursuit of their aims. They take calculated risks, experiment with new ways of working and learning, and create new knowledge, options and choices.

Winners value relationships. They empathise and invite feedback. They question and challenge, and listen and learn. They collaborate with complementary spirits who share their vision and values. They enter into partnering arrangements based upon openness and transparency.

The boards of change winners are competent and confident. They avoid the distractions of trappings. Their game is to inspire, enable and support growth, development and transformation. They cut through blather and hype to get down to the fundamentals of what needs to be done.

Winners prefer simple solutions and direct action. They think before they act, push back the boundaries of what is possible and become sought after business partners. Effective change managers avoid diversions, panaceas and single solutions. They focus on activities that deliver the results they seek.

Change, renewal and transformation should be regarded as normal activities. Work with colleagues to foster winning attitudes and behaviours, and ensure a balance between change strategy and capability. All the pieces of the jigsaw puzzle required for successful transformation and sustained competitiveness should be in place.

Check that colleagues are clear about what they are trying to achieve and are visibly committed to agreed objectives. Make sure that people understand what they need to do and are enabled to act. Ensure barriers to change are identified and tackled. Problems will arise. Their absence could indicate a lack of ambition. Learning from them and celebrating success help to sustain momentum.

Further Information

★ Information about the forthcoming companion volume on transforming corporate performance will be available from www.policypublications.com

'Transforming the Company, Manage Change, Compete and Win' by Colin Coulson-Thomas and published by Kogan Page can be ordered by Tel. 01903 828800; Fax. 020 7837 6348; E-mail: orders@lbsltd.co.uk or on-line at www.kogan-page.co.uk or online from www.ntwkfirm.com/bookshop

The skills needed by directors for achieving corporate transformation are examined in 'Developing Directors, A handbook for building an effective boardroom team' which is published by Policy Publications in association with Adaptation and can be ordered from 00 44 (0)1733 361 149 and also online from http://www.policypublications.com/developingdirectors.htm

A methodology for transforming performance by means of re-engineering key processes and introducing new ways of working, along with the tools and techniques required and illustrative case studies can be found in the three volume cased resource pack 'The Responsive Organization' which is published by Policy Publications and can be obtained from 00 44 (0)1733 361 149 or online from www.policypublications.com

Checklist:

- In relation to corporate transformation do you view yourself and/or your colleagues as winners or losers?
- Do others view you and/or your colleagues as winners or losers?
- Do the people of your organisation have a distinctive, compelling and shared vision?
- Is this rooted in the requirements of customers and prospects?
- Does the vision embrace a more flexible and high performance form of organization?

- Is there a corporate-wide transformation programme in place to bring it about?
- Does it address winning business and the creation of value, 'know-how', opportunities and new ventures?
- Does the programme embrace facilitating skills, enabling processes and supporting technology?
- Is it designed to influence attitudes by changing behaviour?
- How disruptive will it be of short-term customer relationships?
- Are goals sufficently demanding to challenge current assuptions, expectations and practices?
- Are change and transformation objectives clear and measurable?
- Is the board committed and supportive?
- Is there stakeholder buy-in to what needs to be done?
- How committed is top management to achieving the transformation?
- Has this commitment been communicated?
- Have people been given reasons why change or transformation is needed?
- Do they understand these reasons and what they can do to help bring change about?
- Will what is sought benefit them as well as the organisation?
- Are they provided with relevant support tools to enable them to do what is expected of them and make a difference?
- Do these incorporate critical success factors and winning ways for the areas where performance needs to be improved?
- Do the managers of the organization, and particularly the senior managers, behave as role models?
- What will be done to retain the commitment of those who may be disadvantaged at a particular stage in the change process?
- Have all the requirements for a successful transformation been identified?
- What 'building blocks' or 'pieces of the jigsaw puzzle' might be missing?
- In particular, are the necessary enablers in place, and have skill requirements been addressed?
- Is it clear to the people of the organization that the programme has been thought through?
- Is the reward system and remuneration both compatible with and supportive of the changes that are being sought?
- Will obstacles and people issues at each stage of the change and/or transformation process be identified and addressed?

- Will success be celebrated and shared?

Chapter 15
Corporate Communications

Modern corporations are essentially networks of relationships based upon trust. When a reputation for fair dealing and accurate reporting is compromised the consequences can be dramatic. Worldcom imploded.

Executives at Enron went to great lengths to conceal the true state of their companies' affairs. As a consequence, employees have forfeited their jobs and investors their savings. Association with misrepresentation sealed the fate of Arthur Andersen.

Are recent high profile scandals isolated instances of deception? Or is there a wider crisis in corporate communications? What lessons can be learned by boards of ambitious and growing companies who are eager to avoid the public fate of corporate failures? What do the winners do differently?

In this chapter we turn our attention to corporate communications. Corporate value statements advocate openness. Professional codes of practice champion integrity. Managers are expected to have 'communication skills'. Substantial investments have been made in communications processes and technologies. Communicating a distinctive vision, stretching goals and clear objectives can inspire, excite and energise people. However, many companies fall short of these ideals.

Looking at what communicators actually do rather than what they say reveals a wide gulf between corporate rhetoric and commercial reality. People are drowning in irrelevant information. They are overloaded, overworked and insecure. With little time to think many do not see the wood for the trees. Some suspect that corporate communications are all smoke and mirrors.

The author's research programme (see appendix A) has examined the communications practices of a wide range of companies in key areas such as winning business, building relationships and managing change*. Research teams compare the approaches of 'winners', companies that cope with changing circumstances, with 'losers', businesses that struggle or fail. Fundamental differences of attitudes and behaviour emerge.

Let us start with vulnerable companies and practices that should trigger alarm bells. Communications are largely top down and one-way. Communicators simply pass on whatever messages their bosses wish to communicate. They don't question a brief or ask whether information they are handed is accurate or fair.

Losers only communicate when *they* feel they need to. They become preoccupied with messages they would like to put across. Recipients are just targets. Smart communicators in floundering companies pride themselves on their ability to distract, exaggerate or keep a situation under wraps. They avoid speaking to people directly and hide behind technology. Sanitised summaries are posted on corporate Intranets.

The communications of struggling companies are often bland and non-committal. They give little away. Bad news is hidden under the carpet. Slick packaging encourages passive acceptance. Communicators mouth generalisations and repeat slogans. Their work is often of a high technical standard. But the focus is upon form and style rather than relevance and impact.

Communicators in stagnant and dying companies are emotionally detached. They display little personal commitment to corporate messages. Their communications are cold, clinical and bland. Many are sophists and cynics. Communications is a game to be played. Scoring points is more important than helping others to understand.

In ailing companies corporate communications is a distinct activity undertaken by dedicated specialists. They do the CEO's bidding, work mechanically and struggle to highlight what is different, special or unique about their employer. Not surprisingly they fail to connect with key stakeholder groups and spend much of their time rationalising failure. When they stumble few help. People who have been tricked or feel duped look the other way.

People in many companies struggle to explain what they do. Interested parties are referred to a handful of 'experts' and other people leave explanations to 'technical specialists'. It is little wonder so many people in 'loser' companies are insecure and so many procurement exercises are so protracted when available options are not understood by either buyers or sellers.

Many board members do not understand their company's core technologies and struggle to explain the essence of what their company does and the value it adds. This situation seems perverse when experience of developing job support tools suggests the use of clear language and appropriate diagrams and/or animation can enable almost all employees to comprehend the operation and contribution of the most complex technologies.

Multimedia capabilities can improve comprehension and understanding. They usually enhance the portrayal of corporate credentials and capabilities, while animations can bring technology to life. They also ensure sales people focus on value and benefits to the customer, and do not devote too much time to extolling the features of their own company's offerings.

Dana Glacier Vandervell Bearings, a leading supplier of engine bearings, found it very difficult to explain to customers and internal staff the sophisticated technology behind what appeared to be relatively simple products. The dependence of the properties of bearings upon the structure and composition of the materials of which they are made was particularly hard to visualise.

The solution adopted by Dana GVB was to capture, structure and package product information and technological expertise onto a CD that provided audio visual presentations to explain the essential characteristics of bearing materials within the overall design of an engine. Explanations and visual demonstrations of the company's unique technology and advanced manufacturing techniques were also given.

CD-Rom discs are ideal for disseminating job support tools. There is usually space to include a search and information management facility and a presentation wizard to allow tailoring of presentations using pre-approved standard modules. A company may choose to include a photographic library, interactive training modules, and self-assessment tests that identify knowledge gaps and advise on further study. Competitor analysis and response strategies and industry and market knowledge can also be added.

Effective job support tools use whatever formats, from text and graphics to animations, visual images, and video and audio clips, best help understanding. When tools are assembled using a knowledge framework such as K-frame (www.k-frame.com) search and fuzzy search facilities can cover a wide range of formats. Complex material can be more easily communicated, and fewer visits may be required to achieve a sale.

Dana GVB used animations with voice-overs to show what is required in particular circumstances. Customers were found to quickly understand the chemical and engineering technologies involved. The tool was also used to induct new employees. Staff and users could appreciate what the company did without needing to visit its factory.

Foreign language versions of support tools can be relatively easy to produce. There are French and English language editions of Eyretel's sales support tool, while ten different language versions have been issued of a tool developed for Bolero, including Chinese, Japanese, Korean, and Arabic.

Communicators in successful businesses are sufficiently confident to try new approaches to explaining what they do and communicating complex messages. Winners also have less to hide. They behave very differently. They share information, knowledge and understanding with people whose cooperation is needed to achieve corporate aspirations. They engage in two-way communication. They encourage, welcome and react to feedback.

Good communicators are not pre-occupied with themselves. They focus on the people they would like to establish, build and sustain relationships with. They try to understand, empathise with and reflect their aspirations, hopes and fears. They make direct and personal contact. They feel. They may stumble over the words, but they demonstrate they care.

Communicators in winning companies consciously build mutually beneficial relationships. They forge longer-term partnerships. They are both sensitive and flexible. They listen. They monitor reactions and are alert to changing requirements. Communications activities evolve, as changes are made to ensure greater relevance.

Effective communicators identify unmet needs, analyse communications barriers and address problems. They recognise the importance of symbols and are visibly committed. They understand they and their colleagues will be judged by what their actions and conduct. They endeavour to match words with deeds.

In companies with prospects communication is an integral element of management. It is built into work processes and the roles of managers. Communicators think for themselves. They question motivations, probe sources and assess likely implications. They take steps to ensure the veracity of corporate messages. They assume responsibility for what they communicate.

Winners explain with conviction the essence of what they are about. Their communications celebrate and sustain success. They engender allegiance and foster relationships that withstand market shocks and survive the traumas of economic downturn. People trust them and will put themselves out for them.

Investors, employees, customers, suppliers and independent directors should never take corporate communications for granted. The intelligence, standing and bravado of corporate leaders and their professional advisers are no guarantee the full story is being told. Be alert to tell tale signs of whether communication approaches and practices indicate likely failure or herald future success.

Further Information

* Findings relating to effective communication are summarized in the author's forthcoming book on transforming corporate performance (see www.policypublications.com) and in 'Transforming the Company, Manage Change, Compete and Win' by Colin Coulson-Thomas, which is available from Kogan Page: Tel. 01903 828800; Fax. 020 7837 6348; E-mail: orders@lbsltd.co.uk or on-line from www.ntwkfirm/bookshop

The board's role in corporate communications and the communication skills of directors are examined in 'Developing Directors, a handbook for building effective boardroom teams' which is published by Policy Publications in association with Adaptation and can be ordered from 00 44 (0)1733 361 149 and http://www.policypublications.com/developingdirectors.htm

Lessons of the research for communication with customers and prospects are summarised in 'Developing Strategic Customers & Key Accounts', 'Winning New Business, the critical success factors', the 'Close to the Customer' series of briefings and other titles in the 'winning business' series of reports which can be obtained from Policy Publications: Tel: + 44 (0) 1733 361149; Email: colinct@tiscali.co.uk or from www.ntwkfirm.com/bookshop

Information on the use of support tools for corporate communications, and particularly communicating complex messages, can be obtained from 00 44 0870 748 1400 or www.cotoco.com

Checklist:

- In relation to corporate communications do you view yourself and/or your colleagues as winners or losers?
- Do others view you and/or your colleagues as winners or losers?
- Is communication activity within the organisation an integral part of its management and business processes?
- Is communication regarded as a number of specialized activities, or is it the responsibility of every manager?
- Are all employees able to quickly explain what the organisation does, what is unique, special or distinctive about it and the value it adds?
- Does communication activity follow an analysis of the situation?
- Before rushing into various communication activities do people first think through why they are communicating, and what needs to be communicated to whom?

- Have surveys been undertaken to determine the requirements and interests of those with whom the company wishes to communicate?
- Are the messages used compatible with the vision, goals and values of the organization?
- Is the prevailing pattern of communication one way or two way?
- How genuine is the desire to involve, listen and learn?
- What is really happening out there? What do people think and feel?
- Have the barriers to communication been identified, and are action programmes in place to deal with them?
- What is done to monitor and assess the result of communication activity?
- Do the signs and symbols support or undercut change messages?
- Do key people in the organization exhibit role-model behaviour?
- What incentive is there, in terms of reward and recognition, for people to act as role models and positive symbols?
- Are they equipped with support tools that make it easy for them to explain the distinctive features of the organisation's offerings and build mutually beneficial relationships with customers and business partners?
- Are key work groups equipped with support tools that enable them to understand complex issues and do difficult jobs?

Chapter 16
Going Global: Operating effectively in the international marketplace

The horizons of ambitious managers today embrace the globe. Deregulation, privatization and market forces have eroded trade barriers. Budget airlines have reduced travel costs. The end of the cold war has created new opportunities.

Work can follow daylight around the globe allowing 24 hour a day operation. Resources can be accessed and activity undertaken locally, regionally or at global level depending upon requirements and comparative costs. Even sole traders use websites and email to make direct contact with customers all over the world.

However, operating in the international business environment also presents new challenges. There are commercial, legal and financial risks to consider. There are obstacles of distance, culture and time to overcome. In this chapter we will examine how to operate effectively in the international marketplace.

A continuing investigation led by the author (see appendix A) has examined the differing approaches of successful international operators and businesses that find it hard going. Comparing them reveals some lessons for those with aspirations to go global* - 'dos' that successful operators or winners practice and 'don'ts' that trip up losers. But first let us examine what the winners and losers do differently.

Losers prefer common approaches, standard solutions and global products. They attempt to define and impose a single corporate culture independently of their customers and people. They also have naïve expectations of international developments, new management initiatives and organizational changes.

Because they tend to be more preoccupied with themselves, losers keep to themselves, trust no one and operate alone. They are suspicious of foreigners and do not think through the consequences of their actions or equip their people to manage effectively those joint ventures that they enter into. They mouth the rhetoric of internationalization, while ensuring that all key positions are in the hands of nationals of the 'home country'.

'Loser' companies advocate diversity while seeking to export panaceas, slogans, and simplistic models in their eager search for corporate transformation. Their efforts are resisted. Some programmes founder upon the rocks of the very diversity that is being heralded. The natives, whipped up by the talk of involvement, empowerment and customer focus, become restive. Gaps between actions and words make them fidgety.

Winners endeavour to tailor to local circumstances and requirements. They allow people to network and forge whatever cross-border relationships will best enable them to achieve their objectives. They strive to match corporate culture to the cultures of customers and suppliers at local level in order to develop closer relationships.

Because they are more focused upon others, winners think through the implications of whatever it is they are endeavouring to do and anticipate and address likely problem areas. They are realistic and think through likely consequences, outcomes and reactions before they act.

Winners form networks of relationships with various collaborators at home and abroad. They act to reap the benefits of joint ventures and to ensure that they are properly managed. They recruit a diverse and multinational cadre of managers where appropriate and ensure that management positions go to those who are most qualified for each role.

When assessing how 'international' people are losers use measures such as trips of abroad. Mobility may, or may not, be an indicator of internationalization, according to its purpose. The appearance of internationalization in the form of the jet-setting executive could conceal the reality of a lack of localization. More local involvement, not to mention computer- and video-conferencing, might obviate the need for so much travel. The acid test should be the extent to which customer requirements are met.

The flexibility of the network organization can allow major corporations to create internal labour and information markets to overcome the imperfections of external markets. The network can grow or contract organically, according to market opportunities and economic circumstances, without the dramas of starting up or closing local operations associated with the bureaucratic form of organization.

Mobility has its costs. For example, after an initial 'honeymoon period', an adverse reaction may set in, with 'the vision of mountains, sea and sand being replaced by the reality of crime, disease and telephones that do not work. Mobility can be expensive, and may create tensions between expatriates and local managers. On the other hand, staff travelling overseas may obtain opportunities to work with and learn from customers.

Mobility is widely perceived as a means of equipping managers with an international perspective. In reality, it may provide them with some insight into particular countries and cultures, without developing a broader international awareness. Ford has taken the view than an international perspective should precede the assumption of international responsibilities, rather than be left to arise as a consequence of them.

Winners recognize that true internationalization is of attitude, awareness, approach and perspective. It is evidenced by openness, tolerance and active encouragement of cultural and national diversity.

People can be internationalized in many ways, from visits, exchanges, job swaps to joining international project groups, task forces and teams. Moving roles around the organization and managers through various international projects and teams helps to build a multiple perspective. Opportunities to come together across traditional divides expose many individuals to a diversity of viewpoints.

Companies that have thought it through use a combination of approaches, rather than the 'single solution'. Internationalization is also integrated into mainstream processes, rather than regarded as a 'bolt-on for those who need it'.

Thinking global is the first step towards acting global. To take it you need to be aware of what is happening abroad. When you touch down be open to new influences and receptive to alternative ideas. Winners are intuitive, perceptive and observant.

Retain a sense of perspective. Business people around the world can watch the news on cable television and receive regular feeds of stories that interest them direct to their desktops. Global media shape their attitudes and perceptions. But even MTV has its regional offerings, and requirements for products can vary greatly between national markets. The significance of borders will depend upon the business you are in,

Don't be overawed by the claims of others. Many so-called international companies are national enterprises that trade internationally. People who travel a lot sometimes hold onto stereotyped views or exaggerate national characteristics. Living and working abroad can reinforce existing prejudices. Some make an effort to adjust and adapt. Losers don't.

Appearances can be deceptive. A German manager who might seem formal and detached may contribute as much as a more voluble American. Reluctant Britons might observe a consensus outcome while delightful French colleagues may refuse to implement decisions they disagree with.

Many losers name drop and like to appear as citizens of the world. However, knowledge of the best bars in Amsterdam, Barcelona or Venice does not distinguish an 'international manager'. Attitudes, approaches and perspectives do. Internationally aware mangers are alert to developments in the global business environment.

True internationalization requires more than an ability to speak foreign languages. Learn from winners. Respect other viewpoints. Be tolerant of national differences. Actively support cultural diversity. Seek opportunities for foreign travel. Participate in overseas exchanges and job swaps. Join international project groups, task forces and teams.

Companies like countries can have distinct cultures. Be sensitive to differences and similarities in national assumptions, attitudes, and motivations. Try to reconcile conflicting interests, while recognizing that particular local requirements create opportunities for bespoke offerings.

Customer segments may or may not coincide with national borders. Experienced international operators are intuitive and cross-culturally aware. Learn to handle diversity and relationships with overseas colleagues. Mutual expectations need to be realistic and compatible.

Address practicalities such as whether the technologies of the various parties that need to collaborate will connect. If they won't consider the use of job support tools for communicating across national borders and handling challenges such as international new product launches (see chapter 27). As we will see in chapter 26 leading companies are using support tools to communicate complex messages to national and international partners and diverse groups.

People likely to be interested in what you have to offer may be widely scattered. Keeping opportunities to yourself, trusting no one and operating alone will stunt your growth. Form relationships with complementary collaborators in other countries.

Some managers have a distorted understanding of overseas situations and harbour naïve expectations of international initiatives. Be realistic. Think through the implications of what you are setting out to do. Anticipate likely consequences, consider probable outcomes and assess possible reactions. Be prepared to address potential problem areas.

Recognize fundamental national differences and match words and deeds. Don't advocate diversity and variety, and then insist upon common approaches. Don't impose standard solutions that are inappropriate in particular locations. Wherever possible, tailor your approach to local circumstances and individual requirements.

Aim to communicate with customers and prospects in ways that are acceptable to them. Use languages they understand. If your intention is to become an international rather than a European player, you may need to give greater priority to Spanish and Portuguese.

Some executives talk about internationalization but then make sure that all key positions are in the hands of 'home country' nationals. Diversity can be a spur to creativity. If you get the chance, recruit and develop a multinational cadre of managers. Ensure opportunities go to those who are best qualified for each role.

Try not to force internationalization down your colleagues' throats. Let it occur naturally and tackle problems as they arise. Don't sweep difficulties under the carpet or hope they will go away. Allow people to network. Let them forge whatever cross-border relationships will best enable them to achieve their objectives.

Do not foist a single corporate culture on employees, customers and suppliers regardless of differing local conditions and unfavourable circumstances. Match your management style to how people you wish to develop closer relationships with operate.

Before you set up joint ventures with overseas businesses make sure you and your colleagues are equipped to manage them. Be prepared to devote time to making them work. Because of the effort involved select prospects with care. Learn from your mistakes, and from your customers, suppliers and business partners.

Don't be pre-occupied with yourself. Emulate winners. Focus on the people you would like to establish, build and sustain relationships with. Understand them. Empathize with them. Respond to their aspirations, hopes and fears.

Effective international relationships are based on trust and respect. Lasting partnerships depend upon compatible interests. Establish a shared vision, common values, joint goals and agreed objectives. Consciously create mutually beneficial arrangements. Monitor reactions and be alert to changing requirements. And finally, celebrate, enjoy and sustain success.

Further Information

*The findings relating to successful internationalization are summarized in the author's forthcoming book on transforming corporate performance. This will be available online from www.policypublications.com

Internationalization is also covered in 'Transforming the Company, Manage Change, Compete and Win' by Colin Coulson-Thomas is available from Kogan Page: Tel. 01903 828800; Fax. 020 7837 6348; E-mail: orders@lbsltd.co.uk or on-line at www.kogan-page.co.uk

It is relatively easy to produce different language versions of job support tools of the type considered in chapters 26 and 27. Information on the use of support tools to communicate across national borders and with different language groups and cultures can be obtained from 00 44 0870 748 1400 or www.cotoco.com

Checklist:

- In relation to going global do you view yourself and/or your colleagues as winners or losers?
- Do others view you and/or your colleagues as winners or losers?
- Does the organisation have an international vision?
- How international is the perspective of the 'key players'?
- How tolerant are they of cultural diversity?
- Are different language versions of support tools used by key work groups produced?
- Is the membership of the board drawn from a mix of nationalities?
- What does the company do to understand, and respond to, developments in the international business environment?
- Who are the key global competitors?
- Does it have a nationality, or is it an international actor?
- Whose cultural values predominate throughout the organization?
- Are the resources of the organization equally accessible from any point?
- What is done to allow the total resources of the company to be harnessed to deliver value to the individual customer?
- Are customer facing staff enabled to craft and deliver bespoke responses to particular local requirements?
- How is the company responding to regional, global and centralized purchasing?

- How easy is it for the people of the company to work together in groups and teams across the barriers of function, distance, nationality and time?
- Is it realistic for staff at various locations around the world to aspire to senior management positions?
- Are 'head office functions concentrated at a single point, or dispersed around the international corporate network?

Chapter 17
New Ways of Working

People should be able to work at whatever time and place enables them to best harness their potential and be effective at whatever tasks they are undertaking. The right way of working for one role or activity might not be appropriate for another. In some cases 'being there' might be important while other work could be 'location independent'.

Those who follow the advice of the last chapter and 'go global' will encounter many different attitudes to work in various parts of the world. A generation ago IBM, ICL and Rank Xerox operated telecommuting networks. 'Telecoms' companies like BT and Cable and Wireless and the European Commission introduced various initiatives to promote more flexible patterns of work such as teleworking. However, their adoption has been much slower than champions and early enthusiasts predicted. While corporate structures have undergone significant change many traditional ways of working persist.

Too often processes are simplified or re-engineered without fundamentally changing how, where, when or with whom particular tasks are undertaken. Yet a pan-European project team led by the author has developed 'The Responsive Organisation'* framework and methodology for introducing new ways of working during the course of process improvement activities. Doing both at the same time can massively increase the success rate of business restructuring and yield significant benefits for both people and organisations.

In this chapter we look at how to succeed with new ways of working. Flexible operation is the key to the success of many entrepreneurial companies. Hazell Carr offers the services of professional actuaries who work from home. Training services are provided to the freelance knowledge workers, and checks are in place to monitor the quality of calculations resulting from the company's virtual model of operation. Working at night enables RS Communication Services staff to install phone lines in City Offices while their users are asleep or clubbing.

Virgin and easyJet have based their business strategies upon doing things differently. Small companies sometimes give a lead when it comes to adopting alternative ways of working. Although operating in a traditional sector, Swift Construction allows its people to work flexible hours and job-share.

Cisco Systems grew rapidly by providing products that allowed others to use the Internet and embrace ebusiness. New ways of working also create business opportunities for those who help to make it happen. Telework Systems products include software for tracking, monitoring and managing mobile and remote workers.

Innovation is often a question of balance. Naivety can be dangerous, but excessive control can stunt and eventually suffocate. Support tools should enable and release rather than constrict and restrain. If they are to aspire, reflect, dream, initiate, build and create people may need to be set free from mundane distractions and petty constraints.

Achieving shared goals needs to become more important than protecting selfish and vested interests, which can become self-defeating within the context of many forms of collaborative relationship. Corporate policies that encourage openness, trust and mutual respect are more likely to encourage effective knowledge entrepreneurship.

If successful transformation from corporate bureaucracy to incubator of enterprise is to be achieved management approaches must liberate rather than constrain. A decade ago I argued in my 1997 book 'The Future of the Organisation' (published by Kogan Page) that there are ten essential freedoms that should be both adopted and actively championed:

1. Freedom to dream, aspire, build and create.
2. Freedom to enter into mutually beneficial relationships.
3. Freedom to do what is necessary to deliver value and satisfaction to customers.
4. Freedom as a customer to seek new sources of benefit and value.
5. Freedom to initiate debates, explore, question, challenge, innovate and learn.
6. Freedom to understand one's self, be true to one's self, and to develop and build upon natural strengths.
7. Freedom to work at a time, location and mode that best contributes to desired outputs.
8. Freedom to use the most relevant technology, tools and processes depending upon what it is that needs to be done.
9. Freedom to confront reality, identify root causes and tackle obstacles and barriers.
10. Freedom to learn according to one's individual learning potential.

These ten freedoms should form the basis of a new social contract with key corporate stakeholders. They must become a charter for innovation and enterprise.

The hard protective shells of many companies currently act as barriers to enterprise. Boards and management teams must work to ensure they become frontiers that encourage the migration of people and ideas. They must be turned into open arenas of opportunity if new collaborative activities are to be inspired that will fulfil the aspirations of both individuals and organizations.

Too often the workplace is a constraint, an overhead cost and the cause of sick building syndrome rather than an enabler of creativity and flexibility. Offices should be designed to support a variety of relationships, behaviours and patterns of interaction. To encourage imaginative thinking there should be quiet spaces for personal reflection, and activity areas for brainstorming and other group sessions.

What do winners – the more successful companies - do differently in relation to new ways of working? To answer this question we will draw upon the experience of case study companies in the three-volume set of reports 'The Responsive Organisation' and related findings from the author's continuing research programme (see appendix A).* We will start with the approaches of losers before moving onto the winners.

Losers tend to stick with a particular and hierarchical model of operation. The structure is set out in organisation charts. There are probably job descriptions for most positions, and how the organisation operates is set out in a physical or electronic manual. Preparing these and understanding them takes time. Hence people are reluctant to make changes that might involve altering diagrams, updating files and reprinting documents.

Some people become complacent. They believe they have discovered or created a formula for continuing business success. They also swear by particular approaches and enshrine them in standard processes and procedures. The framework solidifies.

Many losers have a weakness for single solutions, panaceas and fads. They believe that this management approach, that technology or a particular consultant's methodology will provide an answer or solve their problems. While struggling to make a chosen course of action work they fail to consider alternative options. They lock themselves in.

Employees who can be trusted to operate in approved ways and observe standard practice are promoted. After some time corporate structures, processes, systems and mind-sets become rigid and inflexible. Subject them to increasing stress and they first creak and groan and then snap.

Increase workloads and transaction flows and people in 'loser' organisations struggle to cope. Rather than operate in new ways or change processes they endeavour to work harder, faster and for longer hours. They quickly become overloaded and break down. Work-life balance is an issue in these companies because people suffer additional pressures without enjoying any of the compensating benefits.

There are often alternative ways of achieving the same objective. Winning corporate cultures are more tolerant of uncertainty and diversity. Their people think in terms of flows rather than structures. They reflect. They are willing to question, review and consider alternatives. Fluid roles, flexible systems and adaptable processes enable these organisations to move in new directions as situations and circumstances change.

Winners avoid blind allies and dead ends. They do not take continuing success for granted and are always open to alternative ways of operating. They are less wedded to precedent and more likely to treat each case on its own merits. They are also willing to re-invent themselves and to learn and work in new ways as the occasion demands. Innovative responses and novel approaches are recognised and rewarded.

Bespoke products and services are offered. Processes and their supporting systems exist to support developing relationships with customers. Learning is built into them. They are updated as required, and individual tasks are handled in whatever ways are thought to be most appropriate. People endeavour to improve and build upon what has gone before rather than merely replicate previous responses.

On the whole, winners are pragmatic, catholic and wary of 'single solutions'. They assemble creative and practical combinations of whatever ways of working and learning and change elements they feel will enable them to achieve their purposes. They are always alert to the possibility of better alternatives and vary the factors selected to improve outcomes and cope with changing circumstances.

Attitudes, processes, systems and ways of working and learning are relatively robust and resistant to stress. Because they flex to accommodate changing conditions and circumstances they do not fall over when the going gets tough. Winners handle new challenges and opportunities by prioritising, adapting and securing flexible access to whatever additional resources are required.

The EU COBRA project which I led examined how to transform performance by means of new ways of working. According to the resulting three part 'The Responsive Organisation' methodology and resource pack if a new pattern of work, such as a telecommuting programme, is to be successfully introduced:

- it must be appropriate for both the tasks to be performed and the people concerned;
- tasks should be defined in terms of supplying a specified 'output' with fixed parameters of cost and time;
- the people selected should be inner-directed, and able to apply their knowledge and skill independent of a particular location;
- those likely to be affected should be both prepared and involved;
- not only the programme participants, but those who work with them and manage them, should also be prepared;
- employees, or network members, should participate in the design and implementation of the programme;
- top management commitment should be secured and retained, and clear objectives and targets set;
- a respected member of staff should be appointed to lead the implementation programme;
- the programme itself should be voluntary, and allowed to evolve naturally; and
- every effort should be made to communicate regularly with the programme participants during both the implementation and operational stages.

If the implementation requires compulsion and needs to be forced, one should question whether it meets the needs and objectives of those concerned.

In summary a new way of working must be appropriate for the tasks to be performed and the people concerned. Tasks should be defined in terms of delivering a specified 'output' with fixed parameters of cost and time. Ideal flexible workers are those who are inner directed and able to apply their knowledge and skill independent of any particular location.

People likely to be involved in a new way of working - and those who work with them - need to be involved and prepared. Clear objectives and targets should be set and health, safety and security issues addressed. Voluntary programmes are far more likely to succeed than those that are imposed. Regular communications with those who are working flexibly are also highly conducive of success.

Further Information

★A framework and methodology exists for introducing new ways of working while restructuring ['The Responsive Organisation' a three volume set of reports covering methodology, a tool kit and case studies] and re-engineering supply chains using the enabling technologies of electronic commerce ['The Competitive Network']. Details from Policy Publications: Tel. +44 (0)1733 361149; Email colinct@tiscali.co.uk; or online from www.policypublications.com or www.ntwkfirm.com/bookshop/

For those attracted by the list of ten freedoms given in this chapter guidance on seeking new directions and assessing alternative options is given in 'Individuals and Enterprise: creating entrepreneurs for the new millennium through personal transformation' and 'Shaping Things to Come, strategies for creating alternative enterprises'. Both can be ordered from Blackhall Publishing by Tel: 00 353 1 6773242, Fax: 00 353 1 6773243, or email: blackhall@eircom.net) or from the online bookshop www.ntwkfirm.com/bookshop

Some findings relating to new ways of working are also presented in 'The Future of the Organisation' and 'Transforming the Company, Manage Change, Compete and Win'. Both are by Colin Coulson-Thomas and published by Kogan Page and they can be ordered by Tel. 01903 828800; Fax. 020 7837 6348; E-mail: orders@lbsltd.co.uk or from www.ntwkfirm.com/bookshop/

Information on the use of support tools to enable new ways of working can be obtained from 00 44 0870 748 1400 or www.cotoco.com

Checklist:

- In relation to new ways of working do you view yourself and/or your colleagues as winners or losers?
- Do others view you and/or your colleagues as winners or losers?
- What importance does the organisation place upon employee involvement and participation?
- Does it measure employee fulfilment and views?
- In addition to commercial objectives is there also an objective to achieve measurable contributions to employee fulfilment?
- What does the company actually do to empower employees?
- Are people allowed to work at a time and location of choice and in ways that best enable them to harness their talents and give of their best?

- Are members of key work groups equipped with support tools to enable them to do difficult jobs?
- Do these incorporate critical success factors and the winning ways of high performers?
- Do members of the management team understand what empowerment means?
- Are the processes that deliver value for customers identified and documented in order that opportunities can be found to speed them up through the empowerment of people?
- As with any support tools do they incorporate critical success factors and winning ways?
- Do all the people of the organization know what they are expected to contribute to corporate objectives?
- Does each person have a 'vital few' list of things to do?
- What use does the company make of self-managed workgroups?
- Does the knowledge and skill management strategy of the company match the needs of its situation and circumstances?
- How flexible is the organization in terms of access to knowledge and skills?
- How tolerant is it of diversity in terms of both people and patterns of work?
- How tolerant are the people of the organisation of different ways of working?
- How moral is the culture of the company, and how might people be made more honest?

Appendix to Chapter 17

Introducing new ways of working

People can be put first in reality as well as rhetoric if changes are introduced primarily to enable them to become more fulfilled as well as more productive. This involves putting their issues, concerns and aspirations at the heart of projects to introduce new ways of working and learning and create an enterprise:

- Draw up a list of work groups and rank these in terms of the potential contribution it is thought they could make to the delivery of value to customers, the creation and exploitation of know-how and/or the achievement of key corporate objectives.
- Examine these groups in terms of the people and personalities involved, and whether or not some of their members are significantly more effective, creative and/or fulfilled than others.

- Consider the factors that distinguish the performance and/or satisfaction of 'superstars' or 'high achievers' from their less effective, innovative or fulfilled colleagues.
- Assess also the extent of any latent potential that is not currently being tapped.
- Identify the groups that offer the greatest prospect for increasing both 'impact' and the realisation of hidden or latent potential.
- Ask a representative selection of the members of these groups to indicate ways of working and learning that would best allow them to give of their best and be true to themselves.
- Identify areas of concern and future aspirations that need to be addressed while evaluating alternative ways of operating.
- If prompting is required, raise possible 'agenda items' such as the nature and quality of the working environment, preferred work locations for different types of work, or the time of day when people feel most productive or creative.
- Consider also whether there are particular approaches, tools, techniques or methodologies that would benefit them.
- Review their information, knowledge and job support tool requirements.
- Examine whether different processes, facilities or reward mechanisms might be more suited to their requirements.
- Agree, scope and cost the introduction of whatever ways of working and learning would contribute the most to the attainment of customer requirements, corporate objectives and individual aspirations, and attempt to quantify the likely benefits.
- Prioritise the identified opportunities in relation to the size and nature of the gap between benefits and costs.
- Develop the business cases for introducing appropriate responses to the most promising opportunities that have been identified.
- Evaluate whether the approach adopted might form the basis of a performance improvement methodology that could yield benefits for both individuals and organizations.

Chapter 18
Managing Virtual Organizations

Organizations used to consist of people we employed working in buildings we owned. No longer. With outsourcing, teleworking and electronic commerce, the 'virtual organization' can embrace people who work in a diversity of ways in widely scattered locations, and collaborating through a variety of contractual arrangements. Continuing the theme of new ways of working we turn in this chapter to how such organizations should be managed.

Developing a business normally involves harnessing and applying collective capabilities to the process of value creation. We are spoiled for choice in terms of where, when, how and with whom to work and learn. There are so many options for securing personal inputs in terms of employment status, place and hours of work, nature and duration of relationships, etc. This is the age of the 'designer organization'.

Emerging technologies can overcome barriers of function, distance and time, to bring together networks of complementary partners. Virtual teams are held together by a common sense of purpose, shared visions, and compatible goals and beliefs. Competition is increasingly between consortia of cooperating organizations, rather than individual enterprises.

Virtual companies composed of 'members' or 'business partners' specializing according to capability and interest compete successfully with larger corporations. Electronic commerce technologies are democratizing opportunities. The internet allows international communication for the price of a local call. Relevant contacts around the world can be accessed in seconds. Global distribution networks can be built in weeks.

Simple peasants producing craft goods can cooperate to provide store buyers with electronic ordering systems superior to those offered by major manufacturers. Virtual operation offers small enterprises flexibility and responsiveness which many larger corporations only dream of.

Being on line is crucial. Not being connected in the relationship age is the equivalent of physical incarceration on a remote island. Entrepreneurs with business visions are no longer frustrated by lack of people, money, or technology. Required capabilities are contracted in, perhaps in return for an equity stake.

No previous generation has had so many options to earn, learn and buy at times and places, and through relationships, of choice. People move between web sites like birds flitting from one water hole to another. When loyalty can be no longer assumed, commercial success may be fleeting. Those who are absolutely outstanding are sought out. The merely very good are ignored.

Virtual operation raises many questions. How stable are relationships? How does one distinguish individual contributions? What are the risks of fraud, etc.? These and many other questions have been asked in an extensive examination of 'The Future of the Organization'★.

The management of virtual organizations - collaborators and contractors held together by electronic links, and by shared objectives and values - presents new challenges. It demands new sensitivities and new skills. Their governance - involving relationships with peers rather than subordinates - may require new people, personalities and practices in the boardroom.

Unsuccessful adopters – or losers – fail to anticipate the consequences of their actions. Wrong choices are made when 'non core competencies' are outsourced. Strategically important knowledge can be 'given away'; windows of opportunity can be missed. Management teams may find they have forgone the capability to respond to changing situations. Cutting out capabilities not directly related to immediate priorities may reduce the capacity to operate in tomorrow's markets.

When distinct areas of activity are contracted out to various organizations on differing timescales, both the discretion to flexibly re-deploy elements of a total capability and 'understanding of the whole' may be lost. Excessive fragmentation makes it more difficult for core values and goals to be shared.

Those forming a virtual organization should agree a common purpose and observe a framework of shared values and rules that will enable them to reap greater benefits from cooperative activities. What a network stands for and is seeking to do, will attract or repel potential members.

Successful adopters – or winners – recognize that self-awareness and honesty make it easier for people to play to their strengths and work cooperatively with others who have complementary capabilities. People need to be encouraged to discover their working and learning preferences.

Experienced learning or transformation partners can advise on the combinations of approaches, processes, technologies and patterns of work which are most appropriate for a particular company and provide counselling, mentoring and facilitation support specifically related to virtual collaboration (see www.ntwkfirm.com). Successful transition to virtual operation requires individual as well as corporate transformation. People may need to acquire networking, relationship and virtual team-building skills.

Virtual organizations, with their multiple relationships and on-line links, are particularly at risk of being intellectually asset stripped. Network security is critical. Many 'loser' boards act to safeguard physical and financial resources, while overlooking risks to intellectual property.

Winners understand that freedom encourages creativity. Thus measures to protect know-how should not stifle its development. The well of knowledge needs to be replenished. Parasites feed upon the supply, leaving renewal to others. It is important to monitor who is contributing to the virtual company and who is 'living off' it.

Information and knowledge can become commodities. When it is 'on the web', and easily and widely accessible, less value is put on knowledge for its own sake. To be harnessed and applied, information, understanding and expertise must relate to the purpose and objectives of an enterprise.

Shared commitment to learning is especially important. It attracts quality members, while the competitive positioning of a whole value chain could be undermined by the failure of particular collaborators to keep up to date. Adherence to certain principles, or signing a formal agreement covering network security, protection of intellectual property, and learning could be a condition of joining a virtual community.

The defeat of corporate giants by virtual SMEs is not inevitable. An EU framework exists for introducing new ways of working while restructuring ['The Responsive Organization'] and re-engineering supply chains using the enabling technologies of electronic commerce ['The Competitive Network'].★ Texas Instruments, Jaguar, Motorola and other companies have built virtual networks that embrace both internal teams and external supply chain partners.

In an uncertain world, continuing relevance requires loyalty, learning and change. To quote from 'The Future of the Organization'★ effective management of virtual organizations begins with people: - 'listening, building relationships and understanding what is important and represents value and opportunity for them. … It should be about empathy, flows, openness, trust and tolerance …

Success requires the matching of individual qualities, competencies, experience and motivation with a corporate environment that provides purpose, resources, commitment and support. Either without the other is likely to lead to frustration'.

Further Information

Further information on 'The Responsive Organisation' and 'The Competitive Network' methodologies for introducing new ways of working and re-engineering supply chains respectively can be obtained from Policy Publications: Tel. +44 (0)1733 361149; Email colinct@tiscali.co.uk; or from www.ntwkfirm.com/bookshop

'The Future of the Organisation: Achieving Excellence through Business Transformation' by Colin Coulson-Thomas is published by Kogan Page and can be ordered by: Tel. + 44 (0)1903 828800; Fax.+44 (0)20 7837 6348; E-mail: orders@lbsltd.co.uk or on-line from www.ntwkfirm.com/bookshop/

Job support tools such as those considered in chapters 26 and 27 can free people from dependency upon particular locations. Instant updates can be obtained whenever and wherever people log on. Information on the use of support tools for enabling and managing virtual operation can be obtained from 00 44 0870 748 1400 or www.cotoco.com

Checklist:

- In relation to managing virtual organisations do you view yourself and/or your colleagues as winners or losers?
- Do others view you and/or your colleagues as winners or losers?
- How effective are your colleagues at managing virtual teams?
- Does the organisation have an international information technology strategy and how compatible is this with its international vision?
- Does the strategy embrace virtual operations?
- How important are speed and intimate and iterative relationships with individual customers?
- How might the company's relationships with its customers, suppliers and business partners be transformed through the use and application of IT?
- Are support tools being used to enable customer facing staff and business partners to assess requirements and bespoke solutions at times and places that are convenient for them and customers and prospects?

- Do the tools incorporate critical success factors for key corporate activities?
- Are they used when activities are outsourced to ensure that new operators can be quickly brought up to speed and enabled to emulate the approaches of high performers?
- Does the company's IT network facilitate multifunctional, multilocation, and multinational team working?
- Does it allow flexible access to all relevant external sources of knowledge and skill?
- Does the company's IT network facilitate the building of understanding, as well as the acquisition of information and knowledge?
- Is it supportive of 'all-channel' communication, and the integration of working and learning?
- Is the technology of the company appropriate to its strategy, organization, people and management processes?
- Can it handle intellectual property in a variety of formats?
- Is it supportive of continuing adaptation and change?
- How 'user friendly' is the technology of the company, ie is it compatible with, and supportive of, the way people naturally work and think, and conductive of 'interfaces' with, or links to, other networks?
- Do people find it easy to access what they need and understand difficult issues and complex messages?
- Are they helped and enabled to do difficult jobs in winning ways?
- What are the main barriers to virtual operations in your company and how might these be overcome?

Chapter 19
Creating an Entrepreneurial Culture

A corporate culture as well as an organisation's ways of working may need to be changed. Companies need to become enterprise colonies that tap, build, and release the entrepreneurial potential within their people and relevant external networks and communities. Ambitious individuals want to work with organisations rather than for them.

Designers of organisations, processes and systems face a dilemma. The standardisation of steps and responses can result in simplification and cost reduction. Induction becomes easier and results more predictable. Yet if taken too far standardisation can result in commoditisation. Differentiation and bespoke responses may enable a premium price to be charged. Also talented people are demanding more discretion. They have an unprecedented range of choice in relation to how, when, where, for whom and with whom they work.

Increasingly, the challenge for companies is to attract potential entrepreneurs and business partners rather than dependent employees. More knowledge workers seek to live life on their own terms. Rather than approach organisations looking for work, ambitious, creative and confident individuals will treat corporations and colleagues as actual or potential collaborators. When comparing attitudes and approaches, there will no longer be such a stark divide between start-up enterprises and established businesses. Entrepreneurship, either alone or with corporate support, will be for the many rather than the few.

Many companies need to become an incubator and enabler of new enterprises. New approaches and processes for the encouragement of entrepreneurship are required. Individuals and teams should be asked to come forward with new business ideas and ask for venture capital support, access to central services, and development and marketing assistance. A growing number of internal employees will emulate potential external partners by also seeking a share of the rewards for successful intrapreneurship.

An extensive examination led by the author has identified key requirements for 'shaping things to come' and achieving both commercial success and personal fulfilment*. People need to consider what they would really like to do and are especially good at as well as what potential customers would most like to have. Many smart people get paid to do the things they love to do. Some turn their hobbies into moneymaking ventures.

Once a business concept and potential customers have been identified the next steps are daunting ones for many would be entrepreneurs. Securing initial funding, finding premises, recruiting staff and 'doing the books' can be time consuming and frustrating for those who would prefer to do other things. This is where collaboration with an established company can help. Yet, too many corporations are bureaucratic and ill equipped to handle new ventures. The emphasis is upon 'consolidation' and sticking to 'core competences'.

As a consequence, many intending entrepreneurs do not think of taking their new business ideas to an existing employer or a local company operating in a related field or with complementary interests. Instead they look elsewhere for support. Maybe they are worried about losing control or feel that a big corporation might not be interested in a new venture.

Attitudes towards entrepreneurship within larger organisations are changing. But much more effort still needs to be devoted to creating more entrepreneurial cultures. Too often restructuring, retrenchment and re-engineering are essentially negative activities, concerned with survival not growth. The mood in some boardrooms is swinging against downsizing in favour of creating greater value for customers and generating additional income streams.

Many people are fed up with the defensive cost cutting practiced by unsuccessful companies – or losers - and tired of being asked to do more with less. Many would like to change direction, reduce their dependency upon others, and lead more balanced lives. Employees used to seek security and a regular income. They undertook repetitive tasks, implemented standard procedures and followed prescribed rules. Today many want more than material rewards. They also want to build, develop and grow.

Customers too are restless. They demand distinctive and bespoke responses that reflect their individual concerns and priorities. People in client facing roles are expected to behave more imaginatively when creating offerings to meet particular requirements.

Market leadership in key sectors will go to winners who innovate, or assemble a novel combination of elements that represents greater value for particular groups of consumers. Rather than refer to manuals, mechanically apply a methodology or provide standard offerings, people have to make choices and take risks. They are required to consider alternatives, and manage resources and expectations. In short, they must think and act like entrepreneurs.

Many existing employees are struggling to make the transition from corporate dependent to intrapreneur and business partner. More companies are likely to recognise that they need external help and that some independent operators of smaller businesses may have the attitudes, skills and experience they require. Of course 'independents' are used to the freedom of operating alone. A clash of cultures could but might not arise as more big company bosses come to understand the requirements for contemporary market success.

Winners are more willing to empower responsibly. Giving individuals the discretion to do what they feel is most appropriate for each customer enables them to play a much more creative role. Their 'solutions' might contain unusual elements, unique features, novel approaches or new knowledge, which could be licensed to others. Opportunities abound for entrepreneurship and innovation in many walks of life.

The rapid adoption of *e*-Business is eroding barriers to entry. The imaginative can offer new ways of working, learning and earning that better match the preferences of those involved, and greatly increase the prospect of them achieving the twin goals of commercial success and personal fulfilment. This desired combination is most likely where personal and corporate aspirations are explicit, aligned and focused upon winning new business, establishing partnerships and benefiting customers.

Independent entrepreneurs and aspiring intrapreneurs will choose corporate patrons, partners and sponsors with care. For example, how much of the training budget is devoted to building entrepreneurial skills and supporting business development? They will consider whether a corporate culture and working environment encourages initiative, innovation and enterprise or stifles them.

Contracts, facilities, processes and systems should allow and enable questioning, resourceful and inventive individuals and business partners to explore and create. The rewards of successful innovation and entrepreneurship should be fairly allocated in proportion to the respective contributions of those involved. Separate incorporation of new ventures allows more people to become directors.

Successful innovation requires individual initiative and creative collaboration within an entrepreneurial culture. The people of loser companies tend to be cautious 'loners'. They work in relative isolation and cling to the familiar. They settle into their role and associated lifestyle and endeavour to avoid significant changes. They 'stick to the brief' and try to resolve issues by themselves. When reviews are held individuals become defensive and protective of departmental interests.

Knowledge workers take pride in their educational qualifications and membership of qualifying bodies. Their professional status is important to them. They tend to resent being 'second guessed' by others and may interpret requests for a second opinion as a questioning of their integrity and competence.

Groups within loser companies keep to themselves and departmental colleagues. They assume they know best and jealously guard their autonomy. Major bids, especially when time pressures are involved, may be dispatched without being subjected to any form of peer review.

People within loser companies play their cards close to their chest and are reluctant to invite external comment. Some avoid networking opportunities. They worry about cost and confidentiality. Paradoxically, they also imagine that 'outsiders' would find it difficult to master the peculiarities of their businesses.

When occasional independent reviews are held of the processes and activities of 'loser' companies, little tends to happen. The pressure of work and preoccupation with non-critical or even trivial matters militates against the adoption of any suggestions or recommendations made.

Winners are more open, self-assured and willing to change. Current contribution and future relevance rather than past achievements define personal standing. Teamwork, interaction and the sharing of information and knowledge are widespread and an integral element of working practices.

Individuals in 'winner' organisations are usually sufficiently secure to seek the opinions of their colleagues and peers. Drafts may be circulated to other departments and external parties for comment. In general, the interventions and contributions of colleagues are regarded as helpful and they are actively encouraged.

Business development teams seek whatever inputs will increase their chances of success. They submit significant proposals to a 'red team' review and listen carefully to any comments and reactions. People who have not been directly involved in preparing a bid response may find it easier to adopt an objective and customer perspective. Hence, their views can be of considerable value.

Winners are more likely to seek and use independent evaluations. They subject critical business processes to external reviews and 'health checks'. Winners also circulate among their peers and look for opportunities to make new contacts and forge additional relationships. Their best defence against others copying them and catching up is to innovate and thus stay out in front.

Intending entrepreneurs should seek out winners - flexible organisations that are tolerant of diversity and allow and enable people to be true to themselves and to play to their distinct strengths. Enterprise flourishes where people are enabled to work, learn and collaborate in ways that best enable them to harness their particular talents, and assemble new venture teams composed of individuals with compatible aspirations and complementary skills.

Confident people will join - and ambitious businesses will seek to work with - organisations that promote enterprise, support intrapreneurship and collaboration, and view them as potential business partners with ideas for new and profitable ventures. Arrangements should be in place to assess their proposals and provide concept development support and venture capital. Practical advice on securing family support, assembling a venture team and winning business should be provided, along with counselling on overcoming inhibitions, pitfalls and constraints, and getting started.

Farsighted companies will approach independent entrepreneurs when lining up the external support required by new ventures. Their internal procedures, processes and contractual arrangements will reflect the distinct and diverse needs of growing businesses. Their reward mechanisms will allow those responsible to participate in resulting financial returns.

Share-ownership, option or profit-sharing schemes may need to be established, to satisfy the increasing desire of individuals to build capital. Energetic and talented individuals who create knowledge rather than merely consume it, and who can innovate and develop tailored solutions, are seeking a greater share of the value that they create.

Investors should avoid losers - companies that do not champion enterprise and entrepreneurship. Their most capable people and most valuable customers will simply walk, and they will not attract the external partners they will require. Companies cannot afford to be excluded from successful new ventures established by independent entrepreneurs and past employees.

The interests of customers, independent entrepreneurs, companies and investors are rapidly converging. We are at a turning point in the relationship between people and organisations and between micro-businesses and larger companies. We have an historic opportunity to reconcile and align individual and corporate goals. If you are a corporate manager, go for it.

Further Information

★'Individuals and Enterprise: creating entrepreneurs for the new millennium through personal transformation' and 'Shaping Things to Come, strategies for creating alternative enterprises' can both be ordered from Blackhall Publishing by Tel: 00 353 1 6773242, Fax: 00 353 1 6773243, or email: blackhall@eircom.net; or online from: www.ntwkfirm.com/bookshop/

Checklist:

- In relation to creating an entrepreneurial culture do you view yourself and/or your colleagues as winners or losers?
- Do others view you and/or your colleagues as winners or losers?
- Does the organisation have a business excellence, transformation and enterprise or entrepreneurship programme?
- In relation to enterprise and entrepreneurship, does it encourage intrapreneurship and act as an incubator of new enterprises?
- Is enterprise and entrepreneirship taking root or running out of steam?
- How does the programme relate to the central purpose of your company, and to its vision, goals and values?
- Are all the members of the board and the senior management team committed to it?
- Who is responsible for the programme?
- Are people aware of it? Is everyone involved?
- Is the company's approach tailored to its own particular situation and circumstances?
- Is the encouragement and support of new ventures an integral part of the company's management and business processes and practices?
- Does the programme embrace other members of the supply chain, whether customers, suppliers or business partners?
- Is there a gap between internal and external expectations, and what has been delivered?
- How much emphasis is attached to the 'softer' elements of management and entrepreneurship, such as the building of quality relationships?
- Is the programme influencing attitudes and behaviour?
- Is know-how being created, packaged, protected and exploited?
- Is top management behaviour, and are board decisions, consistent with the vision?

- Is the output of improvement, change and new venture teams focused upon key customer-related activities?
- Is the reward and performance management system supportive of corporate and stakeholder goals?
- From time to time does the company reassess its approach to business excellence, transformation and entrepreneurship?

Appendix to Chapter 19

Aspiring Entrepreneurs Checklist

Before actively setting out to become an entrepreneur there are certain basic questions that you should address:

- Are you in control of your life? Do you have a sense of mission and purpose? Or are you happy to be a piece on someone else's chessboard?
- How strongly do you want to become an entrepreneur? Have you thought through the implications and requirements for success?
- Are you robust and determined? Do you have the energy and drive to sustain the growth of a business?
- How supportive are members of your immediate family and other people who are close to you? What is their honest assessment of your prospects?
- Where does your drive come from? Are you inwardly motivated and self-directed, or do you depend upon others for direction and motivation?
- Do you cope on your own? Are you self-contained and at ease with yourself, or does your sense of self-worth depend upon the assessments of other people?
- By nature, do you unthinkingly accept and accommodate, or are you a radical or revolutionary who challenges and questions the status quo?
- Are you alert and sensitive to what is happening in the world around you? Do you notice unsolved problems, gaps in the existing provision of goods and services, and needs that are not met?
- At heart are you a leader or a follower? Are you active or passive? Do you initiate or copy? Could you innovate, pioneer and discover?
- Would you rather be an employee or the owner of a business? Do you seek or shun responsibility and accountability? Are you a risk taker or risk averse?

- Are you imaginative, innovative and creative? Do you instinctively search for new and better ways of doing things?
- Are you an 'ideas person', or someone who likes to 'make things happen'? Are you content to make suggestions and come up with new concepts, or do you also like to implement them?
- Do you have a strong desire for personal recognition and achievement? Do you want to change things, and to have an impact?
- How sound is your judgement of requirements, situations, people and opportunities? Are you perceived as shrewd, or do you get taken in?
- Do you actively network with potential customers, and maintain contact with possible business partners? Have you stayed in touch with former employers?
- How acute are your antennae? Are you aware of contemporary trends, alert to threats and sensitive to risks?
- Would you stake your own money and that of others upon a venture that was dependent upon your personal judgement?
- Do you have your feet on the ground? Are you realistic, realistic and imperturbable?
- Are you dogged, persistent, resilient and determined? When the 'going gets tough', is your first instinct to 'cut and run', or do you hold true to the vision and stay the course?
- At the same time, are you flexible and adaptable? When a particular course of action does not work, do you look for alternative ways of achieving your objectives?
- Have you the tenacity to succeed, and the will to compete and win? Ultimately, do you deliver? Do other people regard you a 'talker' or a 'doer'?
- When the time is right do you 'have a go'? Do you wait for a consensus to form or are you prepared to give a lead and act?
- Have you missed attractive possibilities? Do you delay and dither, or take action while windows of opportunity still exist?
- Are you selective? Do you prioritise and focus? Do you tackle the most important matters first, or do you procrastinate when there are difficult decisions to be taken?
- Do you engender trust? Can other people rely upon your word? Do they like and respect you? Can you establish and sustain longer-term relationships?
- Are you a good listener? Do you take advice from others where appropriate?

- How self-aware are you? Do you recognise your own limitations? How willing are you to share opportunities with people who have complementary skills and qualities?
- Are you a leader? Do you involve, inspire and motivate colleagues and partners? Can you get other people to play your game?

Chapter 20
Entrepreneurial Purchasing

'You are what you eat' is a slogan of our time. The corporate equivalent could arguably be 'you are what you buy'. While over indulgent eating can lead to obesity, flabby buying can drain a company's coffers and impair its performance.

In this chapter we shift our attention from sales to spending. The cash generated by a business is the difference between payments into and out of corporate bank accounts. Companies need to be entrepreneurial when buying from their suppliers as well as entrepreneurial when generating revenues from their customers.

Far too many purchasing teams focus on short-term issues and do not contribute to the formulation of corporate strategy or the development of new products. They fail to strike up and sustain relationships with external suppliers that might both help them to control costs and improve the quality of their offerings.

Many purchasing professionals also fail to secure senior management appointments because they struggle to demonstrate the value they are adding. They are perceived as paper processors rather than creative entrepreneurs. The attitudes, competences and approaches of many purchasing professionals need to change.

One of the research teams led by the author found that for almost 70% of the 296 companies surveyed purchases of external products or services amounted to over a half of their total costs, while all companies reported that their purchasing achievements were falling short of their aspirations. Clearly more effective purchasing can have a very significant impact upon the bottom line.

The 'effective purchasing' study of European purchasing was undertaken with the cooperation of the European Institute of Purchasing Management. The resulting 'Effective Purchasing, the Critical Success Factors' report* reveals significant differences between the approaches of winners and losers, the companies that succeed and fail respectively at achieving the benefits of effective purchasing.

Losers tend to view purchasing as an administrative activity of relatively low status that is sometimes a source of both management and quality problems. Purchasing arrangements are often fragmented, and attempts to consolidate them are viewed as empire building by cynical business colleagues. Targets tend to focus upon year on year savings, yet often ignore price movements over business cycles.

Purchases by losers are often ad hoc. Losers like to shop around. They avoid 'getting involved' with particular suppliers. They look for 'deals' and opportunities to make quick savings. They also fail to recognize differences of capabilities among different suppliers, and that one's approach to purchasing may need to vary according to factors such as degree of commoditization, volume, storage, transportation, quality and item importance, value or visibility to end customers.

Compared with effective purchasers losers are less successful at all of the considerations relating to choosing suppliers that were examined by the research team. Sometimes they have so many relationships with different suppliers to maintain that finding the time to assess individual providers and properly distinguish between alternative suppliers becomes difficult, if not impossible.

When negotiating losers play win-loose games. They keep their various suppliers at arms length and endeavour to play one supplier off against another. They tend to be oblivious to the longer-term consequences of their relentless drive to cut costs. The benefits of consolidation, bulk-buying and cooperation elude them.

Losers give a low priority to the ethical employment, environmental and safety records of suppliers. They also seek to avoid the scrutiny of their colleagues, and are slow to assess their own performance. Winners are different. They measure and report their achievements, and demonstrate their contributions to colleagues. Their greater openness encourages others to have more confidence in them.

For winners purchasing is a source of competitive advantage. They work with their suppliers to reduce costs, innovate, improve quality or speed up deliveries. Involving purchasing and preferred suppliers earlier in the new product development process can often reduce the time required to bring new products to market by a quarter or more.

Winners are more likely to be involved in boardroom discussions of business strategy and new product development. Integrated systems are also more likely, that provide group-wide information and monitoring capability. Winners are able to show they are in control and achieving purchasing objectives. Their targets are more likely to include the building of longer-term and partnering relationships with strategic suppliers, and integrating purchasing into group strategy.

In comparison with their less successful peers, winners are also more likely to pursue win-win approaches to negotiations. They recognize that building value can be as important as controlling costs, and that working with certain suppliers might enable the delivery of improvements and innovations that lead to more competitive offerings and benefits for both parties.

Canny winners recognize it is usually in their best interests that strategically important suppliers do well. Squeeze them too hard and they may lack the margins needed to fund the investments that would enable them to stay at the top of their game. Collaboration to find new ways of working together can lead to opportunities to save both sales costs for the supplier and purchasing costs for the customer.

Winners prefer longer-term contracts with reviews, and framework contracts with local call-offs. They are more interested in establishing and building collaborative relationships with a smaller number of strategic suppliers, and monitoring the quality of what is procured. They are also ahead when it comes to using IT and e-business technologies to automate aspects of purchasing, and facilitate methods of purchasing such as 'internet auctions'. Losers play catch up where the winners pioneer.

When assessing suppliers, winners look for a willingness to enter into a partnership, flexibility and senior management commitment. Other considerations when selecting key suppliers are product quality, low cost and delivery track-record, while for building a successful relationship responsiveness, technical support, technical leadership and – once again – flexibility are especially important.

In recent years purchasing has been transitioning from a regional to national and from national to multi-national model. In larger companies it is becoming increasingly continental or global in scope. Winners favour smaller but more able teams, made up of purchasing professional who endeavour to keep their skills up to date.

Losers appear to be some way behind the winners in relation to longer term trends. Thus many of them were still centralizing, while their more successful peers who bought more centrally were devolving responsibilities to operating units within a framework of approved suppliers and group standards. Winners are more willing than losers to trust colleagues to make higher value purchases.

While losers buy a smaller proportion of a wider range of goods, winners are more likely to spend over half their total costs on bought in items. In particular, they enter into more partnership arrangements and are more willing to outsource. While the purchasing costs of losers are sometimes hidden, winners are both more aware of such costs and more likely to allocate them either to benefiting business units or central overheads.

Few companies appeared to have an integrated approach to checking the quality of purchased supplies. Winners were more likely to get the quality checking basics right, while losers tended to 'hope for the best'. Some losers play Russian roulette with quality, neither requiring supplier liability for faults, nor carrying out supplier audits.

Benefits of effective purchasing secured by purchasing winners include control of product quality, the integration of purchasing into group strategy and product plans, minimum costs of goods purchased, the use of standardized components/materials specifications, minimum work in progress stocks, security of supplies, partnerships with key suppliers, and retrospective discounts.

Losers tend to operate in isolation, while winners are more alert to what is happening in the marketplace. Effective purchasing teams aim to beat market prices by continually monitoring what others are buying, and taking immediate action to remedy any divergences of prices paid by competitors. Winners also embrace just-in-time or lean purchasing and benchmark their performance.

Companies with successful purchasing departments are more likely to be engaged in international trade. International sourcing is spreading and more activities are being outsourced, including the purchasing function itself. By adopting a more strategic approach, and acquiring the skills and experience to manage and monitor collaborative relationships, winners are more able to safeguard the intellectual capital and know-how needed for knowledge-based competitiveness.

There are many ways of simplifying procedures and reducing the complexity and cost of procurement. Prospects can fill in templates and place orders online. Configuration or design tools might allow them to assess alternatives when formulating their requirements. Software upgrades can be delivered over the Internet. Online progress chasing, automatic reordering and budgetary control facilities can all be provided. Support tools can be used to help suppliers to quickly and easily satisfy quality and other buying criteria.

It is important you understand where you are in relation to the differing approaches of winners and losers. The 'effective purchasing' database has been constructed to allow companies to benchmark their approaches against their peers in the survey sample and the winners who derive the most benefits from their purchasing functions. The fifteen page bespoke report★ that is produced covers 137 purchasing issues and enables those who complete a questionnaire to identify the areas they most need to improve.

Further Information

★ 'Effective Purchasing, the critical success factors' and related benchmarking reports are available from Policy Publications by: Tel. +44 (0)1733 361149; Fax: +44 (0)1733 361459; E-mail: colinct@tiscali.co.uk, or online from www.policypublications.com or www.ntwkfirm.com/bookshop/

Using the effective purchasing database the research team can generate bespoke benchmarking reports for companies that would like to compare their practices with their peers and high performing winners. These compare corporate performance with the average for both all companies and those companies that win most benefits from their purchasing functions. Details of these and other services can be obtained online from www.policypublications.com and from www.ntwkfirm.com/policy-publications/benchmarking.htm

Buyers can use support tools to ensure that suppliers meet their requirements. Information on the use of support tools for effective purchasing and handling buying and selling documentation can be obtained from 00 44 0870 748 1400 or www.cotoco.com

Checklist:

- In relation to purchasing do you view yourself and/or your colleagues as winners or losers?
- Do others view you and/or your colleagues as winners or losers?
- Is there clarity about the role of purchasing and is purchasing involved in strategic issues at board level?
- Is the puchasing team tight, professionally trained and up to date?
- Are business units involved in purchasing and are directors and managers trusted to make higher value purchases?
- How intimate are partnering and other arrangements with approved and strategic suppliers?
- Are such arrangments covered by long-term and framework contracts?
- How much importance is attached to the willingness of potential suppliers to enter into a partnership agreement, their flexibility in the face of changing conditions and the commitment of their senior management?
- Is there an appropriate focus upon quality, cost and delivery?

- Is quality checked on delivery?
- Is proper attention devoted to responsiveness, flexibility and technical leadership and support when developing relationships with suppliers?
- Is appropriate use made of e-business options and purchasing support tools that make it easier for current and potential suppliers to satisfy quality and other purchasing requirements?
- Whether or not purchasing is outsourced, is performance measured and monitored?
- How effective is your organisation at developing purchaser-supplier partnerships and linking strategic purchasing to strategic planning?
- Is the company learning with suppliers and are key supliers involved in the development of the next generation of offerings?

Chapter 21
The Knowledge Entrepreneur

Many boards and management teams are missing exciting opportunities to transform corporate performance by better exploiting know-how and using job support tools to boost productivity. They are also forgoing unprecedented possibilities for generating additional revenues from new knowledge-based offerings.

Scientific breakthroughs occur in laboratories and innovative thinking abounds in workshops. Yet people drown in irrelevant information. They waste time and money on 'knowledge management' initiatives to capture and share existing know-how that may or may not be relevant to future aspirations. With unexploited intellectual capital all around them executives imitate and copy others.

Companies are adopting managerial rather than entrepreneurial approaches. The focus is upon managing what is currently known, rather than creating new information and knowledge-based services, tools, ventures and businesses. Most knowledge management processes are missing an explicit knowledge exploitation stage.

Yet we stand at the threshold of a new management revolution. There is simply enormous potential for knowledge entrepreneurship, performance improvement and developing the additional knowledge needed to deliver greater customer and shareholder value. Continuing our theme of entrepreneurship we turn our attention in this chapter to the exploitation of know-how.

Most organisations and executives are barely scratching the surface. A recent investigation by the author for the book 'the knowledge entrepreneur'* has examined processes and practices for exploiting knowledge. The findings highlight the scope for both improving the performance of existing operations and creating new knowledge-based products and services.

But first let us examine what the winners and losers do differently. Losers are risk averse. They are 'talkers', not 'doers', passive followers rather than active leaders. If they do act, they blunder about. The silt they stir up prevents them from seeing the bottom. Aimless and rudderless, they run aground on the sands of distraction.

Entrepreneurs take risks. They initiate rather than copy. They have the qualities and will to succeed and win. They are calm, confident and can reflect as well as act. They look below the surface of people and events and steer purposefully towards the shores of opportunity.

Winners are more willing to make use of emerging and available technologies. Knowledge exists in many forms. K-Frame (www.K-frame.com), a knowledge management framework which won the international e-Business Innovations Award for Knowledge Management, can handle intellectual property in a wide range of print, presentation, audio, animation and video formats.

Successful e-business and entrepreneurship requires more than simply putting appropriate technology in place. Investors and management teams need to assess the potential for information- and knowledge-based ventures.

Winners carefully assess opportunities. Gaps in existing provision in terms of content, format, access and reliability should be reviewed. Users might be prepared to pay for specific changes to be made. There might be flows of information, or specific expertise, that could form a commercial package that would meet the needs of particular communities of people in the external marketplace.

There might be alternative and better sources that could be used. Perhaps availability, responsiveness or cover could be improved, the flow speeded up, or 'on demand' access or 'help desk' support provided. Discontinuing services that are no longer required could yield savings.

There should be clear potential to 'add value' by providing a distinct information service to an identifiable group of people who would be willing to pay for it. The costs involved need to be recovered from subsequent user fees or subscriptions. External 'start up' finance may be required to launch a service, and there could be opportunities for collaborative ventures with other entities.

The further work that may need to be undertaken to put information into a form required by end-users should be assessed, and those who could undertake this identified. Business colleagues should have sound judgement of requirements, situations, people and opportunities. Shared values, goals, commitment, information and knowledge can greatly increase the chances of success.

Winners act while windows of opportunity still exist. They prioritize, focus and tackle the most important matters first. They also build winning teams, networks of people to whom they can turn for independent and objective advice. Particular deficiencies can be balanced by the complementary qualities of others.

Reward strategy should support the creation and exploitation of intellectual capital. Processes and procedures should be in place to monitor and measure learning, information and knowledge sharing; and intellectual capital creation and exploitation.

Whereas unsuccessful companies – or losers – were observed to be wasting resources by putting historic information of limited value on corporate Intranets their more successful counterparts – or winners were adopting a different approach. They were working with a combination of information, knowledge and tools to boost workgroup productivity and generate new income streams.

Winners understand that we need to step up from information management to knowledge entrepreneurship. There is an urgent requirement for knowledge entrepreneurs who know how to acquire, develop, package, share, manage and exploit information, knowledge and understanding and introduce related job support tools.

Many experts struggle to explain the nature of their expertise, what they do, and how they can help others. They are not understood and they do not stand out. As a first step towards creating knowledge-based offerings people and organizations need to package their know-how so that others can appreciate their particular capabilities.

Potential clients often find it very difficult to determine the point at which external expertise is required, and assess the qualities and calibre of those who might be able to help. Individual knowledge workers and professional firms can spend a lot of time assessing whether or not the problems people bring to them might form the basis of an assignment and client relationship in an area within which they specialise.

Most experts would prefer to spend their time applying their skills to challenges that justify high charge out rates. Practice development, dealing with initial enquiries, qualifying opportunities and capturing basic information about prospects can all represent 'non-chargeable' time.

So how can knowledge entrepreneurs help? Let us look at an example. The risk management practices of AIG Europe, Clifford Chance, Dames & Moore, Deloitte & Touche, Hill and Knowlton and Kroll Associates tackled this problem by assembling their core expertise in the form of a self-diagnostic toolkit that people could use to carry out an initial risk assessment. The resulting PROMPT-RPS tool, developed by Cotoco a specialist supplier of job support tools, provided an overview understanding of the major areas of corporate risk, and enabled users to capture basic information about their situation and identify where they required specialist help.

A tool such as PROMPT-RPS can be distributed via a website or by direct mailing a CD-ROM disc to a target group. Its focus can be upon a problem that recipients are either known or likely to have. Self-assessment checklists can be included for completion by either the recipient or colleagues to whom they are emailed. Explanations can be provided where appropriate. Once an initial review has been completed the results can be emailed to the expert sources of advice the tool suggests for tackling whatever problems have been identified.

The recipient of a completed review can quickly check that an enquirer has followed a suggested process. If this has happened, any subsequent relationship can be built upon the overview obtained and the understanding gained during the self-assessment process. The expert will not need to spend time collecting basic information and may be able to avoid an iterative process to determine whether or not there is an issue to address and in what area.

A new generation of practical support tools (see www.cotoco.com and chapters 26 and 27) incorporating critical success factors for competing and winning promise dramatic improvements in both understanding and achievement. The experiences of an A B C D E F of companies as varied as Avaya, B&Q, Cisco, Dana, Eyretel and Friends Provident suggest they represent the next 'big idea' in management.

These pioneers have used knowledge-based support tools to transform business win rates, launch new products and build supply chain quality. They can enable greater delegation and more bespoke responses in complex and regulated areas.

In relation to winning business, returns of over 20 times an initial investment have been quickly achieved. In addition to higher success rates, orders have been brought forward and dramatic reductions have been made in the number of specialist support staff required to accompany sales teams in the field.

Overall, much greater effort needs to be devoted to knowledge creation and exploitation. Directors and senior executives should assess the scope for knowledge entrepreneurship, and consider steps they might take to create and enable a community of knowledge entrepreneurs and stimulate and launch new knowledge-based ventures.

The extent to which the enormous potential of stored information and knowledge is realised, and additional revenues are generated, depends upon the energy and imagination of information and knowledge entrepreneurs, people whose calling and practice is the acquisition, development and commercial exploitation of information, knowledge and understanding. Let us look at the competencies required. The knowledge entrepreneur needs to understand how to:

- Acquire, develop, package, share, manage and exploit information, knowledge and understanding, and related support tools;
- Help and enable others to effectively use and apply them;
- Communicate and share information and complex knowledge in ways that assist comprehension and increase understanding;
- Create, badge, protect, manage and exploit intellectual capital and 'best practice' based job support tools;
- Identify and exploit market opportunities for distinctive information and knowledge based products and services;
- Develop and launch new information and knowledge based offerings and services;
- Use combinations of emerging technologies to network people, organisations and relevant sources of information, knowledge and support tools together;
- Handle knowledge in multiple formats, including animation, audio and video material;
- Develop and use appropriate job support tools to increase individual productivity and corporate performance;
- Collaborate with others, and work and learn in new ways in order to create and deliver greater value; and
- Lead and manage knowledge workers, network organisations and virtual teams.

Some knowledge entrepreneurs are instinctive. Others possess specialist expertise - for example, in corporate communications - or know about particular technologies. However, an overview appreciation of how people, know-how and technology can be brought together and beneficially managed, and also how to establish, launch and develop knowledge-based ventures are less widespread. They need to become more common if we are to grasp current opportunities to transform many aspects of our lives.

Individual business executives should aim to emulate winners by endeavouring to be role models when learning and sharing information, knowledge and understanding. They should understand the key requirements for success in the knowledge society and information age. Many boardroom and meeting room discussions would be enlightened by the presence of one or more knowledge entrepreneurs.

Many companies operate in sectors in which know-how accounts for an increasing proportion of the value being generated for customers. Yet they lack an explicit strategy for obtaining, developing, sharing and exploiting know-how. Corporate culture, policies, processes and practices should all be supportive of knowledge entrepreneurship.

Business executives need to ensure effective acquisition, development, sharing and exploitation of information, knowledge and understanding occurs within the areas for which they are responsible, and that their people are supported with appropriate knowledge based tools.

A designated person should be made personally accountable for corporate effectiveness at acquiring, creating, sharing and exploiting knowledge. Specific opportunities need to be assessed and important workgroups equipped with the support tools they need to do their jobs and achieve their objectives.

Just providing people with relevant knowledge may not be sufficient. They may also require tools to help them use and apply it. Practical knowledge-based tools can transform workgroup productivity by increasing understanding, communicating best practice and sharing the essence of how superstars operate.

There is little excuse for further inaction. 'The Knowledge Entrepreneur' provides lists of possible commercial ventures, along with detailed checklists for identifying and analysing opportunities, exercises for assessing entrepreneurial potential and 'scoping' possible knowledge-based services, and guidance on using support tools.

Further Information

★'The Knowledge Entrepreneur' by Colin Coulson-Thomas can be ordered from Kogan Page by: Tel. 01903 828800; Fax. 020 7837 6348; E-mail: orders@lbsltd.co.uk or on-line from www.kogan-page.co.uk or www.ntwkfirm.com/bookshop/

How companies manage and exploit 20 categories of intellectual capital is examined in the report 'Managing Intellectual Capital to Grow Shareholder Value' which is published by Policy Publications. Along with a related title 'Developing a Corporate Learning Strategy' it can be ordered by: Tel. +44 (0)1733 361149; E-mail: colinct@tiscali.co.uk or from www.policypublications.com or www.ntwkfirm.com/bookshop/

Information on the use of support tools for capturing and sharing knowledge in a variety of formats can be obtained from 00 44 0870 748 1400 or www.cotoco.com

Checklist:

- In relation to knowledge entrepreneurship do you view yourself and/or your colleagues as winners or losers?
- Do others view you and/or your colleagues as winners or losers?
- Are information, knowledge and understanding accounting for an increasing proportion of the value being generated for customers?
- Is the core expertise of key individuals captured and shared?
- Are appropriate support tools used to assess potential client needs and identify areas where professional advice is required and can be given?
- Does the company employ or have access to any information and knowledge entrepreneurs?
- What steps are being taken to encourage enterprise and entrepreneurship in relation to corporate know-how?
- Are people encouraged to come forward with ideas for information- and knowledge-based businesses?
- Do they create, share, package and apply new knowledge and understanding?
- Are relevant information, knowledge, tools, techniques and support made available and used?
- Have the various forms of intellectual capital been identified and protected?
- Are they fully exploited and is their revenue contribution monitored and reported?
- Is an appropriate framework used to capture and store intellectual capital in a variety of formats?

Appendix to Chapter 21

Assessing Knowledge-based Opportunities

The nature of any entrepreneurial opportunities for knowledge-based offerings should be carefully assessed:

- Have you identified a real opportunity to 'add value' by providing a distinct service to an identifiable group of people who are, or might, be willing to pay for it?

- In relation to your potential customers or 'prospects', what information and know-how is required, where, when and by whom? What do they intend to do with it?
- What further work needs to be done before the information or know-how in question is likely to be in a form required by end users? Who does or would do this and how much might it cost?
- Could you or your company undertake the additional work more cost effectively than the current arrangements or provide what is required by some other means?
- Have the people involved thought about and articulated their requirements for a different service or additional provision? If not, could you help to facilitate the review process?
- Are there different and better sources that could be used? Have these already been identified and assessed? If not, could you undertake any search and evaluation that is required?
- What is wrong with the existing provision of information or know-how? How could its content, format, access and reliability be improved? Could you review and critique the current situation and practice?
- Are the potential beneficiaries currently in receipt of an alternative offer? In what ways would your offering represent an improvement?
- Is the information or know-how in question always to hand when it is needed? Could you extend the window of availability? Could 'on demand' access be provided?
- Could the supply of information or know-how be speeded up? Could you provide a job support tool that would make it easier for people to use and apply it?
- What steps could be taken to reduce the cost of the current provision? Are there particular services that are 'gold plated' or no longer required?
- What changes to the current formats and further analysis would make the information easier to comprehend and assimilate?
- Would the users be interested in an offering that was tailored or customised to their individual needs? Is this an activity that you or your company could undertake?
- How responsive are existing suppliers to their customers' requests for help and support? Is cover available outside of normal working hours?
- Could you provide some form of on-line 'help desk' service that represents a noticeable improvement on what is currently available?

- What else could be done to add value to what is currently provided and differentiate your proposed offering from those of any alternative providers?
- What value do the current users place upon the information or know-how in question? Would they be willing and able to pay more for an improved service?
- How much extra would the users be prepared to pay for particular enhancements they are seeking? Would they fund the specific changes that need to be made, or would the costs involved have to be recovered from subsequent user fees or new subscribers?
- Who else might be interested in the same information or know-how, or a similar service? Could the provision of what is required generate incremental income?
- What other information, know-how or expertise within the organization, could be brought together to form a commercial package or job support tool that would meet the needs of other communities of people or workgroups in the external marketplace?
- What price levels could be sustained? Could various categories of user be charged at different rates?
- How would external customers pay for the provision of the information, know-how or service in question? Could users be charged at the point and time of access, or while the information is being downloaded?
- How much would the desired information, know-how or service cost to produce? Could it be provided at a profit? Would the returns compensate for the risks involved?
- Will corporate or 'start up' finance be required to launch the proposed service? How might the users or business partners contribute to this?
- Might external sources of finance be interested in the proposition? What forms of security could you or your company provide?
- If a commercial opportunity exists, should you or your company exploit this itself, or should you seek a collaborative venture with another entity?
- Who might suggest an appropriate arrangement or potential partners?
- Could exploitation rights be licensed to other parties?

- Is there a particular role that you or your company could provide within an external arrangement, for example acting as a publisher?
- Are all the capabilities to do what is required available in house, or will additional and external support be required?
- Is anyone within your company or a potential 'partner' organization interested in collaborating with you to exploit the opportunity on a profit sharing basis?
- Who is going to initiate discussions and establish and manage the relationship? Is this something you could undertake?

Chapter 22
Exploiting Corporate Know-how

Could you and your colleagues quickly secure new income streams and transform the productivity of your current operations by better exploiting what is already known? The most promising opportunities for revenue and profit growth are being overlooked in many companies. Processes for exploiting corporate know-how simply do not exist.

Many people ignore relatively easy ways of improving corporate performance and delivering greater shareholder value. They devote insufficient attention to the development, sharing and exploitation of information, knowledge and understanding.

They are also unaware of how relevant knowledge, critical success factors and the approaches of high performers can be built into work processes and support tools.

An investigation of the differing approaches of successful companies (winners) and their unsuccessful competitors (losers) has identified many opportunities for boosting profitability and generating additional revenue streams by better exploiting corporate know-how. The findings are set out in the report 'Managing Intellectual Capital to Grow Shareholder Value' and 'The Knowledge Entrepreneur' a handbook with exercises for crafting new knowledge-based offerings and checklists of questions that individuals and boards need to ask to reveal the full extent of the possibilities*.

In this chapter we will look at what the investigations tells us about the exploitation of corporate know-how – a core responsibility of the knowledge entrepreneur considered in the last chapter. Opportunities for income generation exist at all levels and in many areas of the companies examined. For example, thirty one distinct learning support services were identified that a typical training and development unit could offer external customers.

The investigation reveals how a new generation of knowledge-based support tools can enable key workgroups such as new business and customer relations teams to adopt the approaches of superstars and emulate their behaviours. However, even the most successful of the companies examined are overlooking their existence and potential.

Corporate policies, systems and procedures are heavily biased towards physical assets and tangible activities. Considerable effort is devoted to protecting and maintaining physical assets, keeping records of them up to date, and ensuring they are properly depreciated and fairly valued in annual accounts, and physically verified by the auditors at the year end; while intellectual assets are inadequately managed.

Losers do little to capture, value and protect corporate know-how. In comparison, winners are more aware of how information flows, support tools, knowledge transfer, and the exchange and sharing of relevant understanding impact upon performance. They are more alert to the possibilities for knowledge entrepreneurship.

People in 'loser' companies are preoccupied with competing for today's customer, and focus almost exclusively upon physical assets and tangible aspects of quality and performance. They have a narrow and dated view of what constitutes intellectual capital.

Corporate entities of losers have hard shells. Losers apply management initiatives to people they employ and within corporate premises. They limit quality, re-engineering and transformation projects to the company; and seek to acquire and impose standard management solutions.

Losers are preoccupied with the quality of things. They work hard to satisfy the requirements for obtaining certain kite-marks, and end up with relatively bureaucratic and costly processes for retaining kite-mark registration, that encourage conformity rather than initiative. They struggle to make existing operations more effective, and are laggards when it comes to recognizing and managing intellectual capital.

Reporting systems and performance indicators used by losers focus upon data that is easy to collect rather than the areas that are intrinsically of greatest importance. Few of them systematically assess, monitor and reward learning or the creation and exploitation of new intellectual capital. Many companies would benefit from tracking indicators such as net income from new knowledge-based ventures and offerings in relation to the value of available intellectual capital.

Winners are more aware of certain aspects of knowledge entrepreneurship such as fostering creativity or measuring and reporting intellectual capital. However, even among the more successful companies systematic strategies for creating and exploiting know-how across all functions and areas of operation were extremely rare.

People in 'winner' companies strive to learn, adapt and change more effectively than their competitors and to attract, retain, motivate and develop better people. They address and endeavour to influence intangibles such as attitudes, behaviour, values and relationships; and recognize the wide variety of forms in which intellectual property assets can exist.

The corporate boundaries of winners are more porous and encompass business partners and strategically important customers and suppliers. They extend management initiatives to customers and supply-chain partners; and work with business partners to apply quality, re-engineering and transformation projects to the whole value chain.

Winners are interested in the quality of experiences, ideas and relationships. They develop a variety of approaches to meet the needs of different contexts and circumstances, and work hard to create additional options and extra value for customers. They employ flexible and cost-effective approaches that remain current and relevant, and encourage and support entrepreneurship. They establish new information and knowledge-based ventures, and are leaders in the creation and exploitation of intellectual capital.

The most successful companies develop a strategy for harvesting more value from corporate know-how and measuring its revenue contribution. They focus upon the categories of intellectual capital which offer the greatest opportunities for revenue generation and increasing shareholder value. They also identify and address the people, cultural, process and IT issues which are the key to creating and exploiting corporate know-how and use best practice ways of reporting achievements to shareholders, customers and employees.

The findings of the continuing investigation suggest certain key questions that need to be asked if entrepreneurs, boards and management teams are to create environments that are more conducive of knowledge entrepreneurship:

Does the company operate in a sector in which know-how accounts for an increasing proportion of the value being generated for customers? If so, what are the implications?

Do members of the board and management team understand the requirements for success in the knowledge society and information age? How many of them are knowledge entrepreneurs?

Does the company have a convincing rationale and clear purpose? Is there a shared, distinctive and compelling vision? Does it reflect opportunities for knowledge entrepreneurship?

Have the vision, mission, goals and objectives of the company been effectively communicated and shared? Have the various elements of capability - including relevant know-how - needed to achieve them been assembled?

Is there an explicit strategy for the acquisition, development, sharing and exploitation of information, knowledge and understanding? Who has specific responsibility for it?

Do people have the knowledge-based support tools they need to quickly communicate what is special and distinctive about the company and its offerings? Who ensures that important workgroups have the support tools they need to excel in their jobs?

Are members of the board and management team role models in relation to learning and the sharing and exploitation of information, knowledge and understanding? Is the corporate culture - and are the attitudes, values and perspectives of the people of the organization – conducive of knowledge entrepreneurship?

In particular, what action needs to be taken to break down barriers and overcome obstacles to the acquisition, development, sharing and exploitation of know-how?

Is there effective two-way communication between the corporate centre and business units, and horizontal communication across functional, process and unit boundaries?

Is the organisation moving up or sliding down the information, knowledge and understanding value chain within its sector of operation? Is priority given to the company's customers and the acquisition, development and application of the know-how needed to deliver more value to them?

What explicit steps are being taken to create and support a community of knowledge entrepreneurs, create new knowledge based offerings and build practical support tools that make it easier for people to do their jobs and emulate the success of superstars?

Have the key processes for the acquisition, development, sharing and exploitation of know-how been identified? Do information, knowledge and understanding flow effectively up, across and down the organization and around its networks of relationships?

Are there opportunities for different individuals, work groups, business units, venture teams and business partners to develop ideas for new knowledge-based offerings and seek appropriate support? Are feedback loops built into the company's operating, learning and entrepreneurial processes? Are they regularly reviewed and refined?

Finally, are the intellectual assets of the organization safeguarded as effectively as its financial and physical assets? How effectively and systematically are they being exploited? Is performance in these areas monitored?

The culture, policies, processes and practices of an organization should enable the effective acquisition, development, sharing and exploitation of know-how. Shrewd investors assess how effective companies are in these areas, and the extent to which people derive meaning and create opportunities, value and intellectual capital from various forms of information and knowledge. In essence they assess a board and management team's ability to encourage and enable knowledge entrepreneurship.

Further Information

How companies exploit 20 categories of intellectual capital is examined in the report 'Managing Intellectual Capital to Grow Shareholder Value' which is published by Policy Publications. Along with a related title 'Developing a Corporate Learning Strategy' it can be ordered by: Tel. +44 (0)1733 361149; Fax +44 (0)1733 361459; E-mail: colinct@tiscali.co.uk or from www.policypublications.com or www.ntwkfirm.com/bookshop/

'The Knowledge Entrepreneur' by Colin Coulson-Thomas and published by Kogan Page can be ordered by: Tel. 01903 828800; Fax. 020 7837 6348; E-mail: orders@lbsltd.co.uk or on-line from www.kogan-page.co.uk or www.ntwkfirm.com/bookshop/

One of the reasons why certain categories of intellectual property are not managed or exploited in many companies is that the technologies they use cannot handle the formats in which the know-how occurs. Information on the use of support tools for capturing and exploiting knowledge in a variety of formats can be obtained from 00 44 0870 748 1400, www.k-frame.com or www.cotoco.com

Checklist:

- In relation to exploiting corporate know-how do you view yourself and/or your colleagues as winners or losers?
- Do others view you and/or your colleagues as winners or losers?
- Is the organisation's approach to creating and exploiting intellectual capital regularly reviewed?
- Has the organisation identified the essential management issues and activities that are the key to managing intellectual capital successfully and growing shareholder value?
- How motivated are people to exploit corporate know-how and how successful is the organisation at exploiting its intellectual capital?
- Are people given incentives to create and exploit intellectual capital?

- Do they understand how important developing and exploiting intellectual capital is for future revenue generation and growth in shareholder value?
- Does the organisation measure and monitor the performance of its intellectual assets and their revenue contribution?
- Is the chief executive or managing director, the marketing director and/or business development director and the finance director involved in the management of intellectual capital?
- Do different functions understand their roles and responsibilities for creating and exploiting intellectual capital?
- Is external advice sought where appropriate?
- Does the board encourage the recruitment of good quality people, a culture of innovation, provide board leadership and focus upon know-how as a business opportunity?
- Within the corporate culture is intellectual capital understood and valued?
- Does the corporate environment encourage the creation, sharing and exploitation of know-how?
- Are people equipped with support tools that enable them to create, share and exploit know-how?
- Can these tools handle know-how in a variety of formats?
- Are intellectual assets actively and appropriately valued?
- Is the value of intellectual capital given in the Annual Report and Accounts?
- Is intellectual capital identified as a prime driver of shareholder value?
- Are achievements reported to the board and shareholders, and where appropriate to customers and employees?

Chapter 23
Developing a Corporate Learning Strategy

Could your organisation and its people derive more benefit from training and development? Do they meet personal and professional development requirements and contribute to key business objectives such as winning new business? If all existing courses were closed down would customers notice or care?

Now is a good time to ask such questions. Training and development are at a watershed. Many existing courses and facilities are coming to the end of their useful lives. There are new approaches to learning and knowledge management to consider, emerging technologies to evaluate, and collaborative opportunities to assess.

Those responsible for corporate learning face tough choices and multiple challenges. Should a corporate university be set up? How might a corporate intranet best be used? Could business development and the processes of value and knowledge creation be better supported?

Certain options go to the heart of current operations. Should training and development be made a revenue centre or a distinct business? Could particular activities, or the whole function, be outsourced? What would be lost if 'central training' were closed down?

A two-year investigation by the author of corporate learning plans and priorities has examined these and other questions. It involved corporate visits and 69 structured interviews with those responsible for the training and development of some 460,000 people. The results, presented in the report 'Developing a Corporate Learning Strategy'* and summarized in this chapter, are sobering and demand urgent attention.

Many courses have passed their 'sell by' date. At the same time essential requirements and critical corporate priorities are being largely ignored. Too little effort is devoted to business development, relationship building, knowledge creation, e-business and entrepreneurship.

Overwhelmingly, the emphasis was upon squeezing costs, rather than the generation of incremental income streams. Only one of the organisations surveyed was equipping its people to be more successful at bidding for business, even though the top twenty bidding skills and critical success factors for winning bids have been identified and tried and tested bid management tools are available (see appendix B and chapter 8).

Human resource teams are working hard, but many of them – particularly in struggling or 'loser' companies - do not appear to be connecting with the world around them. Millions have been spent on grandiose initiatives, fashionable concepts such as empowerment, and general 'quality', 'teamwork' and 'leadership' training, while particular requirements of critical importance are overlooked.

Critically, training inputs are not leading to new know-how and intellectual capital outputs. Existing understanding is being shared, but the new knowledge needed to compete and win and secure market leadership is not being created. Presentations on 'knowledge management' abound, but specific initiatives to develop knowledge entrepreneurs or equip people to use *e*-Business are few and far between.

The organisations examined focused overwhelmingly upon the internal development of employed staff. Customers, contractors, suppliers, associates and business partners – and external members of the supply chains and virtual organizations we considered in chapters 12 and 18 - can all have development needs which could, and should, be addressed by shared learning.

Some of the more successful companies - or winners - have recognized that education, learning, training and updating are rapidly becoming global markets in their own rights. They are among the most exciting of contemporary business opportunities. However, in general training and development are not perceived as a source of incremental revenues. Nor are they used as a means of building relationships with key decision makers in strategic customers, suppliers and business partners.

Most losers among trainers appear to 'follow fashion'. Many buy 'off the shelf' rather than think about what would be most appropriate in specific situations. They provide standard programmes regardless of individual interests and needs. They expose people working on very different activities, to common experiences that have little relevance to their particular requirements and priorities.

Opportunities for training collaboration are also being missed. Many companies face similar development problems and challenges.

Maybe the cost of new resources and facilities could be split between several users. There are also shared learning networks such as the Business Development Forum for those wanting to win more business.

Senior managers in losing companies have little interest in integrated learning networks. They have a resigned attitude towards traditional training and development. Expenditure on them is viewed as worthy and an inevitable cost of being in business. However, when cash flow is squeezed they are among the first areas to be cut back.

Losers tend to lack rigour when analysing training requirements. They provide general and standard courses in areas such as 'quality'; 'empowerment' or 'diversity' rather than develop more specific ones aimed at named individuals in order to support the achievement of particular objectives. Such offerings are in the 'nice to have' rather than essential category.

In 'loser' companies offerings may also be made available on a number of specified dates. There is no particular urgency about them and people attend as and when they can. Programmes remain listed in prospectuses and handbooks until everyone has been through them. Long before this happens in larger companies they may already be past their 'sell by' date.

As with areas examined in other chapters, losers imitate and follow fashion. The training furnished tends to reflect what other companies are doing and the areas and topics considered trendy at the time of its inception. What is supplied rarely addresses the different interests, aspirations and priorities of the various people and personalities involved. Nor does it accommodate their individual learning styles and preferences.

The training provided can also be divisive. Employees are welcome but contract staff and 'associates' may be excluded from training and thus made to feel second-class citizens. Home-based and itinerant staff may simply be forgotten. Joint activities are suspended and customer and business partner representatives read the papers, drink tea or delete unwanted e-mails while the 'home team' goes into the conference room.

Losers are essentially selfish. They give reluctantly and only in order to receive. They focus almost exclusively upon their own objectives. Those responsible for training and development are also departmental in their thinking and approach. They wrestle in isolation with problems that feature on many corporate learning agendas. They fail to collaborate and join training consortia and other collective arrangements. Hence they do not benefit from collective purchasing, resource sharing and specialization.

In many companies training and development activities are preoccupied with identifying and remedying deficiencies – the things people are not good at and would rather not do. Great effort is spent raising people to an acceptable level in areas that they are not interested in. In contrast winners are more likely to concentrate instead upon making people even better at the activities they do best and most enjoy. The emphasis is upon strengths rather than weaknesses. Whereas the loser is concerned with bringing people up to par across the board the winner consciously sets out to create super stars in the areas that really matter.

Finally, the aspirations of individuals are often being overlooked. Trainers focus unashamedly upon corporate pre-occupations. Yet many people seek greater control and more balance in their lives. Switching the emphasis to innovation, entrepreneurship, and business building can enhance both corporate performance and personal fulfilment.

Not surprisingly, education, training and development expenditures are still sometimes viewed as a cost, rather than as strategic activities. They are not always considered vital investments in the creation of knowledge, intellectual capital and value for customers. There are exceptions. Glaxo Wellcome views innovation and creativity in the development of new products as a critical business process. Staff are helped to become more effective researchers.

All in all, the current state of affairs cannot continue. Those interviewed are sincere, hard working and personally committed to individual and corporate development. They derive little satisfaction from the situation revealed by the survey*.

So what needs to be done? Winners tend to be pioneers and innovators, rather than observers and imitators. They facilitate, enable and support development. They champion and reward learning and enterprise. Learning should be built into work processes and peoples roles. It should embrace customers, suppliers and business partners.

Winners allow individuals to manage their own learning. They encourage their people to join shared learning networks and achieve breakthroughs in understanding. They establish corporate universities, foster learning partnerships, and keep their learning strategies current, relevant and vital. Standard offerings are abandoned in favour of specific and tailored interventions.

Training teams with the potential should be tasked with becoming profitable businesses in their own right. Training activities should contribute to enterprise, business and knowledge development. Providing individuals with personal learning accounts could create 'customers'.

Winners are more discriminating and selective. They focus development activities on the requirements of key work groups, for example using support tools to make it very easy for them to do difficult jobs. The learning vision of winners is more likely to embrace helping average performers to emulate the approaches of their more successful peers. They adopt bespoke approaches and provide specific support that addresses particular learning needs and is intended to be helpful to those involved.

The learning costs incurred by winners are more likely to be perceived as investments in building strategic capabilities and the creation of knowledge and customer and shareholder value. Plans and policies are designed to enable the organization to accomplish key elements of whatever it is seeking to achieve. Results are carefully monitored and corrective action taken as appropriate.

Winners address individual as well as corporate requirements. Personnel, learning and IT specialists, business unit teams and infrastructure managers work together. They also cooperate with other organizations. They open up learning opportunities to customers, suppliers, associates and business partners. Learning occurs within and across value and supply chains. It is a differentiator and as a source of incremental income becomes an area of business opportunity in its own right.

Demonstrable outcomes should replace input indicators such as 'bums on seats'. For example, by how much has the 'win rate' in competitive bidding situations increased? What proportion of turnover do new products and services account for? What value is ascribed to new intellectual capital? Whenever a direct causal link to additional know-how, greater customer value or extra business cannot be demonstrated, activities should be discontinued.

Whereas losers focus upon input measures such as cost per hour of various forms of 'training' winners are much more focused upon results. Users of support tools - such as those described in chapters 26 and 27 - can rapidly lead to very significant improvements in performance, which can make them much more cost effective than both traditional learning and e-learning.

'Human resource' professionals must work much more closely with their colleagues. Companies need to become incubators of entrepreneurial activity. Working environments should inspire and enable learning, innovation and creativity.

Many corporate learning strategies and practices need urgent review. Training teams are missing an historic opportunity to make a more strategic contribution to knowledge and value creation and the achievement of both personal and corporate objectives.

Further Information

*'Developing a Corporate Learning Strategy' by Colin Coulson-Thomas is available from Policy Publications by: Tel. +44 (0)1733 361149; Fax +44 (0)1733 361459; or E-mail: colinct@tiscali.co.uk. The report and others such as the related title 'Managing Intellectual Capital to Grow Shareholder Value' can also be ordered from www.policypublications.com or www.ntwkfirm.com/bookshop/

The learning of directors and boards is considered in 'Developing Directors, A handbook for building an effective boardroom team' which is published by Policy Publications in association with Adaptation and can be ordered from 00 44 (0)1733 361 149 and http://www.policypublications.com/developingdirectors.htm

'Developing Directors' identifies the knowledge, skills and personal qualities required by directors and defines the competent director and the effective board. It looks at the route to the boardroom and how to become a director, and how directors are and should be prepared.

Information on the use of support tools to increase understanding and make it easy for people to do difficult jobs can be obtained from 00 44 0870 748 1400 or www.cotoco.com

Checklist:

- In relation to developing a corporate learning strategy do you view yourself and/or your colleagues as winners or losers?
- Do others view you and/or your colleagues as winners or losers?
- Is the culture of the organization conducive of learning?
- Is there tolerance and the active encouragement of diversity?
- Do the members of the board and senior management team act as role models in terms of their commitment to learning?
- Are formal education and development programmes focused upon those processes and activities that add value for customers?
- Do these programmes embrace other members of the supply chain, such as customers, suppliers and business partners?
- What, if anything, does the company learn from customers and other supply chain partners?

- How willing is the company to refine and modify its objectives and processes?
- What is done to help the people of the company identify their learning potential?
- Are individuals encouraged to work and learn in ways that match their own preferences and potential?
- Do training and development objectives make explicit the need for knowledge creation and the creation of new and distinct alternatives?
- What proportion of the training budget is devoted to the support of individual development and diversity as opposed to standard courses?
- Is the focus upon building strengths or remedying weaknesses?
- Is each person enabled to play to their particular strengths and to achieve their personal aspirations?
- Are key work groups provided with job support tools that make it easy for users to do difficult jobs and emulate the approaches of high performers?
- Do the tools enable users to learn with each application?
- How much emphasis is placed upon consensus, 'middle way' and 'lowest common denominator' approaches?
- Do training activities help to build the personal qualities and skills needed to develop new knowledge and craft novel offerings?
- Do they address barriers to creativity, innovation and discovery?
- What is being done to support enterprise and entrepreneurship?
- How much emphasis do courses and counselling place upon role model behaviour and conformity to corporate norms?
- How much importance is attached to imitation, benchmarking, competitor analysis and teamworking, as opposed to innovation and individual discovery?
- Does the corporate culture encourage discussion, stimulate thought and foster inspired individuality?
- Are employees, associates and business partners encouraged to question and dissent from prevailing opinions?
- What proportion of training and development resources are devoted to helping them become more effective at playing existing activities and games?
- What proportion is designed to help them create new and alternative activities and games?

- What steps are being taken within the training and development community to make a more significant contribution to knowledge and opportunity creation?

Chapter 24
Integrating Learning and Working

All of us are born with an innate desire and drive to learn. We come into the world restless and curious to explore, and to experience. We search and investigate, open and receptive, eager for the stimuli that will expand our awareness and understanding. At the same time, we are fed, winded and largely left to our own devices.

Later in life, as children, we are confined for several hours a day, during many of our most receptive years, in institutions of education. Ostensibly, a central purpose of schools is the pursuit of learning. And yet, for most people, the efforts of many thousands of well-meaning and committed teachers over a period of years destroy their desire to learn.

In many countries the educational system fails most people. They learn what they are not good at according to one approach to the development of understanding. Most of us will grow old bereft of any real appreciation of our individual learning capability. We can peer into space and speculate about the origins of the universe while much of what happens within our own heads is unexplored territory. The 'non-academic' majority go through life without ever knowing how they might most effectively learn.

In a global marketplace in which the knowledge worker is becoming the critical and limiting resource, the corporation or society that first and wholeheartedly adopts new approaches to learning that allow individuals to tap more of their potential will reap an enormous competitive advantage.

Already leading companies are using tools that incorporate an understanding of how people learn to make it easy for them to do difficult jobs. While different people vary in terms of how they can best learn particular tasks tend to attract those who learn in a similar way. Hence key work groups can be provided with support tools that are specifically designed to enable their members to learn in whatever ways they find most productive.

As more people become aware of the extent to which companies are competing on the basis of their ability to learn and apply what has been learnt, greater use of job support tools that incorporate critical success factors and winning ways and enable users to learn with each application could make the 'learning organization' a reality. Yet 'loser' companies that would hugely benefit from using them are reluctant to adopt them.

Although the critical importance of identifying, attracting, developing, motivating, tapping and retaining human talent has become an article of faith, training budgets are cut back when the going gets tough. As we saw in the last chapter training and development activity is not always focused upon activities and processes that win business or add value for customers, and the skills being imparted may not be specifically relevant to the achievement of corporate goals and objectives.

Whether training is a 'help' or a 'hinder' depends upon its nature and purpose. Some training entrenches losing behaviours. Many companies find it difficult to decide how much to spend on training. The 'heart' wants to believe that training is a 'good thing' while the 'head' suggests that the results of training efforts are often difficult to determine. The reality of 'what is' often differs greatly from the vision of 'what ought to be'. The intention may have been to 'invest', but the results of traditional training can be disappointing.

Development activities ought to reflect the situation and circumstances of a company, its business objectives and its key priorities. Effective learning comes from doing things and observing the outcomes. Group and team learning that introduces critical success factors and winning ways can be particularly beneficial in this respect, although it is rarely as effective as when these are incorporated into job support tools.

Lessons learned on courses can be quickly forgotten and difficult to put into practice. Results can depend greatly upon the motivation of attendees and while people are learning they are not earning. Learning and working should be integrated. Learning is more successful when its purpose and relevance to the work context are perceived. Support tools that make it easy for people to do difficult jobs and learn each time a tool is used can take people as they are and quickly improve performance by enabling them to emulate the approaches of high performers.

Many losers experience intense competitive pressures upon prices and margins. Sharper and more determined rivals undercut them. In response, they pursue defensive or 'me-too' strategies. They fail to innovate, differentiate and build more value into their offerings. Hence they drift inexorably towards 'commoditization'.

Innovation and the creation of new alternatives are a key source of competitive differentiation. We have seen in earlier chapters that losers tend to be consumers rather than producers of knowledge, understanding and intellectual capital. They are fashion followers, not thought leaders. They tend to work almost exclusively on current projects and opportunities, and rarely, if ever, consider how what they do might be packaged to generate additional income flows that are independent of day-to-day operations.

While losers may attempt to manage existing stocks of information and knowledge, little effort is devoted to ensuring that they are relevant and current. People tend to be passive and unquestioning recipients. What is learnt tends to be applied to improving current operations. Learning takes place at defined times in dedicated places. Learning inputs lead to quantified outputs, such as the number of managers put through particular courses.

When they do find themselves owning intellectual capital, we have seen that losers are among the corporate laggards at managing and exploiting it. While some forms of know-how may be packaged, badged and protected, most of their senior managers are unaware of the variety of different forms of intellectual capital that can occur. Most are also ignorant of frameworks such as the award-winning K-frame (www.k-frame.com) that can handle and search for a variety of formats from text, presentation slides and electronic data stores to animations and audio and video material.

Winners are much more likely to develop, document and use their own ideas and approaches. Increasingly they will equip key work groups with support tools that engage them and enable them to react in new and bespoke ways to address the specific requirements of particular situations and opportunities. Learning takes place whenever and whereever such tools are used.

People in 'winner' companies consider how bespoke responses to particular customer requirements might be packaged to form a generic product or service, or a distinctive capability that could be offered to other clients. As a consequence, they create their own intellectual capital that can represent balance sheet value in its own right and be licensed or sold. Capturing, sharing and applying knowledge enables them to move up value chains and achieve higher margins.

People in winning companies are concerned with flows of information and knowledge – innovations, discoveries and breakthroughs that add to and extend what is already known. They learn with and for customers and review, critique and refresh whatever know-how, resources and facilities are provided in the search for new marketplace offerings and alternative ways of operating. Learning and working are integrated and learning inputs are expected to lead to demonstrable business outputs.

Many winners pay particular attention to the capture, valuation and management of intellectual capital. The right support tools can greatly assist this process capturing new designs and solutions as they are created and facilitating their use elsewhere.

Winners are always alert to opportunities to exploit what they know and apply how they go about doing things in other contexts. They are also catholic in their search for possible applications.

Many different types of know-how can be created and exploited. A knowledge management framework such as K-frame which has been used with a variety of support tools can handle know-how in a variety of formats and allow easy and rapid storage, access and utilization without the need for expensive investments in new technologies or specialist support.

Communities of job support tool users often require relatively little in the way of central services, beyond ensuring that content is up-to-date, and this can be achieved by means of automatic updates. Tool users often find they can cover for each other during holidays, illnesses or periods of peak workload. A central unit or specialist adviser such as Cotoco can help companies identify areas in which working and learning could be integrated by equipping groups of users with support tools.

Support tools themselves can monitor their use and learning activities in different locations and if required can generate appropriate reports. They can provide shared resources from virtual classrooms, specialist learning environments and stores to online bulletin boards, presentations and discussion groups could be provided. They can also allow periodic content audits and reviews of knowledge banks, and the extent to which these are being refreshed with the experience of high performers.

Winners recognize that consumer expectations are rising. New ideas can quickly catch on. What is special today may become commonplace by tomorrow. Hence, they devote greater effort to questioning, challenging, innovation and creativity. Rather than merely match the moves of their better competitors, they use support tools to integrate learning and working and create additional choices and alternative options.

Losers tend to ossify. They become typecast and locked into certain roles within their marketplace. They become fenced in by self-imposed restrictions, constrained by prison bars created within their own imaginations.

Many are also confined by the limited expectations that others have of them. People do not suggest improvements or alternative courses of action to them on the assumption that they will not respond. When under pressure losers may simply redouble their efforts to sell their regular offerings, perhaps using traditional methods such as price reductions and special offers to clear stock.

Within companies that lose market share, people are invariably busy. Even when businesses go into liquidation, their employees are usually fully occupied right up until the moment of collapse. They attend meetings and process a steady stream of telephone calls and e-mails. However, much of this activity is reactive, uncontrolled and undisciplined. With the benefit of hindsight it will be judged to have concerned secondary tasks, while vital priorities were ignored.

Redoubling efforts and 'more of the same' may not be enough. Companies operating in sectors in which margins are being squeezed may need to introduce new lines of business while there is still time. Thinking as well as 'doing' is required. However, increased workloads and longer hours reduce the time that many people have available for deliberation and reflection. They lack the intellectual space to create escape routes and envisage viable ways ahead.

The corporate culture of winners is more stimulating, positive and proactive. Their people are alert, open-minded and curious. They are resilient and mentally adventurous. They instinctively strive to push back the boundaries of what is possible. They will have a go and learn as they go. The right support tools enables them to avoid ossification and push the boundaries each time they are used.

Those who deal with people in winning companies expect them to try their hand at 'new things'. They bring problems to them for solution. In addition to differentiating themselves from competitive suppliers of similar products and services, winners launch new ventures and develop additional offerings that give rise to incremental income streams. Some think outside of the box and transform how business is done.

Winning companies remain alert to novel ideas, monitor relevant debates and plug into emerging schools of thought. They recognize that as existing candles burn down, new ones need to be lit if the darkness of marginalization and irrelevance is to be avoided. They also exploit their know-how and recruit or develop and unleash information and knowledge entrepreneurs.

Winners are more likely to achieve a balance between securing further sales of current products and services, and the development of fresh and different offerings that will sustain future growth. Some have specific and demanding new product development objectives. People are allowed the time they may need to reflect and are encouraged to be innovative. The layout of premises may include social and quiet spaces for networking and thinking, respectively.

Learning from both triumph and disappointment is especially important. Some losers invariably deduce the wrong lessons from failure. For example, following an unsuccessful launch of a new product, they may conclude that in future such risks should be best avoided, when a more positive reaction might be to aim to do things differently and better the next time around.

Many losers rarely discuss outcomes – whether the acceptance of an offer or the rejection of a proposal. They do not build learning loops or feedback mechanisms into their processes. They may periodically re-engineer and redesign, but without learning whatever increased levels of performance are achieved may soon be overtaken by competitors for whom innovation is a way of life rather than an occasional challenge.

Winners go to work to learn as well as earn, particularly in the area of business development. They are more curious and resilient. Their culture and management style encourages knowledge sharing and responsible and thoughtful risk taking. Failure often makes their people more determined then ever to succeed.

People in winning companies learn from their experiences. They dissect and analyse what has happened and probe for root causes. Debrief questionnaires are circulated and reviews are held to uncover why a particular approach or proposal worked or flopped. They then discuss what needs to be changed or improved. Winning ways are incorporated into support tools.

Winners do not expect to rest on their laurels. Like adventurous spirits, they look out for new challenges that will stretch them, open up different routes and widen horizons. They try out further options in order to assess whether alternative courses of action and another response might be more effective. An absence of disappointment could indicate a lack of ambition.

Winners keep a careful watch of trends and developments relating to their own performance. For example, they investigate how procurement and bid practices are evolving. They actively monitor the experiences of competitors without becoming fixated or mesmerized by them. They welcome support tools that incorporate critical success factors and winning ways.

Successful business development teams are always open to suggestions for improving their approaches to winning business. They actively invite feedback and comments from staff, associates, business partners, customers and prospects. Having reflected, people in winning companies quickly implement whatever changes may be necessary to seize windows of opportunity and achieve their objectives.

Tools that produce an outcome without revealing why this has occurred can 'deskill'. A more 'transparent' approach that explains what is happening and allows the learner to observe processes at work can increase understanding with each application. For example, when a sales support tool such as those examined in chapter 26 are used windows can open up to explain why certain options might not be possible for technical, commercial, quality or regulatory reasons.

When a cost-saving approach to purchase decisions is taken, the 'commodity' technology that is acquired can sometimes fall short of what would most effectively facilitate team working and create a rich and distinctive learning environment.

A 'user-friendly' technology is required that does not distort too much the way people naturally learn.

In summary, losers consider learning and thinking as exceptional and specialist activities. They regard innovation and learning as distinct and separate activities, assume most people learn the same way, and instruct and teach. They move forward incrementally from what is known, and adopt technologies that automate existing approaches to learning.

Losers attempt to manage the learning of their people. They provide internal training programmes and operate dedicated corporate training centres. They seek support from traditional sources, fail to create and exploit new know-how, and rarely subject their learning strategies and practices to a periodic and independent review.

Winners operate very differently. They build learning and thinking into people's roles. They integrate learning and working, using appropriate support tools for this purpose. They recognize that people do not all learn the same way. They facilitate, enable and support learning.

In 'winner' companies directors and senior managers encourage people to identify links, patterns and relationships and establish the connections that may result in revolutions and breakthroughs in understanding. They adopt technologies and tools that enable new and better approaches to learning. They allow individuals to manage their own learning.

Winners encourage their people to join international, collaborative and shared-learning networks. They provide channel and business partners with appropriate support tools. They establish corporate universities and learning partnerships with pioneers of new approaches to learning. They are active knowledge entrepreneurs, and they keep their learning strategies and approaches current, relevant and vital.

Further Information

'Developing a Corporate Learning Strategy' by Colin Coulson-Thomas is available from Policy Publications by: Tel. +44 (0)1733 361149; Fax +44 (0)1733 361459; or E-mail: colinct@tiscali.co.uk. The report and others such as the related title 'Managing Intellectual Capital to Grow Shareholder Value' can also be ordered from www.policypublications.com and www.ntwkfirm.com/bookshop/

Integrating working and learning is also considered in a forthcoming companion volume on transforming corporate performance. The new book will be available online from www.policypublications.com

Information on how support tools can integrate working and learning may be obtained from 00 44 0870 748 1400 or www.cotoco.com

Checklist:

- In relation to integrating working and learning do you view yourself and/or your colleagues as winners or losers?
- Do others view you and/or your colleagues as winners or losers?
- Are working and learning integrated in key work groups and across the organisation?
- Are job support tools that can increase understanding each time they are used deployed for this purpose, particularly to key work groups?
- What do directors and senior managers do to encourage informal learning?
- Is the reward system and are promotion and performance management decisions conducive of learning?
- Is learning focused on critical success factors for competing and winning?
- How committed is the company to harnessing human talent on an international basis?
- How critical is the concept of the learning network for particular work group communities to the achievement of its vision?
- Does the company understand the learning process and how people learn?
- Who, within the company, is responsible for learning?

- What is being done to ensure that all members of the network discover their learning potential and how they as individuals might best build their understanding?
- Are the learning preferences of the members of particular work groups taken into account when support tools are designed?
- If it has not already done so, should your company appoint a director of learning, understanding or thinking?
- How relevant is more appropriate technology to the facilitation of learning?
- Should the company be more extensively linked up to national, regional and international learning networks?
- Should the use of relevant support tools be extended to channel and business partners?
- Are support tools being used to facilitate learning?
- Do the company's managers and professionals understand how they can be used for this purpose?
- What needs to be done to ensure that the company itself takes on more of the attributes of a learning network?
- Are you prepared to act as a catalyst in encouraging the adoption of new forms of working and learning, and the integration of working and learning?

Chapter 25
Maximising the benefits from IT and e-Business

Information technology (IT) and e-business should support how people would prefer to work and learn, and enable them to operate in new and better ways. But too often it constricts and constrains rather than liberates. Individuals and teams have to compromise and change in order to fit in with the requirements of technology. The successful operation of IT becomes an end in itself.

Poor investments in IT set existing ways of operating in concrete rather than creating additional options, value and choices for customers. IT should support more intimate relationships with customers, suppliers and business partners; facilitate learning, adaptation and change; enable entrepreneurship and integrate learning and working. It should make it easy for people to share information, knowledge and expertise. Smart users employ it to secure operating efficiencies and create new electronic markets.

So what do the winners do differently to make IT and e-Business an enabler rather than a barrier? To answer these questions a continuing research programme led by the author (see appendix A) has examined the corporate experience of over 4,000 companies. This chapter summarises what companies should do to maximise the benefits of using IT and e-business.

The less successful or losers tend to adopt cautious, tentative and half-hearted approaches. They dabble and test rather than fully commit. For example, they may create static websites featuring background information about themselves and then use the lack of visitors that is likely to result as a vindication of the modest nature of their investment. The consequences of their lack of imagination and relative inaction are used to justify further lethargy and inertia.

Losers are technology driven and regard enhanced technology as a laudable goal in its own right. They are attracted by the prospect of upgrading their information technology and using the latest of whatever is available, and they find themselves easy targets for vendors of information technology.

Boards of 'loser' companies are more likely to pursue fashionable and technology-led approaches to corporate transformation. They apply information technology to improve existing activities and focus on internal opportunities. The people of the organisation are expected to change how they would prefer to operate to fit in with the requirements for successfully operating newly acquired technology.

Losers endow information technologies with an element of mystery and entrust them to specialists. They leave decisions about which technologies to adopt almost exclusively to technical experts, and are more likely to maintain separate and central information technology departments. They also tend to develop static Web sites that replicate other channels of communication.

When losers do act they are often naive and give little thought to the likely reactions of others. They decide they too would like a web presence and its establishment becomes an end in itself irrespective of whether it has a purpose or would help achieve certain objectives. Not surprisingly, the sites that result attract few visitors.

The more successful or winners are more positive, considered and open-minded. They use e-business to expand their customer base and provide additional support services to existing consumers. Some replace physical market places with new electronic market spaces.

Winners are objective driven and view information technologies as a means to an end. They endeavour to acquire only the information technology and level of functionality that is relevant to what they are setting out to achieve. They are demanding consumers and users of information technology.

Boards of 'winner' companies implement relevant and objective-led approaches to corporate transformation. They use information technology to undertake new and different activities and work and learn in new ways, and concentrate on opportunities to improve key relationships. The focus is upon enabling people to behave in winning ways and making it easy for them to access what they need and do difficult tasks.

Winners embed relevant information technologies into the fabric of the organization. They encourage people, and particularly key work groups, to adopt whatever technology is most relevant to the achievement of their objectives. They locate responsibility for information technologies where it is most appropriate. They also create interactive Web sites that provide new opportunities and additional possibilities.

People in winning companies get to know website visitors and their interests, and endeavour to provide a complete, personalised and regularly updated service or experience. They start with a problem or opportunity from a user perspective.

Winners think about how new e-business channels might make it easier for customers to access the information and opportunities that *they* need. They examine ways in which selection and purchasing might be made simpler for suppliers, for example by providing on-line search, configuration, pricing and cost-justification tools.

Every effort is made to build iterative relationships with each individual and provide additional value to that which might be obtained from any alternatives. Wherever possible visitors are enabled to help themselves. Electronic templates allow visitors to present their requirements, or any problems they might have, in a way that makes it easier to provide a relevant response. On-line services could range from simple ordering and tracking systems to complex self-design facilities.

Winners invite feedback from users and their people are encouraged to actively consider how they can make more extensive use of *e*-business applications. Reactions, comments and suggestions are sought, obtained and acted upon. The financial costs involved represent a minor element of the total investment of time and commitment in creating services and facilities that meet user needs and lock them in.

Winners create and actively participate in virtual communities. They encourage mutual sharing and support. By enabling interaction and introducing dynamic elements they encourage repeat visits. Regular reviews occur and findings are acted upon to help ensure that whatever is offered continues to be of interest, relevant and vital. Their involvement enables them to monitor trends, identify evolving concerns and spot emerging aspirations and requirements before they crystallise.

E-business technologies and principles are being used to create new markets and change how business is done. For example, procurement is undertaken electronically. Intelligent agents search for suitable suppliers. Opportunities are put out to electronic auction.

A company's web presence can be used in many ways to build closer and interactive relationships with customers. Many IT companies allow their software products to be purchased and downloaded via the Internet. Guinness produced a screen saver version of its Guinness.com website that can be downloaded.

Electronic links can encourage intimacy and enable 24-hour trading and access to information, knowledge and opportunities. Responses can be made within seconds. On-line visitors can be helped to diagnose problems, assess requirements and assemble or develop solutions. E-Business and mobile technologies are profoundly changing relationships between businesses and their customers, suppliers and business partners.

There are so many opportunities to challenge and improve on current practices that all members of staff should be encouraged to consider the possibilities. Ford in the US and Powergen in the UK have provided all their employees with a home computer. Senior managers believe the skills and experience they acquire will benefit their contributions during office hours.

Success can depend upon the extent to which a web presence is accessible, distinctive and memorable. Follow-up fulfilment processes and offerings need to be in place to ensure that after an initial contact interested visitors are converted into buyers and continuing relationships are forged. Support tools along the lines of those considered in the next two chapters can be used to enable customers and prospects to assess their own requirements and evaluate alternative solutions via a company's website or a mobile phone.

Federal Express has redesigned its core business processes to allow the great bulk of its parcel shipments to be ordered, arranged and managed via the Internet. At any time during the day or night customers can log on and see exactly where each item is. The company's most valuable assets used to be its trucks and aeroplanes. Its value now primarily derives from its processes and supporting software.

The trick is to apply technology to the critical success factors for business success. Too many investments are in areas that do not make the difference between winning and losing. Standard packages may be fine for non-critical activities but bespoke development in crucial areas for competitive advantage can differentiate and result in the creation of new intellectual capital.

Intimate and mutually beneficial relationships are the key to bespoke responses and sustained knowledge and value creation. The effective use of IT has become very dependent upon attitudes towards such relationships, especially 'external' parties and customers in particular. The key question is the extent to which they are perceived and treated as full members or citizens of the network.

Further Information

*'The Competitive Network' report and methodology shows how to combine e-business with re-engineering to build value creating supply chains and win new markets. Details and information on the related 'The Responsive Organization' re-engineering methodology 'for introducing new ways of working can be obtained from Policy Publications: Tel: + 44 (0)1733 361149; Fax +44 (0)1733 361459; Email: colinct@tiscali.co.uk or from www.policypublications.com or www.ntwkfirm.com/bookshop

Findings relating to the creation of a network form of organization are presented in the forthcoming companion volume on transforming corporate performance which will be available from www.policypublications.com and 'Transforming the Company, Manage Change, Compete and Win' by Colin Coulson-Thomas and published by Kogan Page which can be ordered by Tel. 01903 828800; Fax. 020 7837 6348; E-mail: orders@lbsltd.co.uk or on-line from www.ntwkfirm.com/bookshop/

Information on the benefits of using job support tools can be obtained from 00 44 0870 748 1400 or www.cotoco.com

Checklist:

- In relation to maximising benefits from IT and e-business do you view yourself and/or your colleagues as winners or losers?
- Do others view you and/or your colleagues as winners or losers?
- Within the organisation, is IT an enabler or a driver?
- Do the IT specialists in the company understand its vision?
- Are their activities supportive of the changes that are sought?
- Is IT used to automate existing activities or enable and support new approaches?
- Have the key cross-functional and inter-organizational processes that enable new ventures, create know-how and add value for customers been identified?
- Have critical success factors and winning ways for key activities been identified?
- Are these incorporated into processes and support tools to enable average performers to emulate the approaches of high achievers?
- Are partnering relationships and tailored responses to individual customers being supported?
- Have particular individuals been made responsible for key processes and the activities of important workgroups?

- Is IT applied to support key work groups such as customer facing staff, or to activities that may or may not be generating value for customers?
- Is the emphasis on grandiose and general initiatives or the practicalities of making it easy for the members of key work groups to excel?
- Are there actual or latent conflicts within the company between the 'core' IT team, and those in new ventures, business units and divisions?
- Does the IT perspective and e-business strategy of the company embrace business and channel partners and other members of the supply chain?
- Does the organization's IT network allow groups and teams to come together and work across barriers of function, distance, nationality and time?
- Does it support the way people naturally work and think, or do people have to distort their preferred behaviour in order to 'fit in' with the technology?
- Is it a learning network, able to integrate learning and working?
- Is it sufficiently flexible to allow various people to work and learn in different ways, and at a variety of locations, according to personal preferences and changing task requirements?
- Are migration and development options preserved?

Chapter 26
Boosting Workgroup Performance and Salesforce Productivity

In the last chapter we learned some general lessons about how to make the best use of IT. In this chapter we will examine a particular application area - using relevant knowledge and the approaches of high achievers to boost workgroup productivity.

A new generation of job support tools are transforming workgroup productivity and corporate performance. Let us look as some examples from an investigation of how to boost the performance of key workgroups such as sales and marketing teams*. As the number of pioneers in this field is still relatively small this particular chapter will include some quotations from those involved.

Your marketing plans look good on paper, but are people in the front line equipped to implement them? Sales support tools can help your people to get your message across and win more orders.

Many companies initiate grandiose knowledge management initiatives but do little to help staff improve their performance. Putting information on an Intranet is not enough. The expertise to do something better, new or different may require additional skills and tools, as well as access to relevant knowledge. Successful companies take practical steps to enable their people to compete and win.

Improved sales of existing products and more successful product launches are the ambition of every board. Practical knowledge-based job support tools can help achieve this aim. They can incorporate critical success factors and how high performers operate, capture and spread best practice and improve product and market knowledge.

Many sales teams are being pressured to win more orders. With competitors snapping at their heels and customers demanding more bespoke responses, prices and margins are under threat. No wonder sales staff turnover is sometimes so high.

While superstars achieve their targets, many average performers rely increasingly upon specialist support. Some ignore regulatory requirements, make errors when pricing, or leave out standard clauses from proposals. They struggle to explain what is special and distinctive about their offerings.

Eyretel whose products recorded and analysed telephone calls found its growth limited by the speed with which it could recruit, induct and train new sales representatives and bring existing staff up to speed with new offerings. According to Marketing Director, Nathan George: "We had to find a way to get knowledge about our sophisticated product line to a large number of sales people quickly".

Cotoco, a supplier of bespoke support tools, developed a laptop based toolkit with animations to explain Eyretel's voice recording solution, multimedia tours of its software, slide presentations, price and cost justification calculators and report generators. The result made such an impact on increasing sales and reducing sales costs that Eyretel won an eBusiness Innovation Award.

Sales support packages developed for 3Com, Cisco, Dana, ICB and The Innovation Group have included interactive presentations, demonstrations of products in operation, decision trees to assist account planning, and tools for developing and pricing solutions. Job support tools can use whatever formats - from text and graphics to animations, visual images and video and audio material - best help understanding.

Sales support tools are particularly suited to the launch of new products. A single repository like K-frame (www.k-frame.com) can hold all the information and knowledge needed. Technical details can be quickly communicated to groups in various locations around the world. Animations and video footage can be used to show offerings in use, and secrecy can be maintained until the moment of release.

The Innovation Group has used support tools to launch a new Local Authority operating system and roll out its project management methodology. 3Com has employed a similar tool to introduce network products to both direct and indirect channels.

A sales support package can gather together the critical information, knowledge and tools a sales person needs. It can incorporate 'best practice' and the approaches used by 'superstars' as well as key success factors for winning business identified by the winning business research programme led by the author. It can also ensure sales people focus on value and benefits to the customer rather than product features.

Even with complex products tools can be used to assess customer requirements and configure solutions. Multimedia capabilities usually enhance the portrayal of corporate credentials and capabilities, while animations can bring technology to life.

ICB uses its 'Navigator' sales support tool to build product knowledge and communicate with customers. According to Marketing Director Janetta Evans "We now rely on the simple but effective tool as the knowledge base for the whole company. Navigator will become an intrinsic part of how ICB works."

Support tools can automate routine tasks and provide support for every stage of the sales process from prospecting and qualification to negotiation meetings. Commercial, quality and regulatory checks can be built in. A library of background information can help users to answer customers' questions on the spot. Marketing materials can include templates, case studies, testimonials and independent endorsements, competitor analysis, and industry and market knowledge.

Don Fuller of Cotoco emphasises: "Seamless links can be provided to web sites and on-line applications. Feedback mechanisms can gather information from the field. Tools can help sales people identify cross-selling and upgrade opportunities."

Support tools can also ensure consistent application of best sales practice and a high standard of proposals. Marked improvements in product and market knowledge can occur. Other benefits include fewer errors, higher win rates, greater customer retention, less support staff, increased order value, and lower sale force churn.

Refining the sales process and making it easy for people to follow can increase sales. Better prospecting and improved qualification can focus effort on the most productive accounts. New staff can be inducted more quickly.

Prospects can use tools to discover new options that better meet their needs. When operating it themselves some customers order more than they would with a sales representative present. They feel in control and can explore alternatives in their own time. Automated calculations enable them to quickly assess the consequences of different approaches.

Sales support tools can be used to secure control over an indirect sales process. Consistent messages can be delivered to market. Training costs can be slashed by ensuring material is easy to learn and use, and instantly accessible. Reliance upon specialist staff can be reduced considerably.

Friends Provident uses a sales development support toolkit called THE MARKiT to assist staff running local marketing campaigns. Stuart Wilson, the company's Marketing Development Manager explains: "The business objective was to deliver an interactive toolkit that would help sales managers and their teams respond to requests for mailshots, local ads, posters and other lead generation material."

Support tools allow managers to maintain quality and avoid risks when delegating responsibilities. The automation of routine tasks frees up time for the greater differentiation and tailoring that may enable a price premium to be charged. Sometimes less experienced and qualified staff can be used.

Don Fuller the Managing Director of Cotoco believes: "Learning through doing is particularly effective. Building knowledge into tools makes it very easy for people to get complex tasks right first time and every time." Using them can be a differentiator. A systematic and customer focused approach enhances a supplier's reputation and helps to build relationships.

Companies should endeavour to avoid using tools that de-skill. According to Don Fuller"Support tools should help people to learn rapidly. They should improve understanding." Cisco's IP Telephony Sales Tool up-skills people working in its direct and indirect sales channels. As users work through prospect qualification and other tools windows open up to explain why certain courses of action are advocated. They learn from each use.

Ease of use is critical to success. Stuart Wilson describes Friends Provident's requirement: "The toolkit had to be simple to use and capable of processing a large quantity of material in an interactive and user-friendly fashion, whilst also being flexible enough to cater for additional information to be added as required quickly and easily." According to Don Fuller: "To encourage take up and change behaviour support tools should provide the easiest way to accomplish desired outcomes."

For Stuart Wilson the impact of THE MARKiT toolkit "has been impressive. We are very pleased with the end result, having achieved and indeed exceeded our original expectations." Janetta Evans of ICB is another satisfied user: "The message, the confidence, the ability to prove what we sell as a deliverable have all been greatly enhanced- this must lead to a great return on investment."

Users of support tools report significant increases in productivity and the ease with which best practice can be spread. As mentioned in chapter 20 quick paybacks of the cost of developing them can be achieved. Returns on investment of 20:1 or more can be obtained – in one case over 100:1 on a single order.

However, the IT losers we examined in the last chapter should be on their guard. According to Ed Thompson, Research Director of Gartner sales technology often fails to deliver: "Seventy five percent of sales application projects are perceived by their users to have failed to meet expectations twelve months after deployment".

Thompson believes that ill-considered sales technology can be bad for you, but as Eyretel found new and less experienced sales staff can benefit enormously. The key is not trying to shave a few percent off administrative time, but in focusing on what happens in front of the customer.

Eyretel's tool helped both its own people and customers to better understand its technology and products. Users felt so confident in the presence of customers that the ratio of support to sales staff was cut by a third. Win rates increased, orders were brought forward and more professional presentations delivered. Eyretel's Founder Roger Keenan described the tool as "by far the most professional piece of marketing Eyretel has ever produced."

Gartner's research suggests the key to success is to improve a process before automating it. Don Fuller agrees: "Improvements based upon the insights of superstar sales people are more likely to get outstanding results than automating current practices." Content is critical. During development review existing approaches and incorporate useful short cuts and how high achievers operate.

Friends Provident considered paper-based guides. However Stuart Wilson and his colleagues: "Recognised that these documents could very easily become shelf-fillers, gathering dust and rarely used. The company had a huge library of available materials. The challenge was finding how to present it in the most user-friendly way".

Successful users of IT or winners generally find that the best results with support tools are usually achieved with relatively homogenous groups of people undertaking similar tasks. They avoid fixed and inflexible tools in areas undergoing rapid change, unless arrangements are made for continuing review and regular updating. Don Fuller insists: "Ongoing maintenance can greatly increase a tool's shelf life."

Gartner's research found that successful projects need clear goals, management commitment, a sound process and sales force buy in. Stuart Wilson confirms that: "Close liaison between the field, our IT, compliance and design departments has been vital."

Too often sales tools focus on management's needs for reports rather than more effective selling and this approach can be disastrous. Ed Thompson explains: "Many companies never recover the impact of six months disruption while the new technology is being adopted". The focus becomes back office administration rather than performance in front of the customer.

"A sales support tool should focus unashamedly upon helping users land more business" Argues Don Fuller "The 80/20 rule is critical. Improve the 20% of the job role that delivers 80% of the business gain."

Once support requirements have been agreed rapid progress can usually be made. Even complex tools can be developed and tested within a few weeks of a go ahead. Winners find that the introduction of a new tool needs to be carefully planned if people are to obtain the maximum of benefit from it. Putting a CD-Rom disc into the post is not enough. Make sure people understand the significance of what is provided.

Stuart Wilson has no doubt the effort of producing The MARKiT was worth it: "We now have a powerful and, within the Financial Services sector, a unique marketing support tool for our Sales management team".

Further Information

*Job support tools are discussed in 'The Knowledge Entrepreneur' by Colin Coulson-Thomas and published by Kogan Page. The book and an accompanying CD-ROM giving further examples can be ordered by Tel. 01903 828800; Fax. 020 7837 6348; E-mail: orders@lbsltd.co.uk or on-line from www.kogan-page.co.uk or www.ntwkfirm.com/bookshop/

Examples of job support tools developed to increase sales force productivity and launch new products are also given on the CD which is part of a four part resource pack 'Winning New Business' published by Policy Publications. The resource pack can be obtained from 00 44 (0)1733 361 149 and www.policypublications.com

Further information on how the use of support tools can make selling easy and increase workgroup performance and salesforce productivity can be obtained from 00 44 0870 748 1400 or www.cotoco.com

Checklist:

- In relation to boosting the performance of key work groups do you view yourself and/or your colleagues as winners or losers?
- Do others view you and/or your colleagues as winners or losers?
- Does the organisation make it very easy for people to locate and understand what they need?
- Are they helped to understand complex issues and to do difficult tasks?
- Are customers and prospects helped to understand their requirements and select and buy what they need?

- Are critical success factors built into key processes and support tools?
- Are people helped to do important jobs in a winning way?
- Is best practice and what high performers do differently captured and shared?
- Have key workgroups been equipped with simple, scalable and cost effective support tools?
- Do these provide the easiest way to accomplish a given task?
- Is there a focus upon the applications that are likely to have the greatest impact upon corporate performance and personal fulfilment?
- Are customer-facing staff enabled to provide a complete, personalised and regularly updated service?
- Are they enabled to build relationships with individual customers and prospects, offer bespoke responses and deliver additional value over available alternatives?
- Do they learn with each use of a support tool?
- Is feedback from users, customers and prospects encouraged and responded to?
- Are technical, commercial, regulatory and quality checks built into support tools?
- Are relevant support tools made available to business and channel partners?
- Are customers enabled to help themselves?
- Is the appropriate use of support tools regularly reviewed?
- Are support tools maintained, refined and kept up to date?
- Can they be automatically updated as and when people are connected and while they are used?

Chapter 27
Launching New Products

Informing different groups about a new product represents a daunting challenge. New - and possibly complex - material has to be communicated to a variety of audiences with distinct information requirements. In particular:

- Sales staff and indirect sales channels must be able to sell new products.
- Service engineers may have to be equipped to service additional offerings.
- Contact centre and other support staff may need to be prepared to competently answer questions about a further product or service.
- Corporate communicators will need to know enough to be able to talk intelligently to the media, analysts, key customers and other publics.
- Technical staff may require a significantly higher level of technical detail than their colleagues.
- Customers may request or expect implementation guides that will help them to gain the maximum benefit from the product.
- Existing users of previous or related products could be informed of up grade or trade in and exchange opportunities.

Communication with all of these groups may need to occur against the background of tight deadlines. People may also wish to either see or visualise a new product in operation. Without some form of demonstration they may not fully appreciate its advantages and benefits, yet this may be difficult or physically impossible to organise in the time remaining and with the available budget or funding.

As a launch date approaches, new product managers face considerable pressure to 'get everything done'. A major challenge is to co-ordinate the largely simultaneous communication of consistent messages to multiple and disparate audiences, some of which may be potentially diverse in terms of their roles, languages and geography.

Budget limitations and resource constraints in relation to the number of different groups that may need to know about a new product can be compounded by a variety of other factors. For example, an instantaneous launch rather than a phased rollout may be required. Messages may have to be communicated globally. A new product might also incorporate features that are difficult to understand.

In some sectors, there may be regulatory constraints and legal requirements to observe, and these may vary from one territory to another. Furthermore, they may have to be implemented by staff unused to them. There might be commercial, quality or technical risks associated with the new product that need to addressed or minimised.

There might also be a competitive requirement to keep the existence, nature or name of a new product secret until the moment of launch, and yet thereafter interested customers and prospects may expect a whole sales channel to be competent to explain and/or demonstrate it. Such a capability has to be quickly created and simultaneously in widely scattered locations.

Having assessed a serious and significant problem, and the requirements of those affected, a new product launch and/or business development team must now create a solution. Losers tend to throw money at the problem. A large company might develop a costly and protracted roll out programme which frustrates customers, business partners and staff who have to wait for an opportunity to learn about new offerings.

Winners tend to be more imaginative. They recognise that early engagement with customers, business partners and staff in scattered locations can help build relationships and a buzz. One option might be to capture all the relevant information and knowledge related to launching new products within a single repository that can handle material in many different formats. Incorporating a search facility would enable people to find what they need for a particular purpose very quickly.

The know-how that is captured could be used to produce a communication tool for each of the groups that need to be informed about the latest offering and equipped to understand and explain, sell, buy or support it. Elements of the content might be common to certain audiences, thus spreading any costs of producing animations, graphics and other audio or visual material. The result could be much more cost effective and quicker to implement than printing several separately designed items.

A family of multi-media communication tools could be produced comprising one or more of: a sales support tool; an indirect sales channel version for dealers, distributors and agents; a service or engineering support toolkit; marketing and/or internal communications tools; an investor relations briefing for analysts and financial institutions; and customer information manuals and interactive training. Each tool could incorporate appropriate quality and other checks.

Putting the contents into formats that make it easy for recipients to comprehend and learn could facilitate assimilation. Interactive tools could also be included to help people understand. All the derived tools aimed at staff and business partners could contain relevant on-the-job training and appropriate competence assessments.

Tools such as those examined in the last chapter could be provided to operate over the Internet, a corporate Intranet or Extranet, and on CD formats. A device such as traffic lighting could be used to build technical, commercial, quality and regulatory checks and controls into work practices. Winners try to make it easy for people to handle complexity. Automation of routine aspects of key tasks could again include configuration, pricing and issuing proposals.

All the information and knowledge required could also once again be held within a single scalable searchable repository to facilitate access and reuse, for example to launch related and other products. A proven and award winning framework such as K-frame (www.k-frame.com) could be licensed and used to manage any material that is stored, and produce the job-support tools required.

Whereas the communications of losers tend to focus on the technical aspects and features of the product winners recognise that stressing clear 'benefits' is the key to selling many offerings, including knowledge-based services. While losers focus upon bringing their own staff up to speed, winners tend to be much more concerned with enabling their people to help customers and prospects understand how new offerings will help them to achieve their aspirations.

A support tool focused upon interactions with customers has many advantages, and addresses the problems identified above. It ensures consistent messages, which may help to build a brand image, and can enable simultaneous and bespoke communication to a diversity of audiences in multiple locations and languages. The result is likely to be more rapid and widespread awareness of a new product, and increased understanding of its value and benefits.

There are likely to be other gains. Job support tools can help people implement change. They can reduce commercial, technical, regulatory and quality risks. Fewer errors may be made. Animations may make it easy for users to understand how a product works, while video footage can show it in operation. People can see a new offering as well as being told about it.

The suggested approach might differentiate a company and enhance its reputation with the various external groups it needs to communicate with. It can provide a base for future relationships with them, e.g. a product launch tool could be augmented to cater for both existing and further new offerings and become a general sales support tool. Feedback mechanisms could be included to initiate a dialogue. Winners recognise that a clear demonstration of a product's value, advantages and superiority over competitive alternatives might allow a premium price to be charged.

To many losers all of this may seem hard work. Having developed new products they simply want them released. Winners recognise that launching something that is not understood is a wasted opportunity, and that support tools to introduce and explain new offerings can be designed and produced in parallel with the new product development process. They are also willing to seek specialist help.

Support from an experienced partner can ease the workload of implementation, and take the pressure off a new product manager during the launch phase. Winners look for pragmatic suppliers of practical solutions. Existing and proven technologies can be used to speed up delivery and cut training times. Reusing and sharing elements of content across the various audiences reduces development effort and cost.

Much of the time that users might otherwise spend looking for relevant information can be saved because it is now all available in one place, within a repository that is easy to update and maintain. The cost of producing, storing and distributing supporting documentation may be significantly reduced. Issuing updates and follow up communication is also relatively straightforward, while working electronically reduces investment in paper that may become out of date. There may be less to pulp.

Overall, substantial savings can be achieved by taking an integrated approach to launching new products to diverse audiences. Some or all of the effort and resource involved might also be regarded as an investment rather than a cost. A central repository can add significantly to an individual or organization's intellectual capital, because know-how can be more easily re-used, re-versioned and exploited.

Winners are realists. They recognise that some prospects might be reluctant to stick their necks out and become an initial or early adopter. Even through there may be a clear 'first mover' advantage, it may be necessary to provide examples of how other people and organizations have addressed similar problems. Hence, when undertaking the monitoring and search activities advocated earlier in relation to understanding the business and market environment it is important to be alert to what others are doing.

Support tools developed by specialist provider Cotoco illustrate what can be achieved. 3Com has brought together - and within a single repository - everything needed to introduce an entire range of networks products to market. The 'one stop' solution enables users to make more productive use of available time.

Bolero used a support tool to launch a new technology across the world. The tool made it easier for prospects to understand what the company's proposition did, and countered a previous and prevailing sense that it was complicated and the assumption that it would be difficult to adopt. The essence of what was on offer could now be communicated in less than three minutes.

Cisco gathered together and packaged all the information, distilled knowledge and interactive tools its sales and indirect sales channel needed, including a market communication CD to explain the value and benefits of the corporation's technology. This consolidated approach has been well received, as previously people sometimes found it very difficult to locate and manage inputs from disparate sources.

Avaya – formerly Lucent - introduced a CD-ROM based after sales Engineers toolkit to help people service and support its growing product range. A dramatic reduction in cost was achieved, compared with printing and distributing the manual that preceded it. Comprehensive information was now available when needed. The company duplicated far more copies of the CD than the number of engineers employed, because people quickly recognised its value and it was adopted in many other areas of the business. The toolkit won an eBusiness Innovation Award.

As with the tools considered in the last chapter, once the concept of a new product launch toolkit is agreed a comprehensive support package can be produced in a matter of weeks, allowing a relatively quick response to a 'go decision'. A solid base can then be established for subsequent initiatives and subsequent corporate communications. This approach appeals to winners who take a longer term view. Compared with losers they are more alert to future possibilities.

Whereas losers endeavour to get items out of their in-trays, winners are more concerned with achieving an impact and enabling their people to make a difference. New product launch experience further confirms that presenting information in appropriate formats can greatly enhance understanding and the speed with which people can assimilate fresh knowledge and apply it. Again, significant productivity improvements can be achieved by supplying people with job-focussed and knowledge-based support tools.

Further Information

Job support tools are discussed in 'The Knowledge Entrepreneur' by Colin Coulson-Thomas and published by Kogan Page. The book and an accompanying CD-ROM giving further examples can be ordered by Tel. 01903 828800; Fax. 020 7837 6348; E-mail: orders@lbsltd.co.uk or on-line from www.kogan-page.co.uk or www.ntwkfirm.com/bookshop/

Examples of job support tools developed to increase sales force productivity and launch new products are also given on the CD which is part of a four part resource pack 'Winning New Business' published by Policy Publications. The resource pack can be obtained from 00 44 (0)1733 361 149 and www.policypublications.com

Customer-facing staff need to be able to help customers and prospects to quickly understand how new offerings could help them to achieve their aspirations. Further information on the use of support tools to launch new products can be obtained from 00 44 0870 748 1400 or www.cotoco.com

Checklist:

- In relation to launching new products do you view yourself and/or your colleagues as winners or losers?
- Do others view you and/or your colleagues as winners or losers?
- What proportion of the organisation's turnover is accounted for by new products that have been launched over the past twelve months?
- What would the proportion be if you included products launched over the past five years?
- Is a new product launch a protracted or overnight process?
- Can all customer facing staff, business partners and key customers be informed of new products at the same time irrespective of physical location?
- Are support tools used for this purpose?
- Do these incorporate critical success factors for the activities covered and the winning ways of high performers?
- Are they easy to use and understand?

- Do these make it easy for people to understand what is unique, special or different about the new offerings, the value they deliver and their advantages in respect of available alternatives?
- Do they allow customer facing staff and business partners to work with prospects when assessing requirements?
- Could selected customers use them to assess their own requirements and evaluate different options?
- Do they make it easy for customer facing staff to develop and offer bespoke solutions to the requirements of particular customers?
- Are different language versions produced?
- Are they automatically updated when users go online?
- Do they facilitate cross-selling and up-selling?

Chapter 28
Working with Consultants

In the last chapter we saw how specialist help is enabling pioneering companies to boost workgroup productivity. However, many business leaders have a love hate relationship with consultants. While they may resent the high cost of 'external inputs' their slimmed down organisations are often more dependent than ever upon bought in advice as a result of no longer carrying a 'float' of resource to cope with unforeseen events or major challenges.

Cynical consultants ingratiate themselves with chief executives, and encourage dependency by encouraging them to doubt the competence of their internal colleagues. Clients can end up paying large sums of money for 'projects' that do them little good, and sometimes cause great harm.

Many external consultants continually peddle new ideas to companies that would benefit from traditional remedies. Tesco has prospered at the expense of rivals by focusing unashamedly on the basics of successful retailing, particularly the creation of greater value for customers, while at the same time moving into on-line shopping and expansion overseas.

Many companies attach excessive credence to the counsel of external and uninvolved experts, while paying little attention to the views of their customers. The Shell.com website provides discussion group facilities that allow the oil company to seek opinions from interested supporters whether they are allies or critics. Their responses can be taken into account when policies are reviewed.

So what do successful companies or winners do differently from losers when working with consultants? This question is among those considered by the research and best practice programme led by the author (see appendix A) which has examined the experience of over 2,000 companies. This chapter summarises what can be learned from the findings★ in relation to building beneficial relationships with consultants.

Let's start with losers in struggling, stagnant and failing companies. They sometimes use consultants because they lack the energy and intellectual rigour to themselves handle issues they are paid to confront. Insecurity may also cause them to hire an outside party who can be blamed if events do not turn out as planned.

Losers become dependents. They end up relying upon consultants to tell them what to do and how to do it. They also take a short-term and project view of relationships with consultants. There is little cross fertilisation and limited learning across and between individual projects.

Many losers are fixed in their views, or think they know best, even though their performance may suggest otherwise. They are resistant to new ideas and alternative courses of action, and are reluctant to learn from outsiders.

Losers tend to fall back upon existing approaches and tried and tested techniques. They adopt standard solutions, methodologies and packages, and seek general improvements in performance rather than the achievement of specific changes.

Rather than demand original and bespoke approaches that could result in competitive advantage, losers employ consultants who work systematically through their firm's methodology manuals and implement 'me-too' solutions. They also become lost in the intricacies of complex mega-projects, and do not understand how the products and services of different suppliers interrelate with each other.

Losers focus upon what is immediately apparent. They do not search for underlying root causes. They are reluctant partners, and they fail to exploit the full potential of their know-how or prevent its gratis use by others, including rapacious consultants.

Winners who succeed in managing change, competing and becoming market leaders are different. They do not mind being challenged. When they seek external help it is not to avoid their responsibilities, but to obtain independent, objective and informed views from carefully chosen consultants with relevant experience and expertise.

Winners remain in control. They retain ownership of change programmes and do not abdicate this responsibility to external parties. They give consultants clear direction and seek specific help and longer-term and partnering relationships with those who share their objectives. They learn from and with external parties they respect.

Confident winners will try new approaches. They are prepared to develop their own methodologies and techniques. They also prefer to secure bespoke approaches to particular problems, and they endeavour to achieve specified outcomes. Deliverables are defined in clear output terms.

Winners are demanding customers, and ensure consultants get to grips with their particular issues and 'deliver'. They use consultants who understand what is at stake, and ensure they address what is unique and special about an individual company's situation and circumstances. They remain focused. They do not allow themselves to be bamboozled by consultants or sold additional services they do not need.

To ensure different elements of a solution are compatible winners endeavour to understand how individual products and external services complement and work with each other. They also attempt to comprehend root causes and ensure consultants address underlying drivers rather than surface symptoms.

At the end of assignments winners try to learn from what has happened in order to increase their internal capability to handle other similar situations. They may put 'knowledge transfer' into a consultancy contract and ensure that it occurs. They form mutually beneficial learning partnerships with advisors, consultants and business partners, and both manage and exploit the know-how that results.

Further Information

*Guidance on working with consultants is found in the author's forthcoming companion book on transforming corporate performance and 'The Responsive Organisation' three volume set of reports on introducing new ways of working and re-engineering. Details can be obtained from www.policypublications.com

Working with consultants is also covered in 'Transforming the Company, Manage Change, Compete and Win' and 'The Knowledge Entrepreneur' by Colin Coulson-Thomas and published by Kogan Page. They can be ordered by Tel. +44 (0)1903 828800; Fax. +44 (0)20 7837 6348; E-mail: orders@lbsltd.co.uk or on-line from www.ntwkfirm.com/bookshop

Checklist:

- In relation to working with consultants do you view yourself and/or your colleagues as winners or losers?
- Do others view you and/or your colleagues as winners or losers?
- Does the company learn from its consultants or vice versa?
- Does the company regard consultants as external suppliers, or as elements of the network organization?
- Do the consultants that the company uses understand its vision, goals and values?
- How flexible and willing to learn are the people who advise the company?

- Do they understand critical success factors and winning ways for important activities like winning business and building customer relationships?
- Do they understand the particular problems of key work groups and how to increase their performance?
- Do they listen?
- Is leaning shared? Does knowledge transfer occur?
- Are consultants willing to share risks and enter into partnering relationships?
- Do they have a holistic view of business problems, or are they 'functional' in approach?
- Do they apply standard tools and techniques, or are they selective in tailoring approaches to your particular problems?
- Do they describe and confront reality?
- Are their 'feet on the ground'?
- Are they 'telling it as it is', or saying what they believe you might wish to hear?
- How many of the things they talk about have been successfully implemented in their own organizations?
- Are they as willing to come forward with 'lessons of failure' as they are with 'success case studies'?
- What value results from the company's relationship with business schools?
- What would be lost if business schools ceased to exist?

Chapter 29
Using Management Methodologies, Tools and Techniques

Many organizations adopt a variety of management approaches, methodologies, tools and techniques for bringing about significant change. However, subsequent experience of their use suggests a considerable gap between expectations and outcomes when they are used in particular corporate contexts.

Many 'change management' and other approaches and techniques are products of particular sets of circumstances. How relevant are they to contemporary concerns? How could or should they be used to better effect?

These and related questions were explored during an extensive and international investigation of corporate transformation experience and practice (see appendix A). The results are summarized in 'The Responsive Organisation' and 'The Future of the Organization: Achieving Excellence through Business Transformation' *.

In the last two chapters we examined the use of job support tools and consultants who are often the source of new management methodologies, tools and techniques. This chapter summarizes the research findings relating to how their offerings - and home grown equivalents - might be effectively adopted and deployed.

While widespread frustration was encountered, we may be closer to success than many have realised. But first we need to put an unhealthy obsession with standard approaches, tools and techniques to one side. They should be an aid to thinking, rather than a substitute for it. Careful selection according to relevance is essential. More thought is sometimes devoted to the choice of tool than to the selection of the problem to address.

Too many applications of existing approaches and tools, particularly in struggling organizations or losers, are concerned with working people harder or the depressing task of downsizing, rightsizing or reducing the organization to its 'core'. The roots of most of the original ideas behind the innovations examined in the course of preparing 'The Future of the Organization' generally lay outside of the world of work, when seeing a link or connection caused someone to ask a simple, yet fundamental, question. Instead of trapping their organizations within a descending spiral of cost-cutting and despair, their proponents focused upon opportunities and capabilities that could sustain a positive spiral of growth and development.

Those applying management tools tend to focus upon the more visible 'formal' factors. Thus processes are documented and re-engineered, and organization charts are redrawn to reflect the latest restructuring. The trickier 'behavioural' or 'informal' arena of attitudes, feelings and values, is often avoided. Changing the architecture of the corporation may have little impact upon its ethos, culture and soul.

The standard approaches adopted by many losers are dangerous when used as an alternative for careful thought about what would be best in a particular context. Too much attention is devoted to 'tried and tested' tools and existing approaches and activities. Identifying missing elements and devising and adopting new approaches may have greater relevance to bringing about what ought to be.

People in pioneer organizations make the transition from consumers to producers of management tools and techniques in order to address the distinctive features of their own situations and circumstances. At some point companies aspiring to market leadership develop new approaches rather than absorb, consume or improve existing approaches. Winners create rather than imitate.

As we have seen in previous chapters providing people with knowledge-based support tools that enable them to be more effective and successful can yield very attractive commercial returns and increase job satisfaction. Within a partnering arrangement the different parties involved can share in the rewards that are generated.

Culture change, re-engineering and knowledge management initiatives introduced by losers to improve corporate profitability often do little to help individuals in key roles improve their performance. Winners take practical steps to enable their people to manage change, compete and win.

Some losers devote much effort to making a wide range of information and knowledge available on a corporate Intranet. 'Winners' are more focused and selective. They recognize that much of the know-how they could capture may not be relevant to current priorities, future aspirations and critical success factors for building their businesses. Also, the expertise to do something better, new or different may require specific skills and particular tools as well as access to relevant knowledge.

One of the most cost-effective ways of quickly improving individual performance and raising corporate productivity is to provide work groups with practical knowledge-based tools. People often need help when applying relevant knowledge. The right job support tools can capture and spread best practice and increase understanding each time they are used. They can also incorporate devices such as traffic lighting that can influence or change behaviour.

Within most organizations there are many areas of know-how that can be packaged to increase understanding and make it easier for people to do their jobs. Retailer B&Q's vendors manual captures and disseminates both information and processes to the company's supply chain.

In the finance and banking sector HSBC has used support tools to package its economics knowledge and help customers implement card programs. Friends Provident uses a sales development support kit to assist staff running local marketing campaigns. Smart companies apply effort where it is likely to yield the greatest returns. Performance improvements will need to cover the costs involved. This is most likely in areas such as sales that contribute directly to the 'bottom line'.

The value of a tool reflects the quality of its individual elements. A component such as a pricing engine will only be as good as the assumptions upon which it is based. Data sets such as a schedule of prices may need to be regularly updated in order to remain current.

There may be a degree of scepticism to overcome. Some companies are initially cautious because past and un-related investments in sales technology, e-learning and knowledge management have delivered questionable results. Such outcomes are not surprising. These other initiatives have usually been excessively general, and they fail to provide people with the practical support tools they need to do a better job.

Within any community of knowledge workers some are likely to be more effective than others. Every opportunity should be taken to review existing approaches during the development phase, and capture effective short cuts and how high achievers operate. Improvements based upon best practice and the insights of superstars are much more likely to get better results than just automating current practices.

Companies interested in exploring the possibilities for providing work groups with new or improved job support tools should seek a demonstration of the possibilities. If better understanding of complex material is required a tool should use visual means of helping comprehension such as animations and diagrams. One or more workshops should be held to examine the applicability of job support tools to the particular context, and to the people, problems and products involved.

Job support tools can represent a much more cost-effective way of improving understanding and increasing work group performance than traditional training and development activities. Rates of return on investment will depend upon the number of people involved. A medium sized company found the cost of creating an effective tool to be similar to that of sending its sales team on a one-day commercial training course. For a major corporation the cost per sales representative may be no more than providing each of them with a bottle of wine.

Losers become intimidated by large-scale requirements and difficult
challenges, and pass up opportunities they cannot afford to address. They suffer from information overload and drown in an excess of e-mails and other forms of communication. They adapt how they operate to match the requirements of management methodologies, tools and techniques and experience a conflict between their demands and the preferences of their people.

The boards of 'loser' companies look for opportunities to replace people with technology. They regard networks as an internal capability, apply technology to structured situations and address the technical problems of introducing new technologies. They are reluctant to extend network membership and services to customers, suppliers and business partners.

Winners are more willing to tackle complex issues and confront demanding situations, and seek collaborators and partners to exploit opportunities that would otherwise stretch their resources. They draw a distinction between information and understanding, and manage the former to enhance the latter.

Our winners are also more focused on user requirements. They adopt management methodologies, tools and techniques that support how they naturally prefer to work, communicate and learn. They view people, processes and technology as complementary and endeavour to achieve a harmonious relationship between them;

The boards of 'winner' companies support people with technologies, methodologies and tools that enable them to excel at difficult activities. They use networks and support tools to facilitate relationships with customers, suppliers and business partners.

Winners adopt technologies and approaches that enable them to deal with both structured and unstructured situations. They address the attitudinal, behavioural and technical problems of introducing new technologies. Crucially they use network membership and support tools to build intimate relationships with customers, suppliers and business partners, and lock them in.

We need the courage to formulate our own philosophies of business and develop our own tools and approaches. Inspiration should be sought from what is simple yet fundamental, and from within rather than from what is trendy. Proactive and flexible innovators and users initiate trends, fashions and opportunities. They have vision and purpose, and adopt pragmatic criteria for development and selection and adapt to changing requirements and contexts.

Too many people are still victims rather than beneficiaries of restructuring and re-engineering. They work ever harder rather than more effectively on the things which really matter. Losers often lack time for reflection. People who 'rush about' sometimes fail to stay in one place long enough to think issues through or make an impact. The Buddha evolved his philosophy by sitting under a tree and thinking. Individual and corporate self-awareness and self-knowledge can help each to establish what they are particularly good at.

Winners understand that it is what we apply management approaches to and for what ends that generally determines whether or not they bite us. The rationale of organizations should be to develop and harness the potential and capabilities of both individuals and teams, and to apply collective capability and commitment to those activities that deliver value to customers and achieve business objectives'. Thus 'BPR' could be undertaken to re-engineer learning processes to improve the quality of working life, introduce new ways of working or learning, widen job opportunities or help create a learning organization.

Tools that encourage learning and development are especially valuable. Shared learning approaches and tools can help to hold groups and networks together. Their refinement and development can become a key benefit of network membership.

Commitment to learning and change, with emphasis upon empathy, openness, trust and tolerance, and knowledge, capability, and competence can enable renewal and relevance in an uncertain, insecure and transient world. These are the very areas often most undermined by corporate change programmes.

Learning can be a critical core competence. The support of learning or transformation partners can help an organization identify and overcome barriers to learning. They can advise on appropriate learning approaches and technologies and generally help to assess and improve the quality of individual, group and organizational learning. Shared learning across functional, project group, business unit and organisational boundaries can be particularly beneficial.

Winners stress the fun of shared learning and future discovery rather than dwell on the frustration, disappointment and pain of past restructuring. People should be encouraged to work and learn in whatever ways suit their circumstances and preferences, match their aptitudes and allow them to give of their best. Social creatures thrive on trust, and the interaction and interdependence that allow individuals to create and negotiate roles that enable them to contribute while being true to themselves.

Mature people who aspire to be winners seek environments that foster creativity, encourage responsible risk taking, and enable them to grow and develop. Variety, tailoring and the tolerance of very different approaches is often the key to corporate success and individual fulfillment.

Building a community of people who are open minded and free thinking may be a more sensible strategy than the adoption of a complete framework such as quality that may end up acting as a protective cocoon. Many people throughout the ages would not have been innovators if they had been equipped with a standard tool-kit that caused them to look at the world and its problems in the same way as everyone else. They had the courage to attract or create whatever capability and competencies are relevant to the opportunities they define and the markets their imaginations create.

In conclusion, the emphasis should be upon values and relationships roles, competencies and behaviours rather then procedures and structures; flexibility and intuition rather than prescriptive and mechanical approaches, the fostering of diversity and creativity rather than the enforcement of standards; learning rather than control. Management also needs to be holistic to understand interrelationships between elements and assemble the combination of them that will deliver multiple objectives and longer-term goals such as renewal and transformation. People should be beneficiaries of change and not its victims.

The options, examples and opportunities examined in the course of preparing 'The Future of the Organization' suggest that, given a shared sense of purpose, supportive learning partners, and an appropriate mix of change elements, renewal and transformation can be achieved. The potential payoffs - both for ourselves and for others - more than justify the incremental effort involved.

★Further Information

Methodologies and toolkits for re-engineering processes ('The Responsive Organisation') and supply chains ('The Competitive Network'), and winning new business (e.g. 'The Contract Bid Manager's Toolkit') and associated benchmarking services can be obtained from Policy Publications via Tel: +44 (0)1733 361 149; Fax +44 (0)1733 361 459; E-mail: colinct@tiscali.co.uk or via www.policypublications.com

'The Future of the Organisation: Achieving Excellence through Business Transformation' by Colin Coulson-Thomas is published by Kogan Page and can be ordered by: Tel. +44 (0)1903 828800; Fax. +44 (0)20 7837 6348; E-mail: orders@lbsltd.co.uk or on-line from www.ntwkfirm.com/bookshop

Further information on the use of job support tools can be obtained from 00 44 0870 748 1400 or www.cotoco.com

Checklist:

- In relation to the use of management methodologies tools and techniques do you view yourself and/or your colleagues as winners or losers?
- Do others view you and/or your colleagues as winners or losers?
- Do the tools, techniques and methodologies used by the organisation provide a creative stimulus?
- Are they relevant to what the organisation and its people are seeking to achieve?
- Are they excessively prescriptive or do they allow high performers to distinguish themselves?
- Do they encourage people to 'go automatic' or do they stimulate thinking and creativity?
- Do people learn with each use?
- Do they automate the more repetitive and routine aspects of work?
- Are the tools, techniques and methodologies easy to use?
- Do they incorporate critical success factors and the winning ways of high achievers?
- Do they enable bespoke responses?
- Are all tools, techniques and methodologies regularly reviewed and kept up to date?
- Are they a source of differentiation and competitive advantage?
- When new tools, techniques and methodologies are introduced are people helped to understand and use them?

- Do they help people to achieve both corporate objectives and personal satisfaction?

Chapter 30
Creating a Competitive Company

In many sectors different companies appear to have similar competitive strategies. As was mentioned in chapter 1, they recruit from the same business schools, buy the same technologies and employ standard processes. Yet some expand and prosper while others decline. Despite a decade of re-engineering, a succession of management fads, heavy investment in IT and extensive use of management consultants many companies struggle to cope. What do the businesses that adapt and grow do differently?

We return to this central question which for more than a decade has inspired a research programme led by the author (see appendix A), which has examined why some companies win new business, build customer relationships, create and exploit know-how and manage change while others stagnate. Research teams compare the approaches and practices of the most and least successful, and isolate critical success factors for competing and winning*. This chapter attempts a summary of what we have learned.

The collective experience of over 2,000 enterprises across many sectors reveals how profitable and expanding companies – the winners - become and remain competitive. People in these businesses don't print money or cheat. Their attitudes, approaches, perspectives and priorities ensure they win the battle to change, re-invent and break free of past constraints.

If you and your colleagues are frustrated and would like to transform the fortunes of your company you can indeed learn from those who succeed. The key lessons - and stark differences between winners and losers - can be expressed in terms of 'do's' and 'don'ts'.

Let's start with what you are setting out to achieve. Survival – getting through the next quarter or twelve months - does not energize and excite. Be positive. Craft and communicate a distinctive vision, a compelling purpose, stretching goals and clear objectives.

Remain relevant and stay vital. Develop additional income streams, enhance capabilities and refresh intellectual capital. Create additional options and extend choice. Launch new ventures and establish new markets.

Display the will to win. Winners are driven to succeed. Their actions demonstrate they care. Read the road ahead. Anticipate events and confront realities. Take a longer-term view and provide strategic leadership. Ensure immediate priorities do not take precedence over longer-term aims.

Inspire and motivate. Lead and guide. Make sure people understand what they need to do, are visibly committed, and are prepared, equipped and enabled to act. Identify and tackle barriers to change. Don't sidetrack critics, conceal disappointments or rationalize failure.

However keen you are to go forward don't make changes for changes sake. Change can be stressful and it may disrupt valued relationships. Think before you act. Assess likely consequences. Balance change and continuity. Distinguish goals, values, objectives, policies and activities that need to be changed from those that should be continued.

Don't expend energy in peripheral areas or bark up the wrong trees. Concentrate your effort where it is most likely to make a difference. Focus upon the critical success factors for achieving key corporate objectives and delivering greater customer and shareholder value.

Understand your customers. Ensure they are not disadvantaged by change. Put yourself out to develop tailored responses. Deliver bespoke offerings to them. Be proactive. Don't wait to be asked. Take the initiative. Identify and approach those you would like to do business with. Push back the boundaries of what is possible, and aim to become a sought after and trusted business partners.

Don't adopt standard approaches or be rigid and inflexible. Think for yourself rather than imitate and copy others. Jumping upon band-waggons and 'me-too' activities are not the route to market leadership. Don't be overly cautious and too wary of commitments. Don't respond belatedly to events or fail to anticipate requirements and implications.

Be confident. Don't be indecisive or oblivious to the needs of others. Build and release talent. Explore, pioneer and discover. Encourage and support enterprise and innovation.

Losers are complacent, secretive and defensive. Don't keep things to yourself or be reluctant to delegate. Trust other people and share information and opportunities with them where this is likely to prove mutually beneficial. Empathise and invite feedback. Question and challenge, and listen and learn.

Build relationships, but select people, business partners and opportunities with care. Don't end up playing other people's games. At the same time, don't focus exclusively upon your own agenda.

Collaborate on the basis of openness and transparency with complementary spirits who share your vision and values.

Be persistent but pragmatic, and determined but adaptable in pursuit of your aims. Take calculated risks. Experiment with new ways of working, learning and collaborating.

The board should help you to compete and win. It should be the heart and soul of a company, the source of its ambition and drive. Without a sense of purpose, a sound strategy and the will to achieve, well endowed corporations wither and die. Whether or not a company achieves and sustains success depends largely upon the attitudes and conduct of its directors.

Don't mouth generalizations, engage in spin or confuse activity with progress. Cut through blather and hype. Get down to the fundamentals of what needs to be done. Wherever possible adopt simple solutions and take direct action. Regard change, renewal and transformation as normal activities.

Don't try to do everything yourself or resist new and external ideas. Work with colleagues to foster winning attitudes and behaviours. Balance strategy with capability and think holistically. Ensure all the pieces of the jigsaw puzzle required for successful transformation and sustained competitiveness are in place.

Directors and senior managers cannot become directly involved in the many and varied activities needed to respond imaginatively to changing circumstances. Empower business units and venture teams to bring about whatever changes are required to enable them to achieve their objectives and deliver value to *their* customers.

New areas of risk can arise as structures, processes and systems are reviewed and altered. Make sure people understand what is at stake and are ready to respond. Problems will arise. Their absence could indicate a lack of ambition. Learning from them and celebrating success help to sustain momentum.

Finally - as has been stressed before - go for it. The prospects of 'loser' companies can be transformed by putting the critical success factors required for winning in place. Achieving success is often easier and is invariably more satisfying than rationalising failure.

★*Further Information*

Details of various reports covering critical success factors in particular areas that are vital for competing and winning, including those listed in appendix B and related benchmarking services, can be obtained from Policy Publications: Tel: + 44 (0) 1733 361 149; Fax +44 (0) 1733 361 459; Email: colinct@tiscali.co.uk; online from either www.policypublications.com or from www.ntwkfirm.com/bookshop.

Information on related book titles, support services and forthcoming publications based upon the continuing research programme can be obtained from Prof. Colin Coulson-Thomas by Tel: + 44 (0)1733 361 149; Fax: +44 (0)1733 361 459 and by Email: colinct@tiscali.co.uk or via www.coulson-thomas.com or www.adaptation.ltd.uk

Checklist:

- In relation to creating a competitive company do you view yourself and/or your colleagues as winners or losers?
- Do others view you and/or your colleagues as winners or losers?
- Have you thought through what you are trying to achieve?
- Has it been expressed in terms of opportunities, requirements and clear objectives?
- Are these agreed by the key players and partners?
- Are they committed to their achievement?
- Is the commitment visible and palpable?
- Can the objectives be measured and performance managed?
- Have the 'vital few' tasks which need to be done been identified?
- Are roles and responsibilities relating to key tasks understood?
- Have key work groups been identified and equipped with appropriate support tools?
- Have the critical success factors for key activities been identified and incorporated into support tools and ways of working?
- Have the opportunities, requirements and objectives been shared with all those who need to contribute to individual and collective achievement?
- Do people understand their individual contributions?
- Have they been empowered, enabled and motivated to act?
- In particular, are they enabled to adopt the winning ways of high performers
- Do they understand the critical factors for becoming and remaining competitive?
- Can and will relevant, productive and shared learning occur?
- Are the rewards and the performance management framework consistent with what you are all seeking to achieve?
- Do people have the knowledge, skills and support tools to make it happen?
- Are they winners or losers?

- What are the likely obstacles and barriers to success and fulfilment?
- What needs to be done about them, by whom and when?

Chapter 31
Achieving Commercial Success and Personal Fulfilment

Earlier chapters of this book have focused upon different aspects of securing profitable corporate growth and business development. This final chapter argues it is possible to make money and be true to oneself, i.e. one can achieve both commercial success and personal fulfilment.

Many people are creating profitable businesses while doing what they enjoy doing and do best. Individuals and organisations can both benefit if they understand personal aspirations and respond appropriately.

From time to time many individuals consider a change of direction. Some seek a more equitable balance between work and life, or want more control over their destiny. Others harbour a desire to become entrepreneurs. They are fed up being a piece on someone else's chess board and want to play their own game.

People can experience a range of emotions from apprehension on starting work to a mid-life crisis. They question what they are doing with their lives. Sometimes imagined or available alternatives seem to bring their own problems and uncertainties. People weigh the advantages and disadvantages of different courses of action. They assess whether the risks and costs involved will outweigh desired benefits. They wonder whether the grass really will be greener on the other side of the fence.

Certain business trends have implications for both individuals and employers. For example, as more customers demand bespoke responses front line staff dealing with them increasingly need to think and act like entrepreneurs. This opens up an historic window of opportunity to reconcile people and organisations.

An investigation into emerging opportunities for entrepreneurship has examined how people can best respond. The findings - along with self-assessment exercises and checklists - are set out in 'Individuals and Enterprise', a guide for intending entrepreneurs*. They reveal the satisfaction and excitement people can derive from discovering their inner selves, breaking free and changing course.

Most people have opportunities to be true to their ideals and beliefs. Most could either start a new enterprise or make fundamental changes in their current organisation. Challenges such as career uncertainty, new forms of working and even redundancy can be turned into exciting opportunities for going it alone or collaborating with an existing employer to create a new offering or launch a new venture.

Let's look as what those who succeed financially while also being personally fulfilled do differently. Firstly, they acknowledge that all is not well with their existing lives. Whether or not they experience demons in the night they recognise what is missing. They assess their current situation and decide that enough is enough.

Life's winners also recognise the dawn of a new era of opportunity. They both search for and recognise what is latent and hidden. They are alert to trends such as falling barriers. They view emerging concerns, current problems and likely changes as potential sources of opportunity. They consider how such developments will affect them and others, and assess what new qualities, careers, lifestyle options, strategies, offerings and markets will be required to cope with them and benefit from them.

Next, our winners look at what it would take to succeed in the new arenas of opportunity they identify. They consider changing requirements, the limitations of current approaches and potential conflicts of interest. They assess themselves and review their current circumstances and obligations in relation to the essence of what will be required for an effective response.

The most fulfilled devote more time to the question: who am I? They are much more self-aware. They seek to understand the person within and assess which opportunities - if pursued - would most allow them to be true to their inner selves. Organisations too need to assess themselves in relation to new requirements and opportunities, and consider the implications for ways of working and future relationships with people whose aspirations may be changing.

Smart intending entrepreneurs consider opportunities for collaboration before they burn their boats, leave their employer and launch out on their own. They explore options for cooperation, buy-out possibilities and the scope of working with rather than for organisations. Confident companies do likewise. They consider whether they should become a sponsor or business partner rather than an employer, and encourage aspiring entrepreneurs to become internal intrapreneurs or joint venture colleagues.

Successful entrepreneurs look at the world differently and retain a sense of wonder and excitement at the possibilities. They question, probe and explore. They bring new combinations of elements together and assemble winning formulae. When the time is right they seize the moment and have a go.

Winners recognise leeches and parasites, but they also appreciate collective endeavour and understand the value of the right networks and relationships. If appropriate, they operate in collaboration with others. They are not afraid to ask for help, but select colleagues with care. They seek soul mates who share their visions. They attract contributors, energetic business builders with complementary qualities.

Rather than imitate and copy others the most fulfilled 'do it their way'. They recognise individuality, both in themselves and in others. They achieve a healthy balance between reflection and action, and secure flexible access to the capabilities they need to turn their dreams into a reality. They avoid siren voices and the vanity of size, seeking a scale of operation that is right for the opportunities they pursue.

Confident leaders view the entrepreneurial aspirations of their people as an opportunity rather than a threat. They call for proposals and back the most promising ones. They provide corporate support services to help intending entrepreneurs get started. In return for a share of new ventures they offer finance, development advice and access to a customer base.

Further Information

★'Individuals and Enterprise: creating entrepreneurs for the new millennium through personal transformation' and 'Shaping Things to Come, strategies for creating alternative enterprises' - a guide for creating new offerings- can both be ordered from Blackhall Publishing by Tel: 00 353 1 6773242, Fax: 00 353 1 6773243, email: blackhall@eircom.net; or from: www.ntwkfirm.com/bookshop/

Checklist:

- Do you view yourself and/or your colleagues as winners or losers when it comes to achieving both financial success and personal fulfilment?
- Do others view you and/or your colleagues as winners or losers?
- Does the organisation consciously aim at personal fulfilment for its people as well as achieving commercial objectives?
- Is it setting out to be unique, special or different?

- Do the members of the board and senior management team understand the aspirations of its people?
- Can people achieve their aspirations by working for or with the organisation, or do the able and ambitious leave?
- Can the organisation attract, motivate and retain highly talented people?
- Do the people of the organisation start every day with a desire to develop and learn as well as work and earn?
- Are people helped to learn and develop?
- Is what is learned shared?
- Do they feel they are in control of their own destinies?
- Do they have opportunities for personal growth?
- Are people equipped with support tools that make it easy for them to understand complex issues and do difficult jobs?
- Do these incorporate critical success factors and winning ways?
- Are customer facing staff helped to develop bespoke solutions to the requirements of individual customers?
- Are they helped to succeed and make a distinctive contribution?
- Are the personal contributions of individuals visible?
- Are their individual contributions recognised and rewarded?
- Do they feel they are working with the organisation rather than for it?
- Do they feel that what they are doing is worthwhile?
- Are they happy or content in terms of work life balance?
- Overall, how fulfilled do they consider themselves to be?
- Do they consider themselves to be winners or losers in terms of both securing material rewards and being fulfilled?

Appendix A
The Winning Companies; Winning People Research Programme

The question of why some people and certain teams are better than others at particular activities is an intriguing one that has spurred a life long investigation into how best to transform individual and corporate performance. Early inter and cross company comparisons suggested that even quite successful organisations usually find it very difficult to be effective across all areas of corporate operation.

Specific research projects were initiated to identify critical success factors for particular activities that are critical to commercial success. These investigations have invariably revealed both a wide spectrum of attainment and considerable differences in the importance those surveyed attached to the factors whose significance were being assessed.

The roots of many – and in some investigations most - of the identified critical success factors appear to be attitudinal and behavioural. The approaches of people who are successful at the various activities that have been examined differ from those of people who struggle and under perform. Put simply, high achievers do things differently.

The findings are consistent across overlapping areas of activity, and their implications are exciting. Building critical success factors and the approaches of high performers into corporate processes and support tools can enable average performers to adopt the approaches of superstars and emulate their achievements. Within every organisation that has been examined there is considerable potential for performance improvement.

This book summarises what superstars do differently, and how others can be helped to adopt their winning ways. But first some background to the Winning Companies, Winning People Research Programme and subsequent dissemination, development and implementation work.

The research programme and the individual research studies have been led by the author. Their aim has been to improve the effectiveness and contribution of corporate leaders, key workgroups and professionals in many parts of the world in important areas such as managing change (including re-engineering and new ways of working), winning business, building relationships, creating and exploiting know-how, and providing corporate direction.

Some of the areas investigated could be said to be general such as 'communication' and the responsibility of many people, while others such as pricing and purchasing could be regarded as more specific and left to particular individuals or teams. They range from setting the strategic direction of an organisation to managing its performance (see diagram in Chapter 1).

The origins of the research programme lay in work concerning professionalisation, corporate leadership and the differing effectiveness of individual directors and knowledge workers during the late 1970s, and the author's roles with a number of professional associations. Early outputs included guide books and the first of a number of management methodologies (for developing new products).

Subsequent participant observer roles with matched pairs of professional bodies formed the basis of a research design for doctoral research into the process of professionalisation and the relative standing of different groups of professionals. Certain occupational groups were found to be more successful than others at securing status and formal recognition.

Within different groups of knowledge workers skewed distribution curves of competence and achievement were also observed. Typically there would be a small number of high performers and a long tail of barely adequate accomplishment. Some organisations were noticeably better than others at identifying their superstars, but so often the most capable worked on similar tasks to those allocated to their less able colleagues. Little if any effort was made to identify and record what they did differently, or use their approaches to improve the performance of others.

The next phase of investigation, involving over 2,000 companies, was concerned largely with different aspects of how to transition to higher performing and more effective and flexible models of operation. A family of studies examined corporate structures and processes, the competence of directors and the effectiveness of boards.

Other areas examined by questionnaire surveys included 'communicating for change' and 'harnessing the potential of groups'. Some of the findings were counter intuitive and challenged prevailing views at the time. For example, the impact of certain types of communication was found to be inversely related to the amount of effort devoted to refining, polishing and packaging them, while many groups were so distracted by operating effectively as a team they would loose sight of their objectives and purpose.

The current phase of the research programme began with an interest in why some directors, boards and professionals are so much more successful than others at certain activities such as winning business, and continues with an ongoing investigation of critical success factors that has now also involved over 2,000 organisations and the development of tools for sharing best practice that are used by leading companies.

The approach adopted is to identify apparent success factors through desk research, visits to representative companies and/or expert consultation, followed by questionnaire surveys and follow-up interviews. Companies surveyed range from major corporations to smaller companies.

Survey questionnaires are sent to those who are directly involved in - and responsible for - the area being investigated. The aim has been to record the views of people who understand both the approaches adopted within their companies and the results achieved. Practitioners appear more prepared to reveal their performance and approaches in some areas than others. Thus while over 300 participated in one winning business study a related pricing survey secured 73 respondents.

Participating companies are ranked according to outcome measures and top and bottom quartiles of attainment (or those above and below an average or mid point in the range of achievements according to the sample size) compared to isolate critical success factors. In some areas outcomes were easier to assess than in others. Thus success at competitive bidding was measured in terms of the proportion of bids won. The top quartile superstars – only 4% of the total – were those winning more than three out of four of the competitive bid races they entered.

In other areas multiple measures of outcomes - or benefits achieved - were used. For example in the study of how companies develop strategic customers and key accounts 16 possible benefit objectives were assessed on a score of 1 to 5 (from 5 for "very effective" to 1 for "not effective") to give a maximum score of 80 (16 x 5) and a minimum of 16 (16 x 1). Among the 194 companies surveyed the highest score was 77 and the lowest 29, a range of 49.

Both the most effective and the least effective companies were to be found right across the size spectrum of the companies participating in the survey. Roughly twice as many (67%) of the most effective companies win more than half of their business from strategic customers compared with the least effective (35%). The most effective (winners) considered nearly four times as many of a possible 14 reasons for developing strategic customers to be 'very important' as the least effective companies (losers).

To illustrate the number of different areas that can be impacted by adopting winning behaviours the possible benefits considered in the effective strategic customer and key account management study were:

- improving key customer satisfaction, retention and loyalty;
- enhancing a company's image;
- acquiring relevant knowledge and know-how;
- enhancing a company's role in its value chain;
- increasing both general and individual customer profitability;
- reducing sales and administration costs;
- generating growth;
- extending global reach;
- improving market share;
- creating new strategic customers from an existing customer base and gaining them from competitors;
- increasing sales of specific products and services;
- funding product development;
- creating entry barriers for competitors; and
- lowering a company's dependence on any individual customer.

Adopting winning behaviours across all the many activities examined offers the prospect of transforming corporate performance. As we will see in chapter 24 there are now practical and cost effective ways of enabling average achievers to raise their game by adopting the approaches of high achievers. Enormous improvements in productivity and performance have been achieved, while implementation and management of change type issues have been avoided by equipping people with tools that make it much easier for them to do their jobs.

Particular 'rules of the game' can sometimes apply in certain sectors even though sector variations might not be apparent in data collected. In the case of the winning business sector studies that have been undertaken panels of expert practitioners within the sectors concerned have been assembled to assess and comment upon the findings. Resulting research reports (see Appendix B) have contained a selection of their views.

Over 4,000 companies have participated in individual research projects that have been undertaken by the author within the 'winning companies, winning people' programme. The research and resulting publications, approaches and methodologies have concerned the leadership, management and implementation of corporate leadership, transformation and business development. Over a twenty year period the programme has evolved and developed across five over-lapping and inter-related streams:

- Corporate communications, and particularly: communication with customers and prospects, communicating for change, and the communications activities of corporate leaders (both individual directors and boards).
- The development of more competent directors and effective boards, particularly in terms of leading corporate transformation, communicating with stakeholders, creating an enterprise culture and putting the critical success factors for competing and winning in place.
- The management of change, corporate transformation, and the improvement and re-engineering of processes, including those for entrepreneurship, winning business, building relationships and creating and exploiting know-how.
- The critical success factors for corporate success in areas such as managing change, winning business, building customer and stakeholder relationships, and creating and exploiting know-how.
- Knowledge creation and exploitation to generate incremental revenues, enhance shareholder value, raise workgroup productivity and improve corporate performance.

The research questions posed at each step have been informed by previous research findings. The adoption of a distinct directorial perspective has helped to ensure a degree of cohesion, cross-referencing and cumulative enrichment and refinement of understanding and the development of more holistic approaches, while the involvement of professional bodies has helped to ensure successive research surveys were focused on contemporary concerns.

The following paragraphs summarise the research findings that relate to each chapter of this book:

Chapter 2 : Understanding the business and market environment

The importance of strategic awareness and an understanding of the business and market environment within which companies operate was highlighted by an initial survey of 218 companies. Three quarters of the responses were from those holding the job titles of chairman or chairman and chief executive. Other surveys have examined certain issues or particular trends and developments in the business environment. For example, a survey of managing the relationship with the environment covered 104 organisations. Overwhelmingly, the responses were from those with environmental policy or implementation responsibility.

Chapter 3: Visioning

The need for a clear and compelling vision has emerged from several surveys within the winning companies, winning people research programme. Surveys of directors and boards, change managers and project managers have all highlighted the importance of visioning. Yet one survey within the programme involving over 60 entrepreneurs failed to uncover a single example of a vision that motivated people internally and focused their efforts or differentiated a company from its competitors. Visioning exercises have been undertaken for over 40 organisations.

Chapters 4 and 5: Creating a Winning Board and Providing Strategic Leadership

Initial investigations of director development and board operation and effectiveness involved 274 organisations. 247 of the survey responses were from chairmen or chief executives. Subsequent surveys have covered the development of IT and personnel directors, the role and development of particular categories directors such as SME directors and NHS directors, and particular aspects of the work of directors and boards. Specific assignments have been undertaken for over 100 boards and mini surveys of communities of directors have been undertaken in a number of countries.

Chapter 6: Corporate Governance

Aspects of the structure and accountability of boards have been examined in the course of a number of the surveys of directors and boards which have been undertaken within the winning companies, winning people research programme. One survey covering 60 boards was designed to secure the views of chairmen and chief executives of predominantly larger organisations, while another involving a similar number of companies has focused upon the governance of SMEs. Another exercise involving a programme of interviews led to a multimedia development package for a community of directors implementing certain government programmes. Good governance, directorial competences and board effectiveness were the main aims of the project.

Chapter 7: Differentiation

Differentiation has been considered in a number of studies within the winning companies, winning people research programme. It emerged as a significant factor - for the achievement of a price premium - in a survey of the pricing strategies, policies and tactics of 73 companies, and - for distinguishing a particular proposal - in the winning business surveys which have been undertaken covering over 300 companies and over 500 professional firms. Over 100 projects have been undertaken involving activities to differentiate an organisation's offerings from its competitors, while a survey of over 60 SMEs revealed a lack of differentiation as a common characteristic of the firms with falling turnover and profitability that were visited.

Chapter 8: Winning Competitive Bids

304 companies with a combined annual turnover of over £65 billion participated in the core winning new business survey. Sectors in which competitive bidding is widespread such as construction, IT and telecommunications, engineering and transport and distribution are well represented. Panels of experts have examined bidding in particular business sectors. In addition, 62 companies participated in a separate study of 20 specific bidding for business skills. Winning competitive bids has also been examined in parallel studies of how over 500 professional firms set about obtaining new business. Specific reviews have been undertaken of the winning business processes and practices of over 100 companies.

Chapter 9: Pricing for Profit

Some of the companies that had participated in other surveys within the winning companies, winning people research programme were reluctant to discuss their pricing strategies, policies and tactics. Nevertheless 73 companies were covered by the pricing for profit survey carried out in association with the Chartered Institute of Marketing. The respondents covered a broad mix of pricing experience and included those selling in both business-to-business and business-to-consumer markets. The turnover of participating companies ranged from under £10 million (26%) to over £1 billion (8%). Another survey covering the chief executives of over 60 organisations corroborated the main findings of the pricing for profit study.

Chapter 10: Developing Strategic Customers and Key Accounts

194 companies with a combined turnover of more than £70 billion participated in the developing strategic customers and key accounts survey which was carried out in association with Marketing Business, the magazine for the Chartered Institute of Marketing. The annual turnovers of the companies ranged from under £50 (39%) to over £1 billion (11%). 45 per cent of the participating organisations were service providers, 42 per cent were manufacturers, and 10 per cent were wholesalers or retailers. Aspects of managing relationships with customers were also examined in the course of other surveys, such as those of over 500 professional services organisations, and project work with particular companies.

Chapter 11: Negotiating Partnering Relationships

The desire for improved collaboration and partnering has emerged in studies of both purchasing and building relationships with customers within the winning companies, winning people research programme. 490 organisations participated in these two investigations. Other studies within the programme - and projects with particular companies - have examined processes, technologies and tools that can support more effective collaboration.

Chapter 12: Managing Supply Chain Relationships

The effective management of supply chain relationships emerged as a key factor in surveys undertaken within the wining companies, winning people research programme of both quality and performance improvement. Over 300 organisations participated in these studies. A survey of how 194 companies build strategic and key customer relationships revealed how supply chain relationships can be used to lock customers in and competitors out. However, the investigation of corporate learning within the programme found that few of the education, training and learning activities managed by the 69 people interviewed embraced business partners within their organisation's supply chains

Chapter 13: Leading and Managing Change

163 companies employing over four and a quarter million people participated in the initial surveys of changing organisations. 79 of the organisations examined had a turnover of over £1 billion, and over

60% of survey respondents were chairmen, chief executives or managing directors. Subsequent investigations have examined particular aspects of managing change, for example the role of communications, teamwork, project management or particular management techniques such as quality or re-engineering. Over 500 companies have participated in these surveys, while parallel studies of directors and boards have also examined their role in leading change and transformation.

Chapter 14: Corporate Transformation

The research undertaken in the area of corporate transformation has drawn upon the studies mentioned in chapter 12 concerning different aspects of leading and managing change, including specific studies of directors and boards. Additional work included involvement in over 100 change and transformation programmes, and a pan-European investigation of differing approaches to bringing about fundamental change. This encompassed an examination of over 40 re-engineering and transformation methodologies. Subsequent workshops have assessed and compared different approaches with a view to determining those which are most appropriate in particular situations and contexts.

Chapter 15: Corporate Communications

Work undertaken within the winning companies, winning people research programme has included different aspects of communications, for example within teams and across national borders. An initial communicating for change survey covered 52 organisations with a combined turnover of some £90 billion and employing 1.2 million people. Over a half of those participating were directors of their organisations, while a third held the job titles of chairman, chief executive or managing director. Other surveys have examined communication skills, and the role of communications within the boardroom and when winning new business and building relationships with customers.

Chapter 16: Going Global

Aspects of going global have been explored by a number of the surveys undertaken within the winning companies, winning people research programme. For example, a European investigation of the human resources required for effective international operation involved 91 organisations employing over 2.7 million employees and with a combined turnover of some £320 billion. Of the survey respondents 38 per cent were chairmen, chief executives or managing directors. Field work with particular organisations has included projects with organisations in North and South America, Europe, Africa, the Middle East and Asia.

Chapter 17: New Ways of Working

In addition to surveys of changing organisations specific studies of particular ways of working have been undertaken within the winning companies, winning people research programme. A pan-European investigation of teleworking involved over 100 organisations and the production of the 21 case studies that appear within one of the three reports within the 'Responsive Organisation' boxed set. Other studies have looked at areas such as teleworking, teleconferencing and telemedicine. New ways of working and tools to support them have been introduced into several organisations. A methodology for adopting teleworking that has been produced by the research team has been used by over 100 organisations.

Chapter 18: Managing Virtual Organisations

Several studies within the winning companies, winning people research programme have been concerned with aspects of building and management of 'network' and virtual organisations, including investigations of virtual team work and the management of distributed teams and teleworkers. Enabling technologies were among the areas examined by one pan-European investigation, while work with support tools has included an exercise involving over 1,000 separate organisations. Interviews with 69 individuals responsible for education, training and development within their organisations suggest many companies may be overlooking key members of the peripheral workforce.

Chapter 19: Creating an Entrepreneurial Culture

Studies of bidding and other ways of winning new business, the exploitation of know-how, and activities such as pricing and purchasing within the winning companies, winning people research programme have revealed a lack of innovation and creativity within many companies. Business development projects have been undertaken for over 100 organisations, and many of these have involved specific activity to build a more entrepreneurial corporate culture. Over 60 entrepreneurs participated in one exercise to develop more entrepreneurial approaches.

Chapter 20: Entrepreneurial Purchasing

296 companies participated in the effective purchasing study which was supported by the European Institute of Purchasing Management. While the pan European survey covered a range of company sizes 44 per cent had a turnover of over one billion Euros and 43 per cent employed over 5,000 people. Business sectors in which purchasing can represent a particularly significant proportion of costs such as food and catering, IT and electronics, machinery and transport equipment, healthcare and pharmaceuticals were well represented in the survey. Purchasing processes have also been examined during projects with particular companies, including those with over 60 owner managers of SMEs.

Chapter 21: The Knowledge Entrepreneur

Studies of entrepreneurs and of information and knowledge entrepreneurship within the winning companies, winning people research programme have involved over 150 companies. A third of the participants have been CEOs of their organisations. The investigations reveal little effort to create and exploit intellectual capital and have been corroborated by other surveys undertaken by the programme team. For example, an interview survey covering 58 organisations revealed corporate learning activities to be focused upon the sharing of existing knowledge rather than the creation and exploitation of new know-how.

Chapter 22: Exploiting Corporate Know-how

51 companies participated in the managing intellectual capital to grow shareholder value survey carried out in association with Financial Director magazine. The information collected was mainly provided by finance directors and financial controllers, but also by a number of managing directors, CEOs, company secretaries and business development directors. Company sizes ranged from less than £50 million (36.7%) to over £1 billion (12.2%). Aggregate revenues from exploiting the intellectual capital of the companies surveyed were in the region of £9.3 billion. This was more encouraging than the findings of another survey within the winning companies, winning people research programme covering 63 SMEs which revealed little effort to exploit intellectual capital.

Chapters 23 and 24: Developing a Corporate Learning Strategy and Integrating Working and Learning

Aspects of corporate learning, including the development of directors generally and particular categories of director, the preparation of people for effective international operation and the development of bidding, project management and team working skills have been examined by different surveys within the winning companies, winning people research programme. The developing a corporate learning strategy survey involved interviews with 69 directors and managers with specific and corporate responsibility for the education, training and learning of more than 460,000 people. The 58 organisations covered had a combined turnover of over £49.5 billion.

Chapter 25: Maximising Benefits from IT and E-business

Within the winning companies, winning people research programme there have been specific surveys of the impact of particular technologies, including e-business and the IT director community. 56 different e-businesses were examined, while the competitive network methodology for re-engineering supply chains using e-business technologies was based upon an examination of over 40 re-engineering methodologies and a pan-European investigation. Innovative applications were encountered across a wide range of organisation sizes, different areas of business and the public sector.

Chapters 26 and 27: Boosting Workgroup Performance and Salesforce Productivity and Launching New Products

Over 1,400 companies have participated in surveys within the winning companies, winning people research programme concerned with identifying critical success factors for particular corporate activities. Projects to incorporate critical success factors and the approaches of the more successful companies within these surveys have been undertaken for financial services, engineering, manufacturing, retailing and telecommunications companies. Evaluation studies have confirmed the significant improvements in productivity that have been achieved.

Chapter 28: Working with Consultants

Studies within the winning companies, winning people research programme concerning particular professional communities, change management and development activities have examined the role of consultants. For example, the 91 participants in the survey covering preparation for international operation were asked about the contribution of consultants, while most of those involved in a study of project management managed teams of consultants. Over 150 consulting projects have been undertaken in the course of the programme, and particular surveys have been supported by groups of consultants, for example the Institute of Management Consultants and the Association of Consulting Engineers in the case of two of the winning new business studies.

Chapter 29: Using Management Methodologies, Tools and Techniques

Initial research concerned quality, with two surveys covering 205 organisations employing some four million people and with a combined turnover of £344.6 billion. Two thirds of the respondents were directors of their organisations, 71 of whom were chairmen or chief executives. Subsequent investigations have examined differing approaches to process improvement and re-engineering, business excellence and the use of emerging technologies and a new generation of job support tools. Specific project work has been undertaken in over 100 organisations, three of which have been among the largest and most complex implementations undertaken during the years concerned.

Chapter 30: Creating a Competitive Company

Most if not all of the surveys carried out within the winning companies, winning people research programme have been concerned with improving competitiveness, including those carried out to identify critical success factors in particular areas. Over 1,400 companies have participated in this group of studies. Projects have been undertaken to increase the competitiveness of over 150 companies, and over 400 organisations are known to have used methodologies and approaches developed within the programme to improve their competitiveness.

Chapter 31: Achieving Commercial Success and Personal Fulfilment

The experience of the 215 companies surveyed in relation to bringing about change suggests the prospects of successful implementation are significantly improved if what is being proposed benefits the people involved as well as their employing organisations.

Similarly a pan-European investigation of new ways of working involving over 100 organisations found that participation and creating benefits for the people concerned speeded up the delivery of projects. Work undertaken to build support tools has consciously included ways of making it much easier for those affected to do their jobs.

Individual research projects have been assisted by a variety of organisations, including the Association of Consulting Engineers, Chartered Institute of Marketing, European Institute of Purchasing Managers, Institute of Directors, Institute of Management, Institute of Practitioners in Advertising and publications such as Financial Director and Marketing Business. Certain of the early individual studies were also funded by Government departments.

Presentation and discussion meetings to explore the implications of findings have been held at various associations, institutes, universities and other locations in Europe, Africa, Asia, North and South America and the Middle East. Workshops (see Appendix C) based upon project findings have also been delivered in Europe, Asia, Africa, the Middle East and North and South America in countries as far apart as South Africa and Russia and Canada and Brazil.

The research programme continues. It has consciously targeted under-researched areas such as bidding, while more recent developments with pioneering companies include work on a new generation of knowledge-based job-support tools that are transforming the performance of workgroups in some of the areas that have been examined. The investigating team is keen to involve further companies in this work.

The surveys of directors and boards undertaken during the period 1998-91 highlighted the need for director development. The work done is this area has recently been updated in the author's companion book 'Developing Directors, a handbook for building an effective boardroom team' with a view to producing guidance and exercises that are accessible to trainers, consultants and practicing directors.

Certain of the research databases covering activities such as winning new business, building customer relationships and purchasing have also been constructed to enable bespoke benchmarking reports to be prepared for those who complete a survey questionnaire. Reports★ compare corporate approaches with those of average and high performing (e.g. top quartile) companies and indicate areas that need attention in order to match the achievements of the 'superstars'. Completed questionnaires refresh the database and facilitate the updating of reports.

Much of the work which has been done has had a European or international dimension. Most of the companies participating in the surveys operate internationally. Among participants in the purchasing survey companies from the UK, France and Germany were particularly well represented, but there was also significant participation from Benelux, Italian and Nordic companies.

The re-engineering methodology that formed the basis of the responsive organisation and competitive network approaches (see www.policypublications.com) covering the introduction of new ways of working while re-engineering and the re-engineering of supply chains respectively resulted from an EU funded element of the programme. This study - Constraints and Opportunities for Business Restructuring, an Analysis (COBRA) – was a pan-European investigation of re-engineering, teleworking and business restructuring led by the author.

The 'COBRA' approach to re-engineering and corporate transformation formed the basis of subsequent EU funded research projects (e.g. ABUITTS, HOCAPRIT, MARCHIVE, COCO), and a further wave of EU funded application projects. HOCAPRIT and COCO were concerned with healthcare processes and healthcare in EU regions respectively. MARCHIVE produced a methodology for re-engineering Government archiving processes.

The involvement of public sector organisations in certain of the EU projects – and indeed some voluntary organisations in the COBRA investigation - revealed that the identification of critical success factors and successful approaches and the development of support tools to transform the performance of average operators and knowledge workers can also occur in 'non-profit' arenas. Adopting a similar approach to that advocated in this book could well achieve significant improvements in public sector productivity.

The research programme also formed the basis of ABUITTS. This particular EU funded project led to four national initiatives (Greece, Italy, Portugal and Spain) involving *inter alia* a programme of workshops for the founders and general managers of high-tech companies. Feedback from participants included a request for particular help with business development processes.

Winning new business, whether from prospects or securing additional orders from existing customers and cross selling to them, remains a top priority for companies surveyed as markets become more competitive and they respond to an Asian challenge. Work on developing support tools has focused upon helping those who are in direct contact with customers and prospects (see www.cotoco.com). Early tools incorporating the principle of capturing and sharing critical success factors and winning approaches won awards at both national and international level.

A by-product of EU involvement in certain projects has been the wider dissemination of programme findings. The emphasis in research programme outputs has steadily shifted from articles to share research findings with academics and senior decision makers to their incorporation in practical approaches, methodologies and tools and helping practitioners to transform the prospects of their organisations.

Outputs from the programme to date include 21 books, 58 research reports, some 500 articles and a programme of Masterclasses and workshops (see Appendix C). Over 300 seminar and conference presentations have been given in over 35 countries, and over 50 radio and TV broadcasts have been used to disseminate findings of the research programme. This book endeavours to provide a concise overview the differing approaches of high performing winners and low achieving losers.

While a summary can loose the detail of individual research reports, the principles set out in this book have been substantiated through a number of in-depth investigations involving particular companies. These have included the review and improvement or re-engineering of processes examined by the research programme, and in some cases the design of new processes for a greenfield situation or new joint venture.

Projects have been undertaken for companies ranging from entrepreneurial businesses to globally operating 'household name' corporations. Much of the work has involved the review of processes and practices for winning business and/or improving the effectiveness of boards and the performance of key directors and their teams. This activity has further underlined the untapped potential that waits to be released in both people and organisations.

Working with teams on different continents has also revealed how people in diverse situations and circumstances can benefit from the programme's findings. While local considerations may influence how an approach can be implemented in a particular context the requirements for success in international markets need to be addressed if a company is to compete and win.

Consultancy assignments have been undertaken for over 100 major organisations, including several Government Departments. If one includes smaller companies, over 100 private and public sector boards have been helped to improve board and/or corporate performance, and winning business reviews have been undertaken for over 100 companies. It is hoped that key lessons which have emerged will be summarised in future new editions of some of the research reports.

Further Information

*Benchmarking services based upon continuing use of research data-bases developed by individual research projects are available covering building customer relationships, purchasing and winning business for both commercial companies and the following professions: accountancy, advertising, engineering consultancy, law, management consultancy, marketing and PR consultancy and IT consultancy. Details of these can be obtained from Tel: +44 (0)1733 361 149; Fax +44 (0)1733 361 459; e-mail: colinct@tiscali.co.uk or from www.policypublications.com and www.ntwkfirm.com/policy-publications/benchmarking.htm

Appendix B
'Winning Business' Best Practice Programme

The 'winning business' best practice programme is identifying the critical success factors for winning and retaining customers in competitive markets. Over 2,000 companies and professional practices have participated. The business practices of 'winners' are being compared with those of 'losers' to reveal why some companies are so much more successful than others. The investigating teams are led by Prof. Colin Coulson-Thomas, an experienced chairman of entrepreneurial and award winning companies, and Professor of Direction and Leadership at the University of Lincoln.

Recent outputs include 'critical success factors' reports, 'best practice' case studies, practical bidding tools and techniques, key business development skills, process and practice reviews, in-house training and consultancy reports, and a benchmarking service which provides companies with bespoke reports highlighting where they most lag behind successful competitors. Published best practice reports that are currently available include:

- *'Winning New Business: the Critical Success Factors'* which examines the processes and practices for winning business in competitive situations of over 300 companies.
- *'Winning Major Bids, the critical success factors'* a study of bidding practices.
- *'Bidding for Business in Construction, IT & Telecoms, Engineering and Manufacturing, etc.,'* best practice resource packs which include reports on critical success factors for winning business in particular sectors.
- *'Bidding for Business: the Skills Agenda'* which covers the top 20 skills required.
- *'The Contract Bid Manager's Toolkit'* containing 30 practical tools for winning contracts.
- *'Winning New Business in Management Consultancy, Advertising, Accountancy, PR & Marketing Consultancy, Engineering Consultancy, IT Consultancy, Law,* etc., *the Critical Success Factors'* covering particular professions.

- *'Developing Strategic Customers & Key Accounts: the Critical Success Factors'* examines the experiences and key customer relationship practices of 194 companies.
- The *'Close to the Customer'* series of 28 management briefings on particular customer relationship management issues and best practice in different business sectors.
- *'Developing a Corporate Learning Strategy'* which examines training and development practices and priorities, and information and knowledge entrepreneurship.
- *'Effective Purchasing: the Critical Success Factors'*, a European study of issues & trends.
- *'Managing Intellectual Capital to Grow Shareholder Value'* an examination of how the better management of intellectual might generate incremental income.
- *'Pricing for Profit'* which shows how 'leader' companies achieve the benefits of effective pricing.

All these reports and the 'Close to the Customer' series of briefings on customer relationship management are published by Policy Publications Ltd. Information about each report, related seminars and benchmarking services, and on special price arrangements can be obtained from Tel: +44 (0)1733 361149; Fax +44 (0)1733 361 459; e-mail: colinct@tiscali.co.uk or www.policypublications.com

Companies can also now assess their own approaches to winning business, building customer relationships and purchasing. Use of the databases assembled by the research team can generate bespoke benchmarking reports for companies that would like to compare their practices with their peers and high performing winners. Details of these and other services can be obtained from www.policypublications.com and www.ntwkfirm.com/policy-publications/benchmarking.htm

Further information concerning consultancy support services, winning business health checks, workshops and details of his books *'Winning Companies; Winning People, the differing approaches of winners and losers'* (Kingsham Press, 2007), *'Individuals and Enterprise, creating entrepreneurs'* and *'Shaping Things to Come, strategies for creating alternative enterprises'* (both Dublin, Blackhall Publishing), *'The Knowledge Entrepreneur'* (Kogan Page, 2003) and forthcoming titles can be obtained from Prof. Colin Coulson-Thomas by Tel: +44 (0) 1733 361 149; Fax: +44(0) 1733 361 459; via www.adaptation.ltd.uk or www.coulson-thomas.com or by Email: colinct@tiscali.co.uk These and his other books can also be ordered from www.ntwkfirm.com/bookshop and/or www.policypublications.com

Appendix C
Courses, Workshops and Masterclasses

The Winning Companies; Winning People support programme helps under performing boards, workgroups and companies to adopt the winning ways of their higher performing peers. The experience of firms adopting individual elements of the programme suggests workgroup productivity and corporate performance can be transformed to deliver commercial success for organisations and personal satisfaction for individuals.

The programme's offerings include presentations, courses, diagnostics, best practice reports, reviews, consultancy and support tools to help companies build critical success factors and how high performers operate into their processes and practices. The approach adopted is summarised elsewhere in this book and the programme has been designed by the book's author Prof. Colin Coulson-Thomas..

The Professor has led examinations of why some people in key roles are so much more effective than others who undertake similar tasks in equivalent circumstances. Investigating teams identify what high achievers do differently in important areas such as visioning, communicating, building relationships, competitive bidding, pricing, corporate learning and exploiting know-how.

Findings to date suggest most companies devote much effort to activities that do not differentiate or make a difference to whether or not particular workgroups succeed or fail at activities that determine corporate profitability, survival and growth. At the same time, every company so far examined is missing opportunities to improve performance and generate incremental revenues.

Over 4,000 organisations from smaller firms to major corporations have participated in the research programme led by Prof. Coulson-Thomas. Some 2,000 of these have contributed to studies to identify critical success factors for key business development activities and the major drivers of corporate performance. The findings are remarkably consistent across sectors, professions and different sizes of organisation.

Areas examined range from understanding the business environment to purchasing and new ways of working. Because most success factors are attitudinal and behavioural, investigating teams can distinguish the approaches of high performers or winners from the practices of low achieving losers. Over two dozen individual books and research reports, many with case studies and checklists have been produced.

The support programme includes a portfolio of over two dozen courses which can be tailored to the particular requirements of individual businesses. Companies in over 35 countries, and locations from South Africa to Siberia, have already benefited from presentations and courses, while several hundred companies have used methodologies and tools produced by individual projects led by Prof. Coulson-Thomas.

Commercial companies and professional firms can also now benchmark important activities such as winning business, building key account relationships and purchasing. Completing a questionnaire enables them to compare their own approaches with those of their peers and most successful competitors as recorded in the database of the continuing investigation led by Prof. Colin Coulson-Thomas. Participating companies receive a bespoke report and confidentiality is observed.

The new support programme brings the various elements together in an integrated package that can transform overall corporate performance. According to Prof. Coulson-Thomas, 'Identified winning ways can be quickly adopted. Every participant in the underpinning research programme could boost performance by embracing additional critical success factors and adopting more winning approaches.'

Creating a Bespoke Development Programme

Boards, directors, senior managers, entrepreneurs and their teams can design events such as Masterclasses and workshops – even whole development programmes – by selecting a combination of the modules below to address particular development needs. Outlines, presentations, exercises and handouts are available for all of the topics listed below. The handouts for each course module include summary comparisons of successful and unsuccessful approaches.

Each module is based upon key findings from one or more of Prof. Coulson-Thomas' recent books or reports and benefits from his continuing work with ambitious boards, senior management teams and entrepreneurs. Details of related publications are given for each module. The modules available include:

Introduction (Setting the Scene)
Learning from best practice
Critical success factors for competing and winning
The strategic opportunity
The key contribution of the board and senior management team

> Colin Coulson-Thomas, *'Winning Companies; Winning People'* (Policy Publications, 2007), chapter 1
> Colin Coulson-Thomas, *'Transforming the Company, manage change, compete and win'* (Kogan Page, 2002 & 2004), chapters 1 and 2

Understanding the Business Environment
Issue monitoring
Issue management

> Colin Coulson-Thomas, *'Winning Companies; Winning People'* (Policy Publications, 2007), chapter 2
> Colin Coulson-Thomas, *'Transforming the Company, manage change, compete and win'* (Kogan Page, 2002 & 2004), chapter 10
> Colin Coulson-Thomas, *'Shaping Things to Come, strategies for creating alternative enterprises'* (Blackhall Publishing, 2001)

Understanding the company's marketplace
Changing aspirations of customers/employees
Matching individual and corporate aspirations

> Colin Coulson-Thomas, *'Winning Companies; Winning People'* (Policy Publications, 2007), chapter 2
> Colin Coulson-Thomas, *'Transforming the Company, manage change, compete and win'* (Kogan Page, 2002 & 2004), chapter 10
> Colin Coulson-Thomas, *'Individuals and Enterprise, creating entrepreneurs for the new millennium through personal transformation'* (Blackhall Publishing, 1999)

Visioning
Establishing stakeholder requirements
Establishing a corporate vision, goals and strategic objectives
Assessing the gap between aspiration and achievement

> Colin Coulson-Thomas, *'Winning Companies; Winning People'* (Policy Publications, 2007), chapter 3
> Colin Coulson-Thomas, *'Transforming the Company, manage change, compete and win'* (Kogan Page, 2002 & 2004), chapter 4

Creating an effective board
Good Corporate Governance
Selecting and Developing Directors

- Colin Coulson-Thomas, '*Winning Companies; Winning People*' (Policy Publications, 2007), chapter 4
- Colin Coulson-Thomas, '*Developing Directors, a handbook for building an effective boardroom team*' (Policy Publications, 2007)
- Colin Coulson-Thomas, '*Transforming the Company, manage change, compete and win*' (Kogan Page, 2002 & 2004), chapter 3
- Colin Coulson-Thomas, '*Creating Excellence in the Boardroom, A guide to shaping directorial competence and board effectiveness*' (McGraw-Hill, 1993)

Leadership
Providing Strategic Leadership
Leading effective teams

- Colin Coulson-Thomas, '*Developing Directors, a handbook for building an effective boardroom team*' (Policy Publications, 2007)
- Colin Coulson-Thomas, '*Transforming the Company, manage change, compete and win*' (Kogan Page, 2002 & 2004), chapter 3
- Colin Coulson-Thomas, '*Winning Companies; Winning People*' (Policy Publications, 2007), chapter 5
- Colin Coulson-Thomas, '*Creating Excellence in the Boardroom, A guide to shaping directorial competence and board effectiveness*' (McGraw-Hill, 1993)

Corporate Governance
Governance Requirements
Corporate Responses

- Colin Coulson-Thomas, '*Developing Directors, a handbook for building an effective boardroom team*' (Policy Publications, 2007)
- Colin Coulson-Thomas, '*Winning Companies; Winning People*' (Policy Publications, 2007), chapter 6

Differentiation
Attracting and engaging good customers, business partners and talented people
Identifying, selecting and developing differentiators

- Colin Coulson-Thomas, '*Winning Companies; Winning People*' (Policy Publications, 2007), chapter 7
- Colin Coulson-Thomas, '*Shaping Things to Come*' (Blackhall Publishing, 2001)

Colin Coulson-Thomas, *'Transforming the Company, manage change, compete and win'* (Kogan Page, 2002 & 2004), chapter 4

Colin Coulson-Thomas, *'Individuals and Enterprise, creating entrepreneurs for the new millennium through personal transformation'* (Blackhall Publishing, 1999)

Creating New Commercial Offerings
Challenging assumptions and identifying opportunities
Creating new options and choices
Packaging what you know
Crafting new knowledge-based offerings

Colin Coulson-Thomas, *'Shaping Things to Come, strategies for creating alternative enterprises'* (Blackhall Publishing, 2001)

Colin Coulson-Thomas, *'The Knowledge Entrepreneur'* (Kogan Page, 2003)

Colin Coulson-Thomas, *'Individuals and Enterprise, creating entrepreneurs for the new millennium through personal transformation'* (Blackhall Publishing, 1999)

Winning Business
Winning new business
Winning competitive Bids

Colin Coulson-Thomas, Carol Kennedy and Matthew O'Connor, *'Winning New Business, the critical success factors'* (Policy Publications, 2003)

Colin Coulson-Thomas, *'Winning Companies; Winning People'* (Policy Publications, 2007), chapter 8

Colin Coulson-Thomas, *'Transforming the Company, manage change, compete and win'* (Kogan Page, 2002 & 2004), chapters 5 and 6

Pricing
Pricing for profit
Justifying a premium price

Colin Coulson-Thomas, *'Pricing for Profit, the critical success factors'* (Policy Publications, 2002)

Colin Coulson-Thomas, *'Winning Companies; Winning People'* (Policy Publications, 2007), chapter 9

Building Customer Relationships
Strategic and key account management
Customer service as a business opportunity

Colin Coulson-Thomas, *'Winning Companies; Winning People'*
(Policy Publications, 2007), chapter 10

Colin Coulson-Thomas, *'Transforming the Company, manage change, compete and win'* (Kogan Page, 2002 & 2004), chapters 5 and 6

John Hurcomb [Executive Editor: Colin Coulson-Thomas], *'Developing Strategic Customers & Key Accounts'* (Policy Publications, 1998)

Collaboration and Partnering

Building effective business partnerships
Partnering with customers, suppliers, consultants and business schools

Colin Coulson-Thomas, *'Winning Companies; Winning People'*
(Policy Publications, 2007), chapter 11

Colin Coulson-Thomas, *'Transforming the Company, manage change, compete and win'* (Kogan Page, 2002 & 2004), chapters 12 and 14

John Hurcomb [Executive Editor: Colin Coulson-Thomas], *'Developing Strategic Customers & Key Accounts'* (Policy Publications, 1998)

Managing Supply Chain Relationships

Networks of relationships
Supply chain collaboration

Colin Coulson-Thomas, *'Winning Companies; Winning People'*
(Policy Publications, 2007), chapter 12

Peter Bartram [Executive Editor: Colin Coulson-Thomas], *'The Competitive Network'* (Policy Publications, 1996)

Process Improvement, Re-engineering and Corporate Transformation

Opportunity seeking and goal setting
Selecting the right approach
Process analysis and redesign
Implementation and evaluation

Colin Coulson-Thomas, *'Winning Companies; Winning People'*
(Policy Publications, 2007), chapters 13 and 29

Colin Coulson-Thomas, *'The Future of the Organisation, achieving excellence through business transformation'* (Kogan Page, 1997 & 1998)

Colin Coulson-Thomas, *'Business Process Re-engineering, Myth & Reality'* (Kogan Page, 1994 & 1996)

Colin Coulson-Thomas, *'Transforming the Company, manage change, compete and win'* (Kogan Page, 2002 & 2004)

Colin Coulson-Thomas et al, *'The Responsive Organisation'* (Policy Publications, 1995)

Change Management
Managing change
Achieving successful corporate transformation
Working with consultants

> Colin Coulson-Thomas, *'Winning Companies; Winning People'* (Policy Publications, 2007), chapters 14 and 28
> Colin Coulson-Thomas, *'Transforming the Company, manage change, compete and win'* (Kogan Page, 2002 & 2004), chapter 6
> Colin Coulson-Thomas, *'The Future of the Organisation, achieving excellence through business transformation'* (Kogan Page, 1997 & 1998)
> Colin Coulson-Thomas, *'Business Process Re-engineering, Myth & Reality'* (Kogan Page, 1994 & 1996)

Corporate Communications
Effective internal and external communication
Communicating for change

> Colin Coulson-Thomas, *'Winning Companies; Winning People'* (Policy Publications, 2007), chapter 15
> Colin Coulson-Thomas, *'Transforming the Company, manage change, compete and win'* (Kogan Page, 2002 & 2004), chapter 7
> Colin Coulson-Thomas, *'Creating Excellence in the Boardroom, A guide to shaping directorial competence and board effectiveness'* (McGraw-Hill, 1993)

New Ways of Working
Understanding and selecting new ways of working
Introducing More Flexible Patterns of Work

> Colin Coulson-Thomas, *'Winning Companies; Winning People'* (Policy Publications, 2007), chapters 17 and 18
> Colin Coulson-Thomas, *'Transforming the Company, manage change, compete and win'* (Kogan Page, 2002 & 2004), chapter 8
> Colin Coulson-Thomas [Principal Author], *'The Responsive Organisation, re-engineering new patterns of work'* (Policy Publications, 1995)

Corporate Learning
Integrating learning and working
Creating a corporate learning strategy

Colin Coulson-Thomas, *'Winning Companies; Winning People'* (Policy Publications, 2007), chapter 23 and 24

Colin Coulson-Thomas, *'Developing a Corporate Learning Strategy, the key knowledge management challenge for the HR function'* (Policy Publications, 1999).

Colin Coulson-Thomas, *'Developing Directors, a handbook for building an effective boardroom team'* (Policy Publications, 2007)

Colin Coulson-Thomas, *'Transforming the Company, manage change, compete and win'* (Kogan Page, 2002 & 2004), chapter 17

Knowledge Management and Exploitation

Knowledge entrepreneurship (making money from what you know)
Capturing and sharing the expertise of superstars

Colin Coulson-Thomas, *'Winning Companies; Winning People'* (Policy Publications, 2007), chapters 21 and 22

Colin Coulson-Thomas, *'Transforming the Company, manage change, compete and win'* (Kogan Page, 2002 & 2004), chapter 8

Colin Coulson-Thomas, *'The Knowledge Entrepreneur'* (Kogan Page, 2003)

Sarah Perrin [Executive Editor: Colin Coulson-Thomas], *'Managing Intellectual Capital to Grow Shareholder Value'* (Policy Publications, 2000)

Workgroup Productivity

Identifying and selecting key workgroups
Job support tools and increasing key workgroup performance

Colin Coulson-Thomas, *'Winning Companies; Winning People'* (Policy Publications, 2007), chapter 26

Colin Coulson-Thomas, *'The Knowledge Entrepreneur'* (Kogan Page, 2003)

Launching New Products

The nature of the challenge
How job support tools can help

Colin Coulson-Thomas, *'Winning Companies; Winning People'* (Policy Publications, 2007), chapter 27

Colin Coulson-Thomas, *'The Knowledge Entrepreneur'* (Kogan Page, 2003)

Business Excellence and Entrepreneurship

Corporate culture and innovation
Creating an entrepreneurial corporate culture

Colin Coulson-Thomas, *'Winning Companies; Winning People'* (Policy Publications, 2007), chapter 19

Colin Coulson-Thomas, *'Transforming the Company, manage change, compete and win'* (Kogan Page, 2002 & 2004), chapter 9

Colin Coulson-Thomas, *'The Future of the Organisation, achieving excellence through business transformation'* (Kogan Page, 1997 & 1998)

Colin Coulson-Thomas, *'Individuals and Enterprise, creating entrepreneurs for the new millennium through personal transformation'* (Blackhall Publishing, 1999)

Colin Coulson-Thomas, *'The Knowledge Entrepreneur'* (Kogan Page, 2003)

Purchasing
Effective purchasing
Entrepreneurial purchasing

Colin Coulson-Thomas, *'Winning Companies; Winning People'* (Policy Publications, 2007), chapter 20

Paddy FitzGerald [Executive Editor: Colin Coulson-Thomas], *'Effective Purchasing'* (Policy Publications, 2000)

Operating in the International Marketplace
Globalisation
Skills and approaches for effective international operation

Colin Coulson-Thomas, *'Winning Companies; Winning People'* (Policy Publications, 2007), chapter 16

Colin Coulson-Thomas, *'Transforming the Company, manage change, compete and win'* (Kogan Page, 2002 & 2004), chapter 11

Colin Coulson-Thomas, *'Creating the Global Company, successful internationalisation'* (McGraw-Hill, 1992)

IT and eBusiness
Getting the infrastructure right
Supporting the network organisation

Colin Coulson-Thomas, *'Winning Companies; Winning People'* (Policy Publications, 2007), chapter 25

Colin Coulson-Thomas, *'Transforming the Company, manage change, compete and win'* (Kogan Page, 2002 & 2004), chapter 15

Colin Coulson-Thomas, *'Shaping Things to Come, strategies for creating alternative enterprises'* (Blackhall Publishing, 2001)

Using Management Methodologies, Tools and Techniques
Traditional approaches
Using job support tools

Colin Coulson-Thomas, *'Winning Companies; Winning People'* (Policy Publications, 2007), chapter 29

Colin Coulson-Thomas [Principal Author], *'The Responsive Organisation, re-engineering new patterns of work'* (Policy Publications, 1995)

Colin Coulson-Thomas, *'The Knowledge Entrepreneur'* (Kogan Page, 2003)

Obtaining Work-Life Balance
Changing direction
Getting control of one's life

Colin Coulson-Thomas, *'Winning Companies; Winning People'* (Policy Publications, 2007), chapter 31

Colin Coulson-Thomas, *'Individuals and Enterprise, creating entrepreneurs for the new millennium through personal transformation'* (Blackhall Publishing, 1999)

Colin Coulson-Thomas, *'Shaping Things to Come, strategies for creating alternative enterprises'* (Blackhall Publishing, 2001)

Next Steps
Creating a competitive company
Achieving commercial success and personal fulfilment
Formulating and implementing an action programme

Colin Coulson-Thomas, *'Winning Companies; Winning People'* (Policy Publications, 2007), chapters 30 and 31

Colin Coulson-Thomas, *'Transforming the Company, manage change, compete and win'* (Kogan Page, 2002 & 2004), chapter 18

Masterclass, Course, Seminar or Workshop Leader

Prof. Colin Coulson-Thomas, an experienced consultant, coach and chairman of award winning companies, the world's first Professor of Corporate Transformation, author of 'Transforming the Company', leader of the 'Winning Companies; Winning People' research programme and also an experienced Process Vision Holder of major transformation projects, has reviewed the processes and practices for winning business of over 100 companies, and helped over 100 boards and management teams to improve board and/or corporate performance. He can be contacted by Tel: + 44 (0)1733 361149; Fax: +44 (0)1733 361459 and by email: colinct@tiscali.co.uk or via http://www.coulson-thomas.com

Further Information

Further information on the director and board support programme can be obtained from Prof. Colin Coulson-Thomas the programme leader by Tel: + 44 (0)1733 361149; Email colinct@tiscali.co.uk and via http://www.adaptation.ltd.uk

'Developing Directors, a handbook for building an effective boardroom team ' by Colin Coulson-Thomas (ISBN 978-1-87298-032-4) is published by Policy Publications in association with Adaptation and available price £34.95 plus p&p (UK: £2.75; US: £3.85; Europe £6.15; Rest of World [Australia, Canada and South Africa]: £7.15) from: http://www.policypublications.com/developingdirectors.htm

Information about other books and reports by Prof. Coulson-Thomas can be found on http://www.ntwkfirm.com/bookshop/ and http://www.wpm-group.com/catalogue/products/publications

Information on the research reports can also be found on http://www.policy-publications.com

Details of the critical success factors identified by his research can also be obtained from http://www.winningnewbusiness.biz/

Information about how critical success factors and winning ways can be built into support tools for key workgroups can be obtained from http://www.cotoco.com

Further information on related and bespoke benchmarking services can be obtained from http://www.ntwkfirm.com/policy-publications/benchmarking.htm

Details of related director and board support services can be obtained via http://www.adaptation.ltd.uk

Information on selected services can also be obtained via http://www.cctequiteq.com

Index

3Com, 166, 176
ABUITTS project, 214
Account managers, 55-57
Account management, 55-57
Achieving commercial success and personal fulfilment, 196-198
AIG Europe, 128
Amazon, 16
Arthur Andersen, 85
Assessing knowledge-based opportunities, 132-135
Association of Consulting Engineers, 212, 213
Avaya, 129, 176
Ballmer, Steve, 16
B&Q, 70, 129, 185
BBC, 16
Bidding for business, 44-47
Bolero, 87, 176
Branson, Richard, 18
BT, 45, 98
Buddha, 187
Building customer relationships, 53-57
Business Development Forum, 56, 144
Cable and Wireless, 98
Chartered Institute of Marketing, 206, 207, 213
Cisco Systems, 70, 99, 129, 166, 168, 176
Clifford Chance, 128
COBRA project, 102, 214
COCO project, 214
Competitive bidding, 44-47
Corporate communications, 85-88
Corporate Governance, 34-36
Corporate learning, 142-147, 150-157, 187-189
Corporate transformation, 79-82
Cotoco, 46, 47, 51, 128-129, 153, 166, 167, 168, 176, 214
Courses, workshops and masterclasses, 220-230
Creating a bespoke development programme, 221-230
Creating a competitive company, 191-193
Creating a winning board, 21-23
Creating an entrepreneurial culture, 111-115
Customer relationship management, 53-57
Dames & Moore, 128
Dana Glacier Vandervell Bearings, 87, 129, 166
Dell, 46
Deloitte & Touche, 128
Differentiation, 39-42
e-Business Innovations Award for Knowledge Management, 127, 166, 176
Enron, 85
Entrepreneurial purchasing, 120-124
Entrepreneurship, 111-115, 117-119, 126-131, 132-135
European Commission, 98
European Institute of Purchasing Management, 120, 210, 213
Evans, Janetta, 167, 168
Exploiting corporate know-how, 136-140
Eyretel, 46, 47, 51, 87, 129, 166, 169
Federal Express, 162
Financial Director magazine, 210, 213
Ford, 93, 162
Friends Provident, 129, 167, 168, 169, 185
Fuller, Don, 167, 168, 169
Gartner, 168, 169
Gates, Bill, 16
George, Nathan, 166
Glaxo Wellcome, 145
Guinness, 161
Guinness.com, 161

Hazell Carr, 98
Henry Boot, 45
Hill and Knowlton, 128
HOCAPRIT project, 214
HSBC, 185
IBM, 98
ICB, 166, 167, 168
ICL, 98
Institute of Directors, 213
Institute of Management, 213
Institute of Management Consultants, 212
Institute of Practitioners in Advertising, 213
Integrating learning and working, 150-157
International operation, 91-95
Introducing new ways of working, 104-105
IP Telephony Sales Tool, 168
Issue monitoring and management, 13-15
Issue monitoring process (IMP), 11-12
IT and e-Business, 159-162
Jaguar, 108
Job support tools, 42, 46, 47, 51, 70, 76, 87, 123, 128-129, 131, 136, 139, 146, 151, 153, 156, 165-170, 172-177, 185-186
Keenan, Roger, 169
Key account management, 53-57
K-frame, 87, 127, 152, 153, 166, 174
Knowledge entrepreneur competencies, 130
Knowledge management and entrepreneurship, 126-131, 132-135, 136-140
Kroll Associates, 128
Launching new products, 172-177
Lucent Technologies, 176
Madonna, 18
Management of change, 73-76
Managing a virtual organisation, 106-109
Managing IT and e-Business, 159-162

Managing supply chain relationships, 67-71
MARCHIVE project, 214
Marketing Business magazine, 207, 213
Microsoft, 16
Motorola, 108
MTV, 93
Navigator sales support tool, 167
New ways of working, 98-102, 104-105
New York, 18
NHS, 205
Partnering and collaboration, 60-65
Policy Publications, 26, 218
Powergen, 162
Pricing, 49-51
PROMPT-RPS, 128-129
Providing strategic leadership, 26-31
Purchasing, 120-124
Quality requirements, 70
Rank Xerox, 98
Redwood Publishing, 45
RS Communication Services, 98
Salesforce productivity, 165-170
Sales support tools, 165-170
Shell.com, 179
Supply chain relationships, 67-71
Swift Construction, 99
Telework Systems, 99
Ten essential freedoms, 99
Texas Instruments, 108
The Innovation Group, 166
THE MARKiT support toolkit, 167, 168, 170
Thompson, Ed, 168, 169
Training and development, 142-147, 150-157, 187-188
Understanding the business and market environment, 10-12
University of Lincoln, 217
USA.net, 16
Using management methodologies, tools and techniques, 183-188
Virtual operation, 106-109
Visioning, 16-19

Wang, 46
Wilson, Stuart, 167, 168, 169, 170
Winning business, 44-47, 165-170
Winning Business Best Practice Programme, 217-219
Winning Business Research and Benchmarking Programme, 44, 46, 47, 56, 217-219
Winning Companies; Winning People Research Programme, 1-7, 200-216
Workgroup productivity and job support tools, 165-170
Working with consultants, 179-181
Work-life balance, 101
Worldcom, 85

Also available from Policy Publications

Winning New Business

A four-part best practice resource pack to increase your success rate consisting of:

- Winning New Business: the Critical Success Factors. A 172 page A4 format report based on the real life experience of over 300 companies which explores the key factors which lead to success in winning new business.

- Bidding for Business: the Skills Agenda. A 70 page A4 research based report which explores the top 20 skills that are important in winning new business.

- The Contract Bid Manager's Toolkit. A set of 30 loose-leaf and inter-linked tools – frameworks, tables, charts, worksheets, checklists - designed to help managers in the practicalities of bidding for business.

- Win More Business. A CD-Rom which contains the above three items together with case studies and other resources designed to help companies win more business.

Bidding for Business

A series of three part best practice resource packs to boost your success rate at winning business in particular commercial sectors such as IT & Telecoms and Engineering and Manufacturing

Winning New Business in the Professions, the critical success factors

A series of seven A4 Winning New Business reports on the critical success factors for winning business in particular professions such as Management Consultancy, PR & Marketing Consultancy, Accountancy, the Legal Profession, Engineering Consultancy, and IT & Telecoms Consultancy.

Pricing for Profit: the critical success factors

A 104 page research based A4 report which shows how some companies are much more effective than others at using pricing management to help achieve business objectives, such as growing market share or improving profitability.

Developing a Corporate Learning Strategy

A 239 page research based A4 report which can be used to review and improve your organisation's learning strategy and practices, decide whether and how to set up a 'corporate university' or centre of learning, and discover ways of generating revenues from corporate learning activities.

Developing Directors, a handbook for building an effective boardroom team

A 367 page guide to director and board development that is packed with exercises and checklists which have been specifically designed for boardroom participation, and provides practical advice on identifying and developing the qualities, competencies, and approaches needed for greater directorial contribution, board effectiveness and corporate success.

Managing Intellectual Capital to Grow Shareholder Value

This 157 page research based A4 report shows how the top management team can build new value into the business by harnessing intellectual capital and "know-how" more successfully.

Effective Purchasing, the critical success factors

Based on in-depth research covering the purchasing functions and activities of 296 European companies, this 175 page A4 report can be used to review your organisation's purchasing strategy and practice, and identify opportunities to derive more value from your purchasing function.

Close to the Customer

A series of 28 briefings on particular aspects of customer relationship management: customer value management; effective data mining; targeting high-value customers; managing frequent traveller schemes; managing complaints and compliments; retail insurance customer management; retail banking customer management; relationship marketing strategy; managing retail customers; building customer relationships: best practice; managing customer service in utilities; relationship marketing: the technology; customer loyalty: best practice; marketing beyond 2000: a new strategy; managing automotive customers; direct mail: best practice; transparent marketing: the implementation; building customer-focused data; best practice customer management; managing good and bad customers; managing customers with e-business; models of customer management; customer management on the move; multiple disintermediation; the intelligent e-business; the intelligent supply chain; time-lapse customer management; and customer management through people.

Benchmarking

Bespoke benchmarking reports (with or without commentary) for companies that would like to compare their winning business, building customer relationships and purchasing practices with their peers and high performing winners.

The Responsive Organization

A three volume boxed set of reports comprising a re-engineering methodology manual, 21 case studies, briefings on teleworking, and notes on 101 re-engineering techniques.

The Competitive Network

This report provides a methodology for the re-engineering of supply chains through the enabling technologies of electronic commerce and e-business.

All reports, briefings and methodologies can be ordered by credit card from www.policypublications.com

For further information on these publications, benchmarking services and forthcoming titles contact Policy Publications at:

Mill Reach, Mill Lane, Water Newton, Peterborough, Cambridgeshire, PE8 6LY United Kingdom

Tel: +44 (0)1733 361 149
Fax: +44 (0)1733 361 459
www.policypublications.com